Robert Frost
and New England

Robert Frost
and New England

THE POET AS REGIONALIST

John C. Kemp

PRINCETON UNIVERSITY PRESS
Princeton, New Jersey

Copyright © 1979 by Princeton University Press

Published by Princeton University Press, Princeton, New Jersey
In the United Kingdom: Princeton University Press,
Guildford, Surrey

All Rights Reserved

Library of Congress Cataloging in Publication Data will be
found on the last printed page of this book

Publication of this book has been aided by a grant from
The Andrew W. Mellon Foundation

This book has been composed in VIP Melior

Design by Laury A. Egan

Clothbound editions of Princeton University Press books
are printed on acid-free paper, and binding materials are
chosen for strength and durability

Printed in the United States of America by Princeton
University Press, Princeton, New Jersey

For **Joyce**

If there is any virtue in Location—
but I don't think I think there is.

—**Robert Frost,** 1912

Contents

Acknowledgments

This book has been long in development. More than a dozen years ago, Robert Lowell's probing comments in a graduate poetry seminar at Harvard aroused my interest in Frost's use of irony to undercut his persona, the speaker in his poems. At that point, I had not taken stock of the various narrative, dramatic, and lyric techniques found in the Frost canon; but when Professor Lowell encouraged me to develop my initial essay for publication, I began an investigation of the strategies this poet used throughout his long career to create convincing, appealing, stimulating speakers in his poetry.

During that year at Harvard, three chance experiences impinged on my interest in Frost: a reading of Daniel Hoffman's *Form and Fable in American Fiction*; attendance in Albert B. Lord's course on bardic convention in oral literature; and the appearance of the first volume of Lawrance Thompson's biography, a work that provides information and a wealth of previously unpublished material concerning forms and fables in the background of New England's own latter-day rustic bard. Then a four-year hiatus of teaching and military service intervened before I returned to graduate study, this time at the University of Pennsylvania, where Daniel Hoffman supervised the doctoral dissertation on which this book is based. His insights and sound criticism were supplemented by counsel from three other Penn professors: Robert Regan (whose advice was especially useful during the dissertation's early stages), Robert Lucid, and Edward B. Irving.

While I am indebted to these persons for definite contributions to my work, I also wish to thank several other teachers and scholars who have indirectly influenced my views on Frost. Kenneth Lynn, Neil Rudenstine, Reuben Brower, A. O. Smith, Johnston Torney, and Thomas A. West have at various times and for various reasons been on my mind as I wrote the book. I hope I have captured some of what they sought to teach about Frost and, more important, about literature and criticism.

In a different way, I am grateful for assistance I received from many individuals and institutions. First and foremost is my wife, who typed countless pages and offered valuable reactions, suggestions, and steady friendship during the development of many drafts preceding this final version. Mrs. Arthur Sherwood and Gretchen Oberfranc gave thoughtful editorial guidance; William L. Howarth and James M. Cox furnished constructive comments on the final draft. Peter Davison, Roy P. Basler, Barbara Crocker, Doris Kirkpatrick, Rosemary Kemp, William Kemp III, Susan Sendrow, Nancy Broadbent, Munekazu Tanabe, and Taketoshi Honma supplied many kinds of support, encouragement, and advice, helping me to acquire material I needed—in some cases, helping me get it halfway around the world. My research was aided by library staff and facilities at Harvard University, the University of Pennsylvania, Kanazawa University, the Library of Congress, the Jones Library in Amherst, Massachusetts, the Amherst College Library, and the Nesmith Library in Windham, New Hampshire. My thinking about Frost benefited from my work with a wide range of students and teachers at secondary schools in Scarsdale, Winston-Salem, and Philadelphia, at the Armor School and the University of Kentucky's Community College in Fort Knox, at the University of Pennsylvania and Kanazawa University, and at several seminars on Frost that I have given in Japan.

I should also mention that all of us with an interest in Frost are beneficiaries of research by Lawrance Thompson and Edward Connery Lathem. I have indicated my specific indebtedness to them and to other scholars and critics in footnotes and at appropriate places in the text itself.

Finally, my thanks are due to Holt, Rinehart and Winston, Publishers, for permission to quote from *Robert Frost: Poetry and Prose*, edited by Edward Connery Lathem and Lawrance Thompson (copyright © 1972 by Holt, Rinehart and Winston), and to Holt, Rinehart and Winston and to Jonathan Cape Ltd. for permission to quote from *The Poetry of Robert Frost*, edited by Edward Connery Lathem (copyright 1916, 1923, 1928, 1930, 1934, 1939, 1947, © 1967, 1969 by Holt, Rinehart and Winston; copyright 1936, 1942, 1944, 1951, © 1956, 1958, 1962 by Robert Frost; copyright © 1964, 1967, 1970, 1975 by Lesley Frost Ballantine), from *Robert Frost: The Early Years, 1874-1915*, by Lawrance Thompson (copyright © 1966 by Lawrance Thompson; copyright © 1966 by The Estate of Robert Frost), from *Robert Frost: The Years of Triumph, 1915-1938*, by Lawrance Thompson (copyright © 1970 by Lawrance Thompson; copyright © 1970 by The Estate of Robert Frost), from *Selected Letters of Robert Frost*, edited by Lawrance Thompson (copyright © 1964 by Lawrance Thompson and Holt, Rinehart and Winston), and from *The Letters of Robert Frost to Louis Untermeyer* (copyright © 1963 by Louis Untermeyer and Holt, Rinehart and Winston).

John C. Kemp
Kanazawa, Japan
1978

Abbreviations

EY   Lawrance Thompson, *Robert Frost: The Early Years, 1874-1915* (New York: Holt, Rinehart and Winston, 1966)

LY   Lawrance Thompson and R. H. Winnick, *Robert Frost: The Later Years, 1938-1963* (New York: Holt, Rinehart and Winston, 1976)

P   *The Poetry of Robert Frost*, ed. Edward Connery Lathem (New York: Holt, Rinehart and Winston, 1969)*

P&P   *Robert Frost: Poetry and Prose*, ed. Edward Connery Lathem and Lawrance Thompson (New York: Holt, Rinehart and Winston, 1972)

RF/LU   *The Letters of Robert Frost to Louis Untermeyer*, ed. Louis Untermeyer (New York: Holt, Rinehart and Winston, 1963)

SL   *Selected Letters of Robert Frost*, ed. Lawrance Thompson (New York: Holt, Rinehart and Winston, 1964)

YT   Lawrance Thompson, *Robert Frost: The Years of Triumph, 1915-1938* (New York: Holt, Rinehart and Winston, 1970)

* Unless otherwise noted, all quotations of Frost's verse are from this edition.

Robert Frost
and New England

One: The Problem of Frost's New England Poetry

We might think—perhaps we should hope—that by now there would be no need for further study of Robert Frost's position as a New England poet. For over half a century, amid wide-ranging discussion of this renowned author, one of the few commonly accepted premises has been that he was indeed "a New England poet, perhaps the New England poet" (to use the words of Mark Van Doren). He has garnered Yankee laurels from such prominent commentators as Ezra Pound, Amy Lowell, William Dean Howells, Bernard DeVoto, W. H. Auden, Cleanth Brooks, and Robert Graves. Furthermore, although some have disparaged his rural vantage point, not even his severest critics—among them R. P. Blackmur, Yvor Winters, Malcolm Cowley, Robert Langbaum, and George W. Nitchie—have questioned his credentials as a major regional spokesman.[1]

[1] Some of the most important commentary on Frost is gathered (and, careful readers should note, frequently abridged) in two collections: *Recognition of Robert Frost*, ed. Richard Thornton (New York: Henry Holt and Company, 1937), and *Robert Frost: A Collection of Critical Essays*, ed. James M. Cox (Englewood Cliffs, N.J.: Prentice-Hall, 1962). For individual publication of the essays alluded to, see: Mark Van Doren, "The Permanence of Robert Frost," *American Scholar*, 5 (Spring 1936), 190-198; Ezra Pound, review of *A Boy's Will*, in *Poetry: A Magazine of Verse*, 2 (May 1913), 72-74, and "Modern Georgics," *Poetry: A Magazine of Verse*, 5 (Dec. 1914), 127-130; Amy Lowell, "North of Boston," *New Republic*, 2 (20 Feb. 1915), 81-82, and "Robert Frost," in Lowell, *Tendencies in Modern American Poetry* (New York: Macmillan, 1917), pp.

While references to the "farmer poet," the "Yankee bard," and the "poet of New England" are now commonplace, the exact significance of such terms remains obscure. Surprisingly, Frost's relationship to the region that dominates his poetry has never been a central subject for scholarly investigation, despite its importance to the standard interpretation of his work. Most commentary proceeds from predictable affirmations of his Yankee identity to unpredictable generalizations about the region, glossed with quotations from the poems and often interlarded with personal opinions for or against what is taken to be New England character. The captivatingly rustic identity Frost presented in his spellbinding performances as poet and public figure apparently enabled him to establish his own definition of his regional importance. He expounded it so persuasively that it has been accepted, echoed, and enlarged upon—but never seriously questioned. Admirers and detractors alike have seized on it as fodder for their critical cannons. Unfortunately, the regional identity has seemed such a convenient assumption that its problematic nature has consistently been overlooked.

The truth is that for the critics, as for the poet himself, New England creates more confusion and uncertainty

79-136; William Dean Howells, "The Editor's Easy Chair," *Harper's Monthly Magazine*, 131 (Sept. 1915), 165; Bernard DeVoto, "The Critics and Robert Frost," *Saturday Review of Literature*, 17 (1 Jan. 1938), 3-4, 14-15; W. H. Auden, "Preface" to *Selected Poems of Robert Frost* (London: Jonathan Cape, 1936); Cleanth Brooks, "Frost, MacLeish, and Auden," in Brooks, *Modern Poetry and the Tradition* (Chapel Hill: University of North Carolina Press, 1939), pp. 110-135; Robert Graves, "Introduction" to *Selected Poems of Robert Frost* (New York: Holt, Rinehart and Winston, 1963); R. P. Blackmur, "The Instincts of a Bard," *Nation*, 142 (24 June 1936), 817-819; Yvor Winters, "Robert Frost: Or, the Spiritual Drifter as Poet," *Sewanee Review*, 56 (Aug. 1948), 564-596; Malcolm Cowley, "Frost: A Dissenting Opinion," *New Republic*, 111 (11, 18 Sept. 1944), 312-313, 345-347; Robert Langbaum, "The New Nature Poetry," *American Scholar*, 28 (Summer 1959), 323-340; and George W. Nitchie, *Human Values in the Poetry of Robert Frost: A Study of a Poet's Convictions* (Durham: Duke University Press, 1960).

than anyone wants to admit. Despite a wealth of local lore, popular stereotypes, and scholarship in the area, we only have to sample a small portion of the material on Frost to realize that the region's fundamental character and its literary tradition are much in dispute. Donald Greiner's recent scholarly survey, *Robert Frost: The Poet and his Critics*, cites the influence of arbitrary notions about New England as a crucial stumbling block for the critics.[2] There is disagreement even on basic facts of geography and climate. Some would exclude urban areas like Boston, Providence, and New Haven from the region and associate Frost only with the farm country to the north and west of the main population centers. Yet others have stressed his affinities with urbane intellectuals and academics like Emerson, Thoreau, James Russell Lowell, Longfellow, and William James. Considering just rural New England, however, we still can find no clear opinion about whether the cold winters, rough farm country, and forested hillsides constituted a challenging and stimulating environment for Frost, or a destructive and debilitating one.

If the region resists definition, the character of its people is still harder to identify. Apparently, the New Englander is qualified as much by spirit or personality as by residence. Paradoxically, however, this spirit does not include a definite sense of allegiance. The Yankee is often characterized as an idiosyncratic and equivocal type, who, if asked, might maintain that *no one* has ever belonged in New England, not the original colonists, not even the Indians who came before them. From this point of view, Yankees are eccentrics more than anything else, aliens wherever they may be.

Despite such uncertainties, received opinion has it that

---

[2] (Chicago: American Library Association, 1974), pp. 181-203. In the section titled "Frost and New England," Greiner questions whether "a single description of New England is possible" (p. 183) and concludes: "The crucial factor remains the particular critic's definition of the New England tradition" (p. 203).

Yankees are an identifiable group. But identifiable as what? It is common to think them plain, simple, down-to-earth folk, yet reputable sources have also labeled them shrewd, devious, and unpredictable. And there is additional disagreement about their social tendencies: some regard them as outwardly warm and affable, while others brand them dour and unsociable.

We have heard much of Yankee ingenuity, but we are not likely to know whether it is motivated by dedication to work or by mere laziness. It might come from perseverance and careful planning, or it could bespeak serendipity and sudden flashes of genius. Furthermore, even if we accept contradictions and paradoxes as part of the legendary New Englander's quaint perversity, we must choose between those commentators who point to an underlying optimism and those who argue that a fundamentally pessimistic outlook is more typical. The former emphasize rustic wit and droll types who savor the comic side of life; the latter find Yankees cold and humorless, living stoically at best, desperately at worst.

To study Frost's regional poetry, we should pay particular attention to the New Englander's distinctive verbal and linguistic traits. But again there is little agreement on the basic character of the local dialect. Extremists on one side assert that it is demotic and enervated, the speech of an impoverished and moribund culture. On the other hand, its proponents claim that it is a lively and colorful language, flourishing with pithy idioms, striking locutions, and vivid figures of speech. In a general way, the popular image of Yankee prudence and taciturnity is hard to reconcile with the garrulous, impulsive country folk whose discursive circumlocutions and whimsical ramblings dominate such characteristic Frost poems as "The Mountain," "A Servant to Servants," and "The Witch of Coös."

So much controversy and confusion about Yankee character is a serious hindrance, especially when Frost's critics—antagonists and apologists alike—seem unwilling to recognize its existence. The problem is further compounded by the absence of reliable definitions of New England poetry. Everyone agrees that Frost wrote it, but in all the vast critical literature devoted to him it is impossible to find systematic analysis of the generic features that distinguish an actual New England poem. (For a chronological listing of commentary on Frost's regionalism, see the appendix.) One is hard put to say whether a given poem is or is not a genuine specimen. Of course, Frost and Edwin Arlington Robinson are considered leading exponents of the tradition, and Emerson, Thoreau, and Emily Dickinson are oft-mentioned nineteenth-century forbears. But there are many famous works by famous Yankee poets: Bryant's "Thanatopsis"; Emerson's "Concord Hymn" and "Brahma"; Whittier's "Barefoot Boy"; Longfellow's *Hiawatha* and "The Village Blacksmith"; Dickinson's numerous lyrics; Lowell's *Vision of Sir Launfal* and *The Biglow Papers*; Holmes's "Old Ironsides" and "The Chambered Nautilus"; and Robinson's Tilbury Town verse. Questions about the relationship of such poems to one another, to a local culture, and to a New England literary tradition are not easily answered. Scholars have been understandably reluctant to confront these issues or to suggest methods by which they might be approached. Commentary on Frost's regionalism, for example, often founders on the lack of a New England setting in well-known pieces like "The Trial by Existence," "Once by the Pacific," "Acquainted with the Night," "Departmental," and "All Revelation." These may be New England poems, but certainly not of the same sort as "The Death of the Hired Man," "New Hampshire," "The Need of Being Versed in Country Things," "The Birthplace," and other works that deal more overtly—and, we may think, more typically for Frost—with the countryside north of Boston.

Perhaps the most harmful aspect of Frost's regional reputation is that it seems to have discouraged critics from attempting to discriminate among his poems. Many scholarly books and articles discuss the regional point of view, the local themes and images, and the message and philosophy of Frost's *oeuvre* while avoiding the basic critical responsibility of evaluating individual poems and particular literary techniques. Consider some frequently discussed examples of New England verse, which will also be central to the present study: "My Butterfly," "The Tuft of Flowers," "Mowing," "The Vantage Point," "Mending Wall," "The Death of the Hired Man," "Birches," "Brown's Descent," "New Hampshire," "Stopping by Woods on a Snowy Evening," "A Drumlin Woodchuck," and "Directive." We can of course distinguish sonnet from ballad and lyric from dramatic monologue, but the important problem—again a problem that has never received adequate attention—is to define significant similarities and differences among poems like these in terms of their specific features as regional works of art. Not only does the literature on Frost neglect analysis of types or categories of New England poem, but it fails to appraise the relative effectiveness of the regional techniques and poetic strategies that Frost adopted. Are we to believe that throughout a career spanning eight decades his relationship to New England and his poetic treatment of it never varied? Were there no changes in form or style, no developments in technique, no high points or meaningful failures?

Although most critics and scholars have been content with the standard interpretation of Frost's regionalism, one notable authority, the poet Archibald MacLeish, offers a pointedly unorthodox view in a recent study titled "Robert Frost and New England." Well qualified by his eminence as a modern author and his long acquaintanceship with Frost, MacLeish stresses the inadequacy of conventional attitudes toward the Yankee poet. If it seems ironic that his essay accompanies a portfolio of photographs in a *National Geographic* Bicentennial tribute to New England, this is only part of MacLeish's unorthodoxy. His obvious intention was to bypass the academic audience and address general readers directly. MacLeish reveals his point of view in disparaging references to "the discomfiture of distinguished scholars who, having used Frost's predecessors among New England poets as keys to his work, have ended up trying to explain why the keys don't fit."[3]

Believing that scholars have been on the wrong track, MacLeish holds them responsible for perpetuating misconceptions about Frost's regionalism: "the trouble is that if you start with the assumption that Frost was a Yankee poet you will expect him to write like a Yankee (which he often, but not always, does), and you will expect his poems to be New England poems, poems not only of the New England scene but of the New England mind, which they may not be at all" (p. 440). At a stroke MacLeish undercuts a good part of the regional commentary on Frost. Yet his essay is regrettably short, and for all its originality and insight, it treats only five poems. While performing the valuable service of challenging a popular but untrustworthy hypothesis, it opens up many areas that demand further study if we are truly to understand the relationship of the poet and his region. For instance, the point that Frost "often, but not always" writes like a Yankee leaves us asking: which are the Yankee poems, which are not, and why have scholars so frequently failed to see the distinction? Equally important, when and why did Frost adopt or abandon the Yankee voice, and what were the poetic effects of his choice?

MacLeish's argument that "it is a mistake to look for the New England mind in Frost's work" (p. 442) strikes at the root of a central problem in the critical literature and raises several issues. We must investigate how such a misconception developed and how it has been perpetuated. Scholars may have erred in seeking keys to Frost's poetry in the work of earlier New Englanders, and

---

[3] MacLeish, "Robert Frost and New England," *National Geographic*, 149 (Apr. 1976), 438-444.

the keys may indeed not fit, but the poet's contribution to this misunderstanding is highly significant. Those most directly influenced by his conversation and personality—Ezra Pound, Gorham Munson, Sidney Cox, and Bernard DeVoto, for instance—have written some of the strongest endorsements of his spokesmanship for New England attitudes.

In probing the origins of Frost's interest in New England, MacLeish also challenges the widespread belief that the poet was an indigenous, dyed-in-the-wool Yankee. He argues that "the relation of Frost to New England was not the relation of the native son" because prior to 1900, when Frost took up farming in Derry, New Hampshire, he was "hardly a Yankee at all in the country sense." Thus, there must have been a decisive turning point that brought him to a sudden new awareness of the region: "when he got safely through the first winter and settled down to writing, his poems became Yankee poems—became famous in time as the Yankee poems of his generation. And it is there, precisely in that curious, almost paradoxical fact, that one finds the real key to his relation with New England" (p. 442). This is a valuable perception, for critics have never grasped the importance of the process through which Frost discovered the artistic potentialities of New England. At the core of the paragraph, however, MacLeish's tantalizing suggestion that Frost's poems "became" New England verse points up another subject for investigation. In reviewing this poet's early work, what kind of evolution do we find? When and under what circumstances did he reach a turning point? What were the causative factors and critical elements in the development of his relationship to New England? What differences can we observe between the pre- and post-Derry pieces, and which poems best exemplify his artistic progress?

For such study, a scholarly, annotated edition providing an accurate chronology of Frost's poems would be highly valuable. Discussion of his development has always been hampered by a paucity of information about dates of composition for many of the early poems. Frost himself was notoriously evasive, even deceitful, concerning such matters, and he delighted in teasing readers, critics, and literary acquaintances with hints about a secret fund of old manuscripts from which he could draw material whenever he wanted to publish a new collection. Indeed, many volumes contain works written decades prior to publication. Thus, confounded by the poet's secrecy and by the difficulty of dating such drafts and manuscripts as are available, commentators have been wary of speculating about his maturation as a writer.

However, through the diligence of two dedicated Frost scholars, Lawrance Thompson and Edward Connery Lathem, considerable information is now available on dates, places, and circumstances of composition for many of the poems. Three years after the poet's death, the first volume of Thompson's "official" biography, *Robert Frost: The Early Years, 1874-1915*, was published. It aroused controversy among readers who were surprised at so much detail and such an unflattering portrait by Frost's personally appointed biographer. Overlooked in the ensuing uproar was a wealth of documentary evidence and previously unpublished verse. Some five years later the second volume, *Robert Frost: The Years of Triumph, 1915-1938*, won a Pulitzer Prize and elicited further arguments for and against the poet's personal character and artistic integrity. Finally, after Thompson's death in 1973, his assistant, R. H. Winnick, completed the last volume, *Robert Frost: The Later Years, 1938-1963*. Meanwhile, Lathem edited *The Poetry of Robert Frost* (1969), which includes helpful bibliographical and textual notes for each of the poems. There are still gaps in the record, and some important questions remain unanswered, perhaps unanswerable; but the text and copious notes of these works—along with several recent volumes of supplementary material—provide an adequate basis for thorough study of the poet's artistic growth.

Accordingly, the present examination of Frost's relationship to New England will involve a close reading of those poems through which one can best discover the poet's shifting attitudes toward the region. Instead of approaching the issue of regionalism through historical or sociological estimates of Yankee character, I shall explore Frost's own perception of the rural world and his position in it. Using biographical sources, the poet's letters, essays, incidental writing, and, of course, the poems themselves, we can assemble a reasonably complete record that will enable us not only to investigate the evolution of his stance toward New England, but also to see how concern with his own identity as a Yankee influenced the development of his art.

In order to focus the discussion and establish a concrete frame of reference, the remainder of this first chapter is devoted to a comparison of two apparently similar New England poems, "Mending Wall" (1913) and "Christmas Trees" (1915). Written within a few years of each other during a crucial phase of Frost's career, both pieces can be classified as medium-length (forty-five and sixty lines) dramatic narratives; both center on a regional object (wall and trees); and both involve a country ritual that provokes a conflict of values between the speaker and a second character. Despite these similarities, the poems exhibit a significant contrast in the stances taken by the poet toward the rural world of the poem. In "Mending Wall" we can see how Frost's highly imaginative treatment of regional incident, local character, and rustic imagery contributes to the unusual power of this well-known piece. "Christmas Trees," on the other hand, is of interest chiefly for what it reveals about the liabilities inherent in his self-conscious adoption of a Yankee identity.

After this introductory suggestion of what was at stake for Frost as a regional poet, the second chapter will investigate the poet's early years, giving special attention to literary evidence that his youthful development was not firmly grounded on a commitment to New England perspectives or to a rustic identity. Chapter Three will then explore the curious process through which his removal to England in 1912 influenced his first extensive use of regional material in the poems gathered in *North of Boston* (1914).

Successive chapters will discuss the period of Frost's most pronounced regionalism, the years following his return to New England in 1915. Chapter Four probes the significance of his role as the Yankee farmer poet, analyzing particular elements and devices dependent on it and evaluating its overall effect on his career. Finally, Chapter Five seeks to show that Frost's best New England poems transcend the limitations of local-color writing and attain a complexity and universality not inherently regional.

"Mending Wall": Vision at Play in the Region

Although dating from 1913, when Frost was still an unknown poet living in a kind of self-imposed exile at Beaconsfield, England, "Mending Wall" is one of the ten or fifteen poems on which his reputation as a great New England author unquestionably rests. For more than sixty years now it has been interpreted, anthologized, and applauded as one of his most successful and representative compositions. Quantifiable proof of its importance can be found in the continuing efforts of scholars and critics to explicate it and account for its extraordinary power.[4] Although the poem has stimulated much con-

[4] Thompson discusses the composition of "Mending Wall" in *EY*, 432-433. For interpretation and criticism, see James K. Bowen, "The Persona in Frost's 'Mending Wall': Mended or Amended?" *CEA Critic*, 31 (Nov. 1968), 14; John C. Broderick, "Frost's *Mending Wall*," *Explicator*, 14 (Jan. 1956), 24; G. R. Elliott, "The Neighborliness of Robert Frost," *Nation*, 109 (6 Dec. 1919), 713-715; Carson Gibb, "Frost's *Mending Wall*," *Explicator*, 20 (Feb. 1962), 48; Graves, "Introduction," *Selected Poems of Robert Frost*, p. xiii; Robert Hunting, "Who Needs Mending?" *Western Humanities Review*, 17 (Winter 1963), 88-89; Frank Lentricchia, *Robert Frost: Modern Poetics and the Landscapes of Self* (Durham: Duke University Press, 1975), pp. 103-107; John F. Lynen, *The Pastoral Art of Robert Frost* (New Haven: Yale University Press, 1960), pp. 27-31; Mar-

troversy, its basic appeal is unmistakable and results from the skillfully presented relationship of a speaker, or persona, and his neighbor, the farmer from "beyond the hill" who believes "Good fences make good neighbors."

The spirited discussion of the poem bears witness to its moving evocation not only of the two characters, but also of the paradoxically linked themes that their conflict dramatizes: neighborliness and isolation, open-mindedness and prejudice, dependence and independence. Ever since G. R. Elliott contended in 1919 that "Mending Wall" is testimony to Frost's neighborly spirit, commentators have explored the poem's implications and argued about just who is neighborly (or unneighborly) to whom. The variety of interpretations has been remarkable. By concentrating on one of the two characters, by making more or less of the poem's symbolism, its irony, or its connection with Frost's other work, readers have found ways to condemn the speaker as well as to defend him, and they have been equally ingenious in presenting arguments for and against the farmer's adage about good fences.[5]

Despite all the speculation about the characters and

---

ion Montgomery, "Robert Frost and His Use of Barriers: Man vs. Nature Toward God," *South Atlantic Quarterly*, 57 (Summer 1958), 339-353; Nitchie, *Human Values in the Poetry of Robert Frost*, p. 92; Richard Poirier, *Robert Frost: The Work of Knowing* (New York: Oxford University Press, 1977), pp. 104-106; Floyd Stovall, "Robinson and Frost," in Stovall, *American Idealism* (Norman: University of Oklahoma Press, 1943), pp. 184-185; Allen Tate, " 'Inner Weather': Robert Frost as a Metaphysical Poet," in *Robert Frost: Lectures on the Centennial of his Birth* (Washington, D.C.: Library of Congress, 1975), pp. 57-68; Lawrance Thompson, *Fire and Ice: The Art and Thought of Robert Frost* (New York: Henry Holt and Company, 1942), pp. 107-109; and Charles N. Watson, Jr., "Frost's Wall: The View from the Other Side," *New England Quarterly*, 44 (Dec. 1971), 653-656.

[5] Among the commentators cited previously, Thompson, Elliott, Stovall, and Graves applaud the speaker's skepticism about walls and fences, while Montgomery admires just the opposite quality: his supposed respect for barriers. Bowen, on the other hand, finds him pathetically passive and ineffectual and Watson concludes that he "moves in darkness" even more than the farmer does. Hunting alleges that he is the "real villain of the piece" ("Who Needs Mending?" p. 89).

what they stand for, not enough has been said about the different approaches Frost took in portraying them. The redoubtable, wall-loving neighbor, though figuring directly in only twelve of the forty-five lines, seems to dominate the poem because he is so conspicuously recognizable as a conventional Yankee. Laconic, sententious, hide-bound, down-to-earth, he is imposing simply by virtue of his familiarity. In presenting his persona, on the other hand, Frost relied on distinctive language rather than stereotype, gradually revealing an anomalous individual whose central role as a sensitive, reflective observer is somewhat obscured by the immediate impressiveness of the obstinate neighbor.

Although the farmer may appeal to readers as a quaint local figure, his deep impact on the imagination results less from his regional attributes than from the persona's stimulating perception of him. The poem's strength lies in its unusual vision; it is a masterpiece not simply because of its piquant Yankee, but because of the speaker's piquant response to him. It is a mistake to think that the countryman's vigorous presence makes the poem a regional sketch like Robinson's "Reuben Bright," "Richard Cory," and "Aaron Stark" or Masters's "Lucinda Matlock" and "Anne Rutledge." The concentrated focus of such pieces is inconsistent with the complexity of Frost's poem and with the force he achieved by evoking dramatic conflict between the observer and the character observed. Ironically, his artful handling of his speaker's reflections has probably contributed to the critical confusion, investing the farmer with so much dramatic power that he seems more dominant than he really is. Indeed, when Frost returned from England in 1915 and began to present himself as a Yankee farmer, his performance—both in public appearances and in verse—lent credence to a vague, unfounded association in the popular mind between himself and the neighbor of "Mending Wall."[6]

[6] Perhaps the extreme instance of the mistaken identification of Frost and "Mending Wall's" Yankee farmer was the inclusion of the "Good

Of course, as Marion Montgomery has noted, the "good fences" philosophy is echoed in later poems like "Trespass," "Triple Bronze," "From Iron," and "A Considerable Speck." But whatever this shows about Frost's development, it is highly unreliable as evidence that he originally sought to express his own convictions through the farmer's aphorism. In fact, the speaker's skeptical tone undercuts the appeal of the "good fences" adage so effectively that Montgomery's moral judgments distort the emphasis of the poem, exaggerating the didactic purpose of the poet: "Something wants all walls down so that individual identity may be destroyed. The wise person knows that a wall is a point of reference, a touchstone of sanity, and that it must be not only maintained but respected as well."[7] Quite revealingly, Montgomery attributes his own belief that walls must be "maintained" and "respected" neither to the farmer nor to the persona—nor even to the poet (though he implies that the poet agrees)—but to an unspecified "wise person." The problem is that the poem makes no allusion to a "wise person" and offers no conclusive testimony, despite Montgomery's confident exegesis, on the wisdom of maintaining and respecting walls.[8]

Many of Frost's New England poems after 1915 involve a "wise person," directly or indirectly, in the guise of the Yankee sage ("Birches" and "Christmas Trees" are the earliest of such poems); but "Mending Wall" does not en-

---

fences make good neighbors" aphorism in a Latin speech celebrating the poet's 1957 honorary degree at Cambridge University: "Ubi boni limites, ibi boni vicini." See Elizabeth Shepley Sergeant, *Robert Frost: The Trial by Existence* (New York: Holt, Rinehart and Winston, 1960), p. 411.

[7] Montgomery, "Frost and His Use of Barriers," p. 350.

[8] For proof that Montgomery's philosophy is his own and not "Mending Wall's," see the diametrically opposed views in Robert Graves's "Introduction" to the *Selected Poems*. Finding a pun buried in the opening lines, Graves maintains that what "doesn't love a wall" is frost—and "its open-hearted namesake, Robert Frost." Like Montgomery, Graves claims to have discovered the poet's philosophy in the poem; but for him the poem prescribes contempt instead of respect for walls.

courage the reader to regard either the speaker or his neighbor as a source of absolute wisdom. Frost's unassuming comment that the poem simply contrasts two types of people demonstrates his awareness that the strengths of the piece lie in its dramatic conflict (and in the characterization requisite for such conflict) rather than its philosophy.[9]

The conflict in "Mending Wall" develops as the speaker reveals more and more of himself while portraying a native Yankee and responding to the regional spirit he embodies. The opposition between observer and observed— and the tension produced by the observer's awareness of the difference—is crucial to the poem. Ultimately, the very knowledge of this opposition becomes itself a kind of barrier behind which the persona, for all his dislike of walls, finds himself confined.

But at the beginning, the Yankee farmer is not present, and the persona introduces himself in a reflective, offhanded way, musing about walls:

Something there is that doesn't love a wall,
That sends the frozen-ground-swell under it
And spills the upper boulders in the sun,
And makes gaps even two can pass abreast.

(1-4)

Clearly, he is a casual sort. He broaches no difficult subjects, nor does he insist on talking about himself; yet Frost is at his best in a sentence like this. Through the language and rhythm of the lines we gain a faint but unmistakable sense of the poem's conflict. Like the "frozen-ground-swell," it gathers strength while lying buried beneath the denotative surface of the poem. From the start, we suspect that the speaker has more sympathy than he admits for whatever it is "that doesn't love a wall."

Frost establishes at the outset his speaker's discursive

[9] Frost, interview with *Harvard Service News*, 16 May 1944, reprinted in Edward Connery Lathem, ed., *Interviews with Robert Frost* (New York: Holt, Rinehart and Winston, 1966), p. 112.

indirection. He combines the indefinite pronoun "something" with the loose expletive construction "there is" to evoke a ruminative vagueness even before raising the central subject of walls. A more straightforward character (like the Yankee farmer) might condense this opening line to three direct words: "Something dislikes walls." But Frost employs informal, indulgently convoluted language to provide a linguistic texture for the dramatic conflict that develops later in the poem. By using syntactical inversion ("something there is . . .") to introduce a rambling, undisciplined series of relative clauses and compound verb phrases ("that doesn't love . . . that sends . . . and spills . . . and makes . . ."), he evinces his persona's unorthodox, unrestrained imagination. Not only does this speaker believe in a strange force, a seemingly intelligent, natural or supernatural "something" that "sends the frozen-ground-swell" to ravage the wall, but his speech is also charged with a deep sensitivity to it. The three active verbs ("sends," "spills," "makes") that impel the second, third, and fourth lines forward are completed by direct objects that suggest his close observation of the destructive process. He appreciates the subterranean dynamics of the frost, he knows how spilled boulders look in the bright winter light, and he seems so familiar with the gaps that we suspect he has walked through more than a few (evidently with a companion).

The first line of "Mending Wall" is also notable because it functions effectively as a counterpoint to the farmer's "good fences" apothegm, which appears once in the middle of the poem (l. 27) and then again in the final line. The farmer is summed up by his adage, fittingly his only utterance; his reiteration of it is an appropriate ending to the poem because it completes a cyclical pattern to which the speaker has no rejoinder and from which he cannot escape. Beyond expressing an attitude toward walls, it evokes the farmer's personality through its simplicity and balanced directness. The basic subject-verb-object syntax of the five-word maxim is reinforced by the repeated adjective and by the symmetrical balance and rhythmic similarity of subject ("Good fences") and object ("good neighbors") on either side of the monosyllabic verb "make." The persona's initial observation, "Something there is that doesn't love a wall," with its hesitations and indefinite circumlocutions, conveys not only a contrasting opinion, but also a different way of thinking from the tight-lipped Yankee's. Significantly, though the speaker's observation too is reiterated later in the poem (1. 35), it is not a self-contained statement. Unlike the farmer's encapsulated wisdom, it is a protest, a complaint leading into a series of tenuously linked explanations, digressions, and ruminations.

Throughout the first half of the poem the speaker contemplates the deterioration and repair of walls, strengthening our awareness of his two central traits: his whimsical imagination and his fine sensitivity to detail. He digresses (ll. 5-9) to describe hunters who actively tear walls apart in search of rabbits. Then he returns to his own interest in a more mysterious, unseen, unheard, destructive power. With relaxed, conversational irrelevance, he launches into a discussion of the rebuilding ritual, shifting from objective physical description (ll. 11-17) to a light tough of fantasy "We have to use a spell to make them balance" (1. 18)—which is likely to be noticed only because of the suggestive hints made earlier to the strange force responsible for the gaps.

Frost's control of tone during this desultory ramble is responsible for the speaker's ability to hold our attention and pique our interest. Even on successive readings, we are surprised by the implications of a given line or phrase, and we find ourselves gauging how much of a smile or frown accompanies each sentence. The imagined spell of line 18 dissolves in the jocularity of line 19: " 'Stay where you are until our backs are turned!' " Yet, just as quickly, the concrete, sensory images in the following line remind us of the real effort such work requires: "We wear our fingers rough with handling them."

Having touched on the seriousness of wall building, however, the speaker indulges in another irreverent speculation:

Oh, just another kind of outdoor game,
One on a side. It comes to little more.

(21-22)

The unceremonious sentence fragment and the deprecatory offhandedness of "just another kind" and "comes to little more" are unsuited to the earnestness of the preceding line; yet by now we are accustomed to incongruities, and we suspect that behind his capriciousness there is something on the speaker's mind. The allusion to an "outdoor game" evokes rivalry and competition, not only in wall repair but also in wall destruction. This persona shows great appreciation of playfulness and recognizes many kinds of sport. If the wall builders participate in one "kind of outdoor game" together, then they surely play another game against the wall destroyers: the hunters and those mysterious underground forces that wait strategically until the workers' backs are turned before spilling any more boulders. Hints of opposition and competitiveness soon gain strength in lines that effect a marvelous blend of natural fact and fanciful fabrication:

He is all pine and I am apple orchard.
My apple trees will never get across
And eat the cones under his pines, I tell him.

(24-26)

This telling passage indicates how far the persona's imagination can carry him. It is true that the acidity of pine duff would prevent apple seeds from taking root, but simple aboricultural observation leads to a fantastic—and deeply revealing—personification. Although the speaker seems merely facetious, his imagery betrays antagonism as he ridicules the farmer, implying that he is too foolish and stubborn to see the incongruity of a rapacious invasion of apples (which are edible) seeking to devour pine

cones (which are *not*). While attacking his neighbor's lack
of open-minded amiability, the speaker is the one who
exhibits antisocial tendencies. He is quick to think the
worst, presuming that the farmer's concern with the wall
is motivated by base selfishness, despite the latter's ex-
pressed interest in being "good neighbors." Furthermore,
it is not the farmer but the speaker who initiates the mend-
ing-wall ritual (l. 12). Thus these lines heighten a still un-
defined tension and reveal surprising complexities while
preparing us for the Yankee farmer's blunt precept: "Good
fences make good neighbors." Such a forceful line crystal-
lizes the poem's dramatic conflict by standing in salient
opposition to everything the persona has said and, in-
deed, to his mode of speech. It is a remarkable and
memorable line, not because of its inherent truth or quot-
ability, but because of Frost's effective anticipatory pre-
sentation of an extraordinarily imaginative antagonism to
"good fences."

Just as the twenty-five lines preceding the farmer's
aphorism contribute to its impact, so do the sixteen suc-
ceeding lines that lead up to its reiteration. But once the
conflict of farmer and observer has been made overt, the
last section of the poem develops a contentiousness that
further elucidates the differences between the two charac-
ters and reveals how little sociability there is between
them. As the poem draws to its close with a chimerical vi-
sion of the farmer as "an old-stone savage" (l. 40) the term
"neighbor" seems increasingly ironic. The farmer looms
not as an associate or coworker but as an alien being
whom the speaker observes, criticizes, and reflects upon
while maintaining his distance and objectivity.

The two men—farmer and observer, insider and out-
sider—are separated by deep differences in perception,
differences that the speaker does not fully appreciate. He
thinks they are building a wall, but to his neighbor it is
merely fence mending. A more significant contrast is sug-
gested by the Yankee farmer's reliance on shibboleth (a
form of mental enclosure). Confident in his beliefs, he re-

lies on traditional wisdom to suppress inquisitive or speculative tendencies. He concerns himself not with the whys and wherefores of walls but with the simple, practical fact (to *him* a fact) of their efficacy. His unwillingness to explain or debate his position implies that he feels there is nothing to be gained through communicating or exchanging ideas. If fences are good, then, conversely, too much closeness between neighbors must be undesirable. Indeed, there is no evidence that his "neighborly" relations with the speaker extend much beyond the laconic yearly ritual described in the poem. Satisfied to confine himself behind his personal wall of self-assured taciturnity, he never converses with the speaker. He only repeats the aphorism he learned from his father, as if to keep from saying something original (or as if incapable of saying something original).

The persona, for his part, does not equate thinking with resorting to adages; instead of accepting parental or neighborly authorities, he seems willing to "go behind" (l. 43) anyone's sayings, including his own. Even his tendentious investigation of whatever it is "that doesn't love a wall" is inconclusive, shifting as it does from the mysterious instability of walls to the foibles of the barrier-loving neighbor before finally dissipating in bitter complaints. But conclusiveness can hardly be the major concern of a speaker so given to equivocations (ll. 21-22, 36-38), digressions (ll. 5-9), questions (ll. 30-34), suppositions (ll. 28-29, 32-35, 41-42), and outright fantasies (ll. 18-19, 25-26, 39-40).

After ranging from careful description to seemingly frivolous speculation, from shrewdness to willful illusiveness, and from subtle irony to urgent sincerity, the persona grows diffident toward the end of the poem about his own perceptions. He is particularly uncertain about how he should respond to his neighbor. Though wanting to "put a notion" in his head, he goes no further than conjecture: "I wonder / If I could" (ll. 28-29). His claim that "Spring is the mischief in me" (l. 28) recalls the mischievous force "that doesn't love a wall," yet he does not try to make gaps in the farmer's mental fortifications. He indulges only in speculative, figmental "mischief," contemplating the crucial question he dares not ask: "*Why* do they make good neighbors?" (l. 30). He even undercuts his strongest comment with a qualifier: "He moves in darkness *as it seems to me*" (l. 41; my emphasis).

Ironically (and there is much irony in this poem), although the speaker complains about his neighbor's unfriendliness, his own susceptibility to subjective vision and his willingness to let his imagination run away with him predispose him also to prejudicial attitudes. He sees the wall, and its symbolism virtually overwhelms him. By contrast, the farmer, who surely knows that "fence" is a misnomer for the country-style stone wall they are working on, sees no sinister implications in it and evidently uses the slightly imprecise adage to show his desire *not* "to give offense" (l. 34). It was a brilliant touch by Frost to use wordplay in exposing his persona's central misjudgment. For wordplay is the mark of the poet, and it is a poet's sensibility that so delightfully plays this speaker false. It is only in the imagination that the fence gives offence, and it is only this visionary speaker who insists that a wall cannot be innocent, cannot be the benign fence of the farmer's precept.

Ultimately, the persona's imaginative and indecisive disposition renders him incapable of challenging the Yankee's confident maxim. But Frost has shrewdly made him both un*able* and un*willing* to settle on an argument that might demonstrate what it is that wants a wall down. The allusion to elves (l. 36), though meaningful to the persona, would never appeal to the hidebound farmer; it is such a hopeless suggestion that it leads to a kind of surrender: "I'd rather / He said it for himself" (ll. 37-38). Yet this concession only reaffirms the personality displayed earlier. The speaker's sensitivity to what he sees may excite his desire for action, but he is neither capable nor desirous of didactic argument. Though the Yankee farmer says little in the poem, we may not notice that the persona actually has less to say to break down those walls he finds so detestable. He can only imagine saying something, for he is an observer and a commentator, not a reformer or a philosopher.

In the closing lines of "Mending Wall" the Yankee farmer may seem to get the last word and leave his antagonist circumscribed—indeed, walled in—by an alien philosophy. But truly, the speaker has mended the walls of his own personality, and instead of combating an opponent, attempting moral or philosophical sallies, and worrying about victory or defeat, he has again taken an observer's approach to his neighbor. At the end he presents a highly imaginative and appropriately climactic response to the Yankee, envisioning him as a shadowy "old-stone savage." As he completes this portrait, he brings his own drama to its denouement. His deep feelings about walls have led him to challenge what he takes to be his neighbor's antithetical position; but after recognizing the futility of debate, he returns to his original contemplative outlook.

This study of Frost's treatment of his persona in "Mending Wall" should be sufficient to establish that the poem is not primarily an expression of moral views on neighborliness. Contrary to the burden of critical opinion, it is less about neighborliness than it is about modes of thought, about language, perhaps even about poetry itself. To the speaker, the farmer is antipathetic because he seems so antipoetic: he distrusts the flow of words, ideas, and feelings. Lacking a playful imagination and the willingness to "go behind" a saying or a concept, he seems cut off from the poetic. But we must not forget that the failure of communication in the poem is mutual. And in truth, Frost's persona is the less communicative and the more hostile of the two. His portrait of an intractable neighbor involves feverish speculation that makes us doubt the reliability of his point of view. On the surface of it, at least, the Yankee's brief adage bespeaks more amiability than do the speaker's speculations and suspicious conjectures. Yet Frost offers no answers in "Mending Wall," no clues about who is right or wrong. He does not moralize: he demonstrates. And what he demonstrates is a conflict that commands our attention because in its origin and development it exhibits the power of imagination in flight.

When we consider regionalism, we think of setting, of characterization, and of a regional message—some point of view or philosophy growing out of, or founded on, life in a specific locale. Clearly, this is inappropriate for "Mending Wall." We find a brilliantly realized New England scene and an indelibly etched Yankee farmer, but the region provides only the world of the poem, not the point of view. The point of view is that of a persona gifted with an exploring mind and a lyric voice. An extraordinarily complex and impressionable observer, he possesses a verbal facility for evoking subtle and poignant moods. He is anomalous, unorthodox, inspired by what he sees—a poet, ultimately, as all poetic persona must be.

While "Mending Wall" deserves its reputation as a regional masterpiece, its success depends chiefly on the speaker's voice. And this voice is central to Frost's greatest regional work. It is capable of carrying the reader forward through a succession of striking images, surprising and stimulating observations, and deeply felt emotions. But such an idiosyncratic voice can not be made to serve regional traits or local philosophy. On the contrary, it involves an element of fantasy, an occasional diffidence, and a touch of uncertainty. Frost's best poems center on a moment of doubt, a moment that gives depth and complexity to the work (as it does in "Mending Wall") by evincing the fragility of the persona's imaginative perception.

In contrast to this imaginative, meditative, uncertain observer, another persona appears frequently in Frost's work, with more self-confidence as well as more predictability. Not merely an observer of rural New England, this figure is also a spokesman for the region, a spokesman whom Frost first exploited fully in "Christmas Trees" and to whom he returned frequently thereafter.[10]

"Christmas Trees": Regional Vision at Work

When Frost returned from England in 1915, he enjoyed considerable vogue as a Yankee poet. Though he purchased a farm in New Hampshire's White Mountains, he spent much time visiting the city. With *North of Boston*, his second collection and a best seller, he was feted by such connoisseurs as Amy Lowell, Walter Lippmann, Nathan Haskell Dole, and Ellery Sedgwick. When he finally secluded himself in New Hampshire just before Christmas 1915, "Christmas Trees" was one of the first works he produced from the new farm.[11] The poem was not an overt expression of a turning point in his career, and it has never elicited much critical commentary. Yet it merits special attention because it was his earliest use of a persona characterized by traits traditionally ascribed to the Yankee farmer, traits that took on special importance in the last part of his career.

"Christmas Trees" was also his first published occasional poem, explicitly identifying the poet with his persona. That his debut as a writer of occasional verse coincided with his new approach to the Yankee farmer is significant. In fact, not only his composition of this doubly innovative poem but also his decision to publish it prominently at the beginning of *Mountain Interval* (1916) demonstrated a new confidence in the acceptability and propriety of his role as a poet. Frost had outgrown the

[10] It should be noted that my view differs significantly from James M. Cox's argument, in "Robert Frost and the Edge of the Clearing," *Virginia Quarterly Review*, 35 (Winter 1959), 73-78, that " 'Mending Wall' . . . marks the full-dress entrance of the farmer poet" (p. 76). Viewing the farmer poet as a lover of aphorism (p. 77), Cox seems to misinterpret the speaker of "Mending Wall."

[11] The original version (*RF/LU*, 20-21) differs significantly from the published text (*P*, 105-107).

self-deprecation and secretiveness so obvious in his early verse and was turning toward a more public poetry.

The stock character of the Yankee farmer, which dates to eighteenth-century folklore, was established in nineteenth-century drama and regional fiction.[12] It must have been a vivid figure to a poet who had observed provincial behavior and local custom in Salem, Derry, Plymouth, and similar small towns in New Hampshire and Vermont, and who was also familiar with the rustic characters favored by local-color writers in turn-of-the-century magazines like *The Independent*, the *Atlantic Monthly*, *New England Magazine*, and *The Youth's Companion* (magazines to which the young Robert Frost was an aspiring contributor).

To be sure, Yankee stereotypes had been important in several of Frost's poems prior to "Christmas Trees." But the persona in such poems was a neutral character who stood apart, observing recognizable Yankees like the cantankerous field hand in "The Code," the frustrated wife in "A Servant to Servants," the tight-lipped farmer in "Mending Wall," and the wry, quizzical one in "The Mountain." The few speakers directly associated with farming in the early poems (for example, in "Storm Fear," "Mowing," "The Tuft of Flowers," and "After Apple-Picking") show little affinity with the conventional New England farmer, displaying aesthetic sensibilities, tendencies toward irresolution, and a metaphysical curiosity—all of which differentiated them from stereotypical local figures.

The reader of "Christmas Trees" soon learns that the poem expresses the experience and sentiments of an un-

[12] The background of the Yankee in literature and folklore has been traced in Constance Rourke, *American Humor: A Study of the National Character* (New York: Harcourt, Brace and Co., 1931), pp. 3-32; R. M. Dorson, "The Yankee on the Stage—A Folk Hero of American Drama," *New England Quarterly*, 12 (Sept. 1940), 467-493; L. P. Spingarn, "The Yankee in Early American Fiction," *New England Quarterly*, 31 (Dec. 1958), 484-495; and Daniel Hoffman, *Form and Fable in American Literature* (New York: Oxford University Press, 1961), pp. 33-82.

mistakably rural figure. It is the Yankee farmer both in voice and manner who says,

> there drove
> A stranger to our yard, who looked the city,
> Yet did in country fashion in that there
> He sat and waited till he drew us out,
> A-buttoning coats, to ask him who he was.
>
> (4-8)

Not only is this speaker knowledgeable about "country fashion," but he also has a countryman's assumptions about anyone "who looked the city." Furthermore, Frost draws on rural speech patterns. The farm family comes out "A-buttoning coats" rather than—in a more conventional locution—"buttoning our coats."

As the poem proceeds, both the speech and the personal traits of the rustic Yankee are reinforced. Of course, as several scholars have demonstrated, Frost was never a dialect poet.[13] His theories on the sound of sense and his belief that "we must go out into the vernacular for tones that havent [sic] been brought to book" (SL, 159) are reconcilable with James Russell Lowell's "Introduction to the Second Series of Biglow Papers" (1867); yet, compared with The Biglow Papers, with the New England local-color fiction for which Lowell provided a rationale,[14] or even with Amy Lowell's dialect poems

[13] Reuben A. Brower, The Poetry of Robert Frost: Constellations of Intention (New York: Oxford University Press, 1963), pp. 9-11; Lynen, Pastoral Art of Robert Frost, p. 86; William H. Pritchard, "North of Boston: Frost's Poetry of Dialogue," in Reuben A. Brower and Richard Poirier, eds., In Defense of Reading: A Reader's Approach to Literary Criticism (New York: E. P. Dutton & Co., Inc., 1962), p. 55.

[14] Lowell's essay, one of the major theoretical works in the tradition of New England literature, corroborated the trend toward artistic reproduction of local speech. It was preceded by considerable experimentation and exploitation of local dialect in the plays of Royall Tyler, Samuel Woodworth, and C. A. Logan, the poetry of Whittier, Thomas Green Fessenden, and Robert Dinsmore, the humorous sketches of Seba Smith and Thomas Chandler Haliburton, and the New England fiction of Susan Warner, Rose Terry Cooke, and Harriet Beecher Stowe.

(which have been called "a counterpoint" to *North of Boston*),[15] Frost's poetry exhibits very few of the extreme linguistic peculiarities believed typical of New Englanders since the first "Jonathan" or "stage Yankee" was derided for his "indelicacy of diction" in 1787.[16] John F. Lynen, in fact, asserts that there are "only five or six localisms in the whole of Frost's work."[17]

Nevertheless, in the context of the speaker's self-evident country residence, many phrases in "Christmas Trees" have a Yankee ring perhaps all the more effective for its subtlety. Without the distractions of eccentric spelling and vocabulary, Frost evokes his speaker's country character even in the simple sentences of his reply to the merchant's offer to estimate the value of his trees: "You could look. / But don't expect I'm going to let you have them" (ll. 31-32). The conditional "could look," though surely not a local form, evinces the Yankee's conventional impassivity and laconic inscrutability. The speaker grants such tentative, unemphatic permission that it is as much a warning as an invitation. Then the omission of the relative pronoun "that," in "don't expect I'm going to let you" is an unusual compromise between the formal, "do not expect *that* I am going to let you," and the conversational, "don't expect me to let you"—a hint of provinciality that may convey the Yankee personality as effectively as any number of glaring solecisms or archaisms.

Several other phrases in "Christmas Trees" have this same faint unorthodoxy or irregularity. The speaker's description of the trees is especially noteworthy:

Pasture they spring in, some in clumps too close
That lop each other of boughs, but not a few

[15] Louis Untermeyer, "A Memoir," in *The Complete Poetical Works of Amy Lowell* (Boston: Houghton Mifflin Company, 1955), p. xxiv.

[16] Royall Tyler, "The Contrast," in A. H. Quinn, ed., *Representative American Plays*, 6th ed. (New York: Appleton-Century Company, 1938), p. 63.

[17] Lynen, *Pastoral Art of Robert Frost*, p. 86.

> Quite solitary and having equal boughs
> All round and round.
>
> (33-36)

The sentence opens with "Pasture" shifted from its expected position as the object of the preposition "in." Then the next line uses "lop" most idiosyncratically. Since in regular usage only *limbs* get lopped and not the trees themselves, the clause would normally read "that lop the boughs off each other." But Frost makes "each other" an aberrant object for the verb. Finally, he concludes with a compound modifier in which the coordinated elements are not properly balanced: "Quite solitary and having equal boughs." In an early version of the poem sent to Louis Untermeyer, the original draft of this line (*RF/LU*, 21) had a more parallel—and hence less distinctive—structure: "*Stood* solitary and *had* equal boughs" (my emphasis). In revising the line, as in composing the rest of the poem, Frost sought no exaggerated rusticism that might echo the proverbial Jonathan's ludicrous "indelicacy of diction." He did, however, succeed in setting his speaker apart as a rustic figure.

If the language of "Christmas Trees" suggests local speech instead of caricaturing it (as was usually the case in New England literature), the personality of Frost's persona is more obviously related to traits traditionally ascribed to Yankees. Reserve and taciturn independence, shrewdness and keen wit, and underlying wisdom and goodness are all evident in this poem, and in displaying them, Frost at several points verges on cliché.

By focusing on the bargaining process, he revived one of the most familiar elements of New England folklore and literature. The Yankee has always been known for his ability to drive a good bargain,[18] and the farmer of

---

[18] Constance Rourke discusses the Yankee trader at length in *American Humor*, pp. 3-32. Significant literary use of the stereotype can be found as early as the 1820s in Washington Irving, "The Devil and Tom Walker," in *Irving's Works* (New York: G. P. Putnam's Sons, 1880), IV,

"Christmas Trees" is quick to recognize a trading situa-
tion. He affirms his faith in the "trial by market everything
must come to" (l. 24), and there is much of the barterer's
indirection in his initial response to the merchant's in-
quiry about the purchase of trees. Like the sharp trader
who veils his intentions to buy or sell, he tells the mer-
chant, "There aren't enough to be worth while" (l. 29).
The same exchange that hints of New England speech also
reveals canny strategy in the farmer's dour suggestion,
"You could look. / But don't expect I'm going to let you
have them." Then the two characters undertake the well-
known trading ritual of inspecting and judging the goods.
The tree merchant nods routinely at well-formed, sym-
metrical trees and responds with what the farmer knows
is only "a buyer's moderation" to even the best speci-
mens, begrudging them nothing more than an insouciant,
"That would do" (l. 38).

In early versions of "Christmas Trees" the climax of the
bargaining activities is dominated by the merchant, but
when Frost revised the poem for publication, he strength-
ened his portrait of the speaker's bartering instinct. Origi-
nally there was no mention of the farmer's reaction to the
merchant's brusque appraisal, "That would do"; in the
final text, however, Frost added line 39—"I thought so
too, but wasn't there to say so"—reminding the reader of
the farmer's highly developed sense of trading tactics. Al-
though conversant with the seller's habit of talking up his
wares, this Yankee "wasn't there" for any such purpose.
He had the wit to see that the merchant's professed lack of
enthusiasm was only a gambit, and the added line reveals
that he also had the self-control not to fall for it.

449-467. Later instances include: Thomas Chandler Haliburton, *The
Clockmaker: or, The Sayings and Doings of Samuel Slick of Slickville*
(Philadelphia: Carey, Lea, and Blanchard, 1837); E. N. Westcott, *David
Harum: A Story of American Life* (1898; rpt. New York: Dover Publica-
tions, Inc., 1960); and Alice Brown, "A Righteous Bargain," in her
Meadow-Grass: Tales of New England Life (Boston: Houghton Mifflin
Company, 1895).

A few lines later, Frost made a similar addition. The version sent to Untermeyer gave only the farmer's question about price and the merchant's reply:

"A thousand Christmas trees!—at what apiece?"
"A thousand trees would come to thirty dollars."

The published text adds a line of astute commentary by the farmer that brings the trading story to an effectively understated, but much more droll and satisfying, close:

"A thousand Christmas trees!—at what apiece?"

He felt some need of softening that to me:
"A thousand trees would come to thirty dollars."

(42-44)

The Yankee knows what the city slicker is up to and why he has offered thirty dollars for the lot rather than quoting a price *per tree* (as asked), but he is not taken in. Despite his interest in the "trial by market," he has his own sense of the value of his trees, and he perceives that the merchant's "need of softening" the three-cents-per-tree price is a final indication of a bad bargain. With typical Yankee reserve, however, he is careful, as he reaches a decision, not to betray his feelings:

Then I was certain I had never meant
To let him have them. Never show surprise!

(45-46)

The bargaining procedures that dominate the central portion of "Christmas Trees" enable Frost to exhibit the laconic hardheadedness of his Yankee speaker; yet these vividly presented traits do not seem entirely appropriate to the spirit of the occasion that the poem celebrates or to the moral values for which the persona ultimately stands. At the beginning and end of the poem, Frost portrays not the shrewd trader but a different representative of traditional Yankee character: the virtuous, homespun philosopher. The poet's adoption of this role deserves careful analysis.

"Christmas Trees" opens with the opposition of city and country:

> The city had withdrawn into itself
> And left at last the country to the country. . . .
>
> (1-2)

The countryman's viewpoint is implicit in the phrase "at last," and so is the assumption that the country is better off for its separation from the city. This assumption, this preference for the rural world, was to appear frequently in Frost's work after "Christmas Trees."[19] It is also an assumption that had been made by many New England writers before him: originally, of course, by Emerson and Thoreau, and then by local-color writers such as Harriet Beecher Stowe, Sarah Orne Jewett, and Alice Brown.

The opposition of city and country in "Christmas Trees" contributes to the appeal of the persona by calling to mind the traditional noble countryman of New England and by distinguishing his "country ways" from the crowded, unwholesome thoroughfares of the city. Frost heightened the contrast when he revised the poem. The original fifth line, for instance, introduced the stranger without the crucial detail that he "looked the city." And in line 9, "town"—an indeterminate word, as applicable to urban or suburban centers as to rural villages—was changed to "city," creating a stronger and more consistent personification:

> He proved to be the city come again
> To look for something it had left behind
> And could not do without and keep its Christmas.
>
> (9-11)

Of course the merchant has come merely to purchase trees the city needs to "keep its Christmas." But the figurative

[19] See, as chief examples, "New Hampshire," "A Brook in the City," "The Kitchen Chimney," "The Egg and the Machine," "A Lone Striker," "Not Quite Social," "A Roadside Stand," "Build Soil," and "A Masque of Mercy."

language suggests "something" more important that urbanites have "left behind" and cannot "do without." Since the Christmas tree is associated both with nature and with reverence and spirituality, these lines hint at modern man's alienation from the natural and spiritual worlds. Frost intimates, as writers like Jewett and Brown did before him, that what the city has left behind is its soul. Thus this Yankee farmer values his trees as a spiritual refuge, a heavenly city antithetical to the commercial world represented by the merchant:

> My woods—the young fir balsams like a place
> Where houses all are churches and have spires.
>
> (13-14)

The conclusion of "Christmas Trees" offers further proof of the speaker's virtue and wisdom. His aversion to the merchant's offer, his reluctance to strip his pasture of trees, his distaste for the paltry remuneration he would receive and the high price purchasers in the city would pay—all these reactions in the final lines bespeak his good sense, and his good heart is manifest in his wish to send a tree as a Christmas present to the reader. Since he can not "lay one in a letter" (l. 58), the poem itself seems a cordial token of his generosity.

Surely the virtuous sentiments of "Christmas Trees" are worthy of the simple, honest countrymen who appear in nineteenth-century literature. Even prior to 1800, in J. Hector St. John de Crèvecoeur's *Letters from an American Farmer* (1782) and Timothy Dwight's *Greenfield Hill* (1794), the wise farmer had been a source of moral and philosophical instruction. In the 1820s the advent of New Hampshire's first "rustic bard,"[20] Robert Dinsmore (1757-1836), showed that the Yankee farmer could be poetic (very much after the fashion of Robert Burns) as well as wise and noble. Dinsmore's poetry, and especially his

[20] This epithet appears on the title page of Dinsmore's (originally spelled Dinsmoor) *Incidental Poems accompanied with Letters* . . . (Haverhill, Mass.: A. W. Thayer, 1828).

stance as a farmer poet, influenced one of the major figures in New England literature, John Greenleaf Whittier, encouraging the latter's Burnsian interest in rural life and affection for local detail.[21] In essays published fifty years apart,[22] Whittier extolled Dinsmore because, as "farmer poet" and "rustic bard," he was "part and parcel of the rural life of New England":

> one who has grown strong amidst its healthful influences, familiar with all its details, and capable of detecting whatever of beauty, humor, or pathos pertain to it,—one who has . . . the large experience of an active participation in the rugged toil, the hearty amusements, the trials and the pleasures he describes.[23]

Although Dinsmore, the living specimen of the noble Yankee farmer, made little impact on literary history (save for his influence on Whittier), a procession of similarly heroic figures maintained the tradition of rural virtue in nineteenth-century fiction and drama.[24] One such charac-

[21] Whittier's first published poem was a testimonial "To the 'Rustic Bard,' " in Dinsmore's *Incidental Poems*, pp. 248-250. For further discussion of the relationship between these two New England poets, see Theodore Garrison, "The Influence of Robert Dinsmore upon Whittier," in John B. Pickard, ed., *Memorabilia of John Greenleaf Whittier* (Hartford, Conn.: The Emerson Society, 1968), pp. 55-60.

[22] The first essay, "The Farmer Poet of Windham," in *The Stranger in Lowell* (Boston: Waite, Peirce and Company, 1845), pp. 124-135, after much revision and enlargement became "Robert Dinsmore," in *The Complete Writings of John Greenleaf Whittier*, VI (Boston: Houghton Mifflin Company, 1894), 245-255.

[23] Whittier "Robert Dinsmore," *Complete Writings*, VI, 248.

[24] Among the many heroic Yankees of simple, honest virtue in the nineteenth century, one might mention the saintly hermit, John Mountain, in Catharine Maria Sedgwick's *A New England Tale: or Sketches of New England Character and Manners* (1822); the "simple-hearted . . . great soul" (p. 137), Mrs. Todd, in Jewett's *Country of the Pointed Firs* (1896; rpt. Garden City, N.Y.: Doubleday and Company, Inc., 1956); the rough but reliable Silas Foster in Hawthorne's *The Blithedale Romance* (1852); the "long-headed Yankee" of "acute common sense" (pp. 202, 209), Seth Plumfield, in Susan Warner's *Queechy* (1852; rpt. Philadel-

ter who made an impression on Frost (*YT*, 261) is Ernest in Hawthorne's "The Great Stone Face" (1851). This patient, humble hero becomes the moral leader of his region largely because, the allegory implies, he eschews ambition and pretension and stays home cultivating his rustic garden. Contrasting his modest farmer with worldly heroes like banker Gathergold, General Blood-and-Thunder, and statesman Stony Phiz, Hawthorne establishes essentially the same tension between rural and cosmopolitan that Frost uses in "Christmas Trees."

Unfortunately, while stressing the opposition of city and country in "Christmas Trees," Frost counts so heavily on his speaker's aura of Yankee virtue that the poem lapses into insipidity and predictability. Particularly in view of its occasional nature—from the subtitle, "A Christmas circular letter," to the direct, personal address to the reader in the closing lines—this work seems to be more self-indulgent, self-assertive, and self-glorifying than any of his previous poems. Never before had Frost created such a blatant advertisement for his own identity as a Yankee. The result is an unsuccessful poem. He had written bad poems before, of course, but somehow he had outgrown them or progressed beyond them. "Christmas Trees," however, was the first bad poem he never transcended. He apparently never recognized its weaknesses, and he failed to see the tendencies displayed within it, which from that time forward jeopardized his New England poetry.

By adopting the stance of the Yankee farmer, Frost committed himself to conventional poses and slighted his original, imaginative impulses. Despite his considerable skill at managing tone, innuendo, and dramatic charac-

---

phia: J. P. Lippincott Company, 1894); and the shrewd but philosophical Reuben Camp in William Dean Howells's *A Traveller from Altruria* (1894). The stage Yankee, R. M. Dorson observes, lost his comic aspect after the Civil War and evolved into a down-to-earth, often sentimentalized hero of "dry wisdom . . . crusty humor . . . and a heart of gold" ("The Yankee on the Stage," p. 484).

terization, his presentation of himself as countryman was ill-conceived and unrewarding. "Christmas Trees" alternates unconvincingly between the crafty trader and the noble farmer. The emphasis on "trial by market" and bargaining procedure undercuts the Christmas spirit conveyed in the final lines and compromises the simple, rustic virtue that both the opening and the closing evoke. A further problem is that the bargaining story never develops a valid conflict and suffers from stale predictability. The opening sentences establish the speaker's attitudes, and the reader guesses all too easily what is going to happen. From the first description of the trees, the insufficiency of the merchant's offer is surely expected, and so is the farmer's self-righteous refusal.

Compared with "Mending Wall," "Christmas Trees" fares poorly because it truckles so obsequiously to the persona, a figure who may be deserving (although that is debatable) but who, for all his Yankeeness, offers no flashes of unpredictable wit or vision, no thoughts to excite our curiosity, no impressions to stimulate our deepest emotions. His chief character traits are familiar Yankee virtues: shrewdness, rustic independence, honesty, noble simplicity, and a strong sense of moral rectitude. The earlier poem, however, benefits from sustained tension between the decisive, wall-loving neighbor and the questioning, disquieted speaker. Frost keeps the opposing attitudes and moral values in an intriguingly dynamic equipoise. He does not permit his speaker to get the better of his antagonist the way the farmer in "Christmas Trees" does. Since the victory in the latter poem is too easily won, the speaker's self-congratulatory tone becomes obtrusive and cloying. But "Mending Wall" continually surprises; the speaker gradually reveals new facets of a captivating personality, and at the same time introduces new attitudes and perceptions about the crotchety neighbor, about walls, and about communication and human relationships.

While concentrating on the persona's regional identity

in "Christmas Trees," Frost seemed to lose much of the imaginative force of his poetic response to the rural world. He employed New England as a moral counter instead of responding to it with the heightened sensitivity displayed in "Mending Wall." It is a sad reflection on his development between 1913 and 1915 that the Christmas trees of the title, despite their potential imagistic richness, remain a trite accessory in the poem. Only a few years earlier he had shown his ability to translate the natural world into the realm of poetry and to make the local object—the stone wall, apple-picker's ladder, or woodpile—an integral part of the poem.

The contrast between "Christmas Trees" and "Mending Wall" shows that Frost's approach to New England was neither consistent nor infallible. Despite many surface similarities, these are radically different regional poems. And the difference significantly effects their success. We must therefore ask how a poet capable of an artistic triumph like "Mending Wall" could within a few years have been satisfied to give such a weak treatment to the broadly similar material of "Christmas Trees." How could he have come to consider the latter poem a worthy successor to the former? To answer such questions, we must investigate Frost's poetic output attentively, and we must scrutinize his letters and pertinent biographical information in order to understand the background and the development of his attitudes toward New England and his interest in regional poetry. In the following chapters I shall demonstrate that his evolution as a Yankee poet had three stages: the early years of experimentation and uncertainty (roughly 1890-1912); a stage of transition (1912-1914) that involved the development of a focus on rural New England and culminated in the adoption of a regional identity; and finally, beginning in 1915, a period of steady association with the farm country of New Hampshire and Vermont.

Frost's situation in 1915 seems an ironic proof of Thomas Wolfe's dictum, "You can't go home again." Attempting to relocate himself in New Hampshire, he surrendered uncritically to the dominating stereotype of the Yankee farmer. His decision to publish an inferior poem like "Christmas Trees" prominently in *Mountain Interval* suggests that the appeal of an imposing and popular literary identity had begun to take its toll. Although he remained capable of writing brilliant New England poems, his creativity does not seem to have benefited from his willingness to write and do what he thought was appropriate for the traditional Yankee.

Returning to the New England farm country in 1915 and adopting the role of the rustic Yankee were crucial steps in Frost's successful campaign for recognition and popularity. So effective was his performance as a regional figure that he was soon identified with the Yankee farmer whose voice he used in "Christmas Trees." And so convincing was this identity that it prevented recognition of momentous changes he had undergone in the preceding years. The acclaim for the poet of New England in the years following 1915 established once and for all the notion—now a foregone conclusion in the literary histories—that "Frost was always, as any textbook will declare, a regional poet."[25] Yet, as the following chapter makes clear, he did not start out as a Yankee poet, and his early poetry had little in common with the traditions of New England regional literature.

[25] Willard Thorp, in Robert E. Spiller et al., *Literary History of the United States*, 4th ed. rev. (New York: Macmillan Co., 1974), p. 1190.

Two: The Poet in the Making (1874-1912)

A central element in discussion of Frost's regional reputa-
tion has always been his practical experience on a farm in
Derry, New Hampshire. In truth, the image of the Derry
farmer has gained so much force over the years that it has
become difficult to visualize this poet without his regional
identity. Throughout his life, Frost cultivated a Derry
myth—what Thompson describes as a "mythic idyll of
self-regenerating isolation"[1]—and he did it well enough
to divert readers from the difficulties and complexities of
his background. To support the myth, he devised a per-
sonal history attributing his poetic development to his
experiences in Derry between 1900 and 1909 and dis-
counting the influence of his reading, previous education,
and personal relationships.[2] That the New England envi-
ronment could be conducive to the spontaneous genera-
tion of literary talent had always been an appealing sup-
position. From the Olympian brow of John Greenleaf
Whittier (as noted in Chapter One) the rustic bard could
spring full grown, panoplied with nothing more literary

[1] YT, 322. See also Thompson's indices for "Myth-Making" (EY, 623)
and "Myth-Maker" (YT, 722-723).

[2] See YT, 321, and SL, 158-160, 222-224, 454, 500-501, 522. It should
be noted, however, that as early as 1917—only a few years after the in-
ception of the Derry myth—Frost was upset to see a cultured critic like
Amy Lowell use it to suggest that he was a limited poet (SL, 219-221,
226).

or intellectural than hoe or pitchfork to symbolize "an active participation in the rugged toil" of rural life.[3] Frost took advantage of this tradition, "spoon-feeding" (Thompson's term, YT, 632) quaint details about his life on the farm to interviewers and literary acquaintances so adeptly that the Derry myth has generally been accepted as gospel.

Although Frost lived only nine years on the Derry farm (compared with about forty years in Vermont and twenty in Massachusetts), the world still sees him as the Derry farmer, a vision perpetuated nowadays through the machinery of American bureaucracy. The New Hampshire state legislature has budgeted $80,000 to make a shrine of "the Frost homestead," and on 26 March 1974, the poet's one-hundredth birthday, the U.S. Postal Service designated Derry a "First Day City," where, with much philatelic ceremony, Robert Frost commemorative stamps received their official date-of-issue cancellations. Ironically, for years after the Frosts left Derry, local folk persisted in calling the farm "the Magoon place" after its previous owner.

In order to understand the unusual nature of Frost's association with New England we should not only reexamine his early years but also recognize that the Derry myth may be as meaningful for what it disguises and conceals about him as for what it ostensibly shows. A contemporary Orphic myth, it established a suitably bardic past and provided a sacred grove to sanctify his singing. But even as it invested him with a forceful and distinctive identity, it was also a way of repudiating—and simultaneously distracting attention from—the indecisive and undistinguished late-Romantic poet he had been until just a few years before his sudden rise to fame as the newly consecrated rustic bard of New England.

By discarding the myth-induced vision of Derry as the

---

[3] Whittier, "Robert Dinsmore," in The Complete Writings of John Greenleaf Whittier, VI (Boston: Houghton Mifflin, 1894), 248.

prime source of Frost's art, we can appreciate the extent of his development prior to 1912. There are many traces of a long and earnest apprenticeship, though this training had little to do with Whittier's prescription for the "large experience of an active participation in the rugged toil" of rustic life. Instead, Frost's background was more urban and cosmopolitan, more literary and sophisticated than he usually indicated. Suggestions about his descent from "folk who lived close to the soil" are highly misleading;[4] in an age when most Americans were still down on the farm, his family had been among the first to leave the country and enter the urban, industrial society that was just beginning to transform the American cultural landscape.

The young Robert Frost never regarded the New England farm country as home. Indeed, his *lack* of a regular home is one of the most basic aspects of his early life concealed by the Derry myth.[5] He liked to claim a regional heritage, like the Maine coast (Gardiner and South Berwick) of Robinson and Jewett, or like Hardy's Wessex or Faulkner's Mississippi.[6] But he was neither born nor reared in the rural world he wrote about, and his movement from the city back to the country—a reversal of his family's pattern and a rejection of what was generally considered social progress—involved problems and ten-

[4] Alfred Kreymborg, "The Fire and Ice of Robert Frost," in Kreymborg, *Our Singing Strength: An Outline of American Poetry 1620-1930* (New York: Coward-McCann, Inc., 1929), p. 317.

[5] For details of Frost's unsettled childhood see *EY*, 487 passim. The family moved so frequently both before and after his father's death in 1885 that biographers are uncertain of precise dates and addresses, but Frost apparently moved no less than seven times in his first nine years (and this does not include a half-year cross-country trip that he took with his mother when he was two). Then, between 1885 and the move to Derry in 1900, he lived in fourteen residences, most of them in or near Lawrence, Massachusetts.

[6] Thompson, who uncovered numerous instances of this myth making, observed that Frost "often gave slightly fictitious information" when asked about his background. For examples, see *SL*, 454, 552, and *YT*, 470.

sions that he often overlooked once he gained recognition as the poet of New England.

It is significant that in creating his mythical background Frost always glossed over the distance between country life and the social position his family had attained by the end of the nineteenth century. The Frosts were well-established townsfolk by then, and their cultivation was *not* of the soil. The family home, to which Frost's mother returned after his father's death in 1885, was in Lawrence, Massachusetts, a highly industrialized city for its day and one of the world's leading textile centers. The paternal grandfather, William Prescott Frost, an important figure in Frost's early life, was a bespectacled, stylishly bearded patriarch who had worked his way up to an overseer's position at the Pacific Mill. Though not a rich man, he could afford a respectable three-story house and a Harvard education for his son. In the 1880s he retired comfortably enough to be able to do some traveling and to support his grandson Robert at Dartmouth and Harvard before buying him the farm in Derry. Frost's grandmother, with her interest in feminism and her role as "an early leader in the local suffragette movement," was perhaps even more attuned than her husband to the sophistication and the new style of life that was developing in urban America.[7] Certainly her son William Prescott Frost, Jr. (the poet's father), seemed well suited to the frenetic spirit of a booming city like San Francisco.[8] By temperament and education, he was ambitious, impatient, and iconoclastic, in some ways closer to the twentieth century than his son would ever be. He loved excitement and action, threw himself into politics and journalism, and sought acquaintance with stimulating figures like Henry George. Too much exertion, along with too much liquor, hastened

[7] *EY*, 49. I have drawn on this work for specific details pertinent to Frost's youth and family background.

[8] Thompson comments, "It is doubtful if any other place on earth could have been more congenial to his tastes than this raw city built on chance, this new metropolis . . ." (*EY*, 7).

his death at age thirty-four. Very much a part of "all this now too much for us," he would have had little sympathy for his son's "Directive" back into the rural past.

If Frost learned little about tilling the soil from his father's side of the family, his mother, Isabelle Moodie Frost, was still less familiar with rural life—and with New England rural life in particular. She never got on well with the Massachusetts Frosts. Her Scottish background, her interest in poetry, and her intense mysticism all set her apart from her in-laws, and hence her influence on her son—which is generally thought to be considerable[9]—did not encourage his sense of identity as a Yankee. An orphan, she had spent her first twelve years with her grandparents in Edinburgh before being taken in by a well-to-do uncle in Columbus, Ohio, a banker and graduate of the University of Edinburgh. Although not a college graduate herself, she was sufficiently educated to gain employment as a teacher, in which capacity she met her husband.

Like her husband, Belle Frost was unfamiliar with country life and unsuited to it. She preferred boarding in hotels to living in a house of her own. She disliked cooking, housekeeping, and washing[10]—chores that only a well-to-do, urban woman could avoid in the late nineteenth century. Deeply interested in literature, she even had ambitions as a writer, publishing reviews and poetry in the *San Francisco Daily Evening Post* during the 1880s. Though she liked to reminisce about meeting William Dean Howells, her tastes in poetry were extremely Romantic. Thompson mentions many nineteenth-century authors she introduced to her children.

That Mrs. Frost contributed much to her son's appreciation of literature has been recognized. Regrettably, however, her actual effect on his poetic development has never been analyzed carefully, probably because the in-

[9] See *EY*, Chaps. 3, 4, and 7, for evidence of Belle Frost's importance in her son's life and her "lasting influence on his literary career" (p. 488).

[10] Louis Mertins, *Robert Frost: Life and Talks-Walking* (Norman: University of Oklahoma Press, 1965), p. 7.

terests and tendencies she encouraged are not entirely appropriate to the mythical, homespun Yankee in whom Frost persuaded his readers to believe. Even Thompson's *Robert Frost: The Early Years*, justly esteemed for its scholarly accuracy and scrupulous separation of man and myth, blurs the relationship between her literary values and those for which Frost became known. Thompson repeatedly links Wordsworth, Emerson, and Bryant as Belle Frost's "favorite romantic poets" (*EY*, 70). After speculating at length about her Swedenborgian attraction to them, he suddenly shifts his attention from mother to son, making much of the latter's ability to recite Bryant's "To a Waterfowl" at age thirteen. As if this one detail proves Frost's assimilation of his mother's preferences, Thompson concludes: "Of these three poets to whom his mother had first exposed him—Emerson, Wordsworth, Bryant—his favorite was hers: Ralph Waldo Emerson" (*EY*, 71). A lengthy footnote supports this assertion, summarizing Frost's admiration for the Sage of Concord and quoting from his essay "On Emerson."

Having done so much to portray Frost as a teen-age Emersonian (or at least as a young devotee of the Wordsworth-Emerson school of Romanticism), Thompson abruptly, and almost as an afterthought, adds a brief paragraph noting that Edgar Allan Poe was also "among Mrs. Frost's favorites" and suggesting that she did not respond to his poetry as *poetry*, but as philosophy: "Mrs. Frost had the capacity to discover in Poe's romantic lines certain mystical and metaphysical correspondences which helped her illustrate some of her favorite Swedenborgian truths . . ." (p. 71). Surprisingly, and perhaps revealingly, the paragraph never refers specifically to Frost; instead, a subordinate clause indicates that both Frost children knew "several of [Poe's] poems by heart before they entered high school." Single-mindedly, Thompson focuses only on Mrs. Frost, neither estimating Poe's impact on her son nor pausing to consider the crucial differences between the incipient Aesthete, Poe—with his poetry of beauty, his concern for sound and technique, and his rejection of morality and truth—and the arch-Transcendentalist, Emerson—for whom the "true poet," as opposed to the mere "lyrist," was distinguished not by his skill with "metres," but by the high moral truth of his "Metre-making argument."[11]

It seems an easy step from Emerson to the mature Frost. The rustic poet on his isolated New Hampshire farm appeared to be following Emerson's injunction that "the poet's habit of living should be set on a key so low that the common influences should delight him." This indeed was a poet who seemed to understand (as the poem "New Hampshire" attests) what the Sage of Concord meant when he proclaimed: "If thou fill thy brain with Boston and New York, with fashion and covetousness, and wilt stimulate thy jaded senses with wine and French coffee, thou shalt find no radiance of wisdom in the lonely waste of pine woods."[12]

Unfortunately, despite the oft-noted and noteworthy relationship between these two writers, there is no solid evidence that Emerson was as highly favored by the *youthful* Robert Frost as Thompson implies. To begin with, Frost wrote his essay "On Emerson" in 1958 as a speech for his acceptance of the Emerson-Thoreau Medal. By his own admission, it was an attempt to make himself "as much of an Emersonian" as possible.[13] Of course it conveyed sincere admiration. Yet, especially as it does not refer to Emerson's poetry but only to the *Essays* and *Representative Men*, it is hardly reliable as evidence of Frost's boyhood interests.

Thompson's emphasis on Emerson is particularly misleading in conjunction with his comparatively insouciant

[11] Emerson, "The Poet," in *The Complete Works of Ralph Waldo Emerson*, ed. E. W. Emerson (Boston: Houghton Mifflin and Company, 1876), III, 9.

[12] *Ibid.*, 29.

[13] Frost, "On Emerson," *Daedalus: Journal of the American Academy of Arts and Sciences*, 88 (Fall 1959), 212.

treatment of Frost's enthusiasm for Poe. From what he says, one would be tempted to conclude that the young Frost, devoted to Wordsworth, Emerson, and Bryant, was only lukewarm to Poe—whom he just *happened* to know because of his mother's weakness for mysticism and otherworldliness. There is significant evidence to the contrary. Two letters, written almost twenty years apart, record Frost's recollections of his adolescent interest in poetry. The first, written to Lewis N. Chase on 11 July 1917, contains a breathless summary:

> The first poetry I read for myself and read all to pieces (this was at fourteen) was Poe, the next E. R. Sill the next Browning (of the Dramatic Lyrics and Romances only), the next Palgrave's Treasury (I *did* read that literally to rags and tatters. This was in 1892.) the next Matthew Arnold, the next T. E. Brown (as late as—not sure of date, but say 1910.) . . . Somewhere in there I had a great time with Emerson. . . . Oh and there was Keats minus Endymion! I'd like to know what I haven't liked. [A footnote expresses indifference to Shelley and Swinburne.] I suppose I had the first copy of Francis Thompson's poems in America. Even Dowson! But before all write me as one who cares most for Shakespearean and Wordsworthian sonnets.[14]

Had Emerson been as much a favorite as Thompson suggests, surely Frost would have accorded him a more precise and imposing position in this lengthy list. Bryant is not mentioned, and Wordsworth is introduced only in the context of his craftsmanship with the sonnet, a form for which Frost showed little interest until he was over thirty. By and large, the poets listed did not write with Wordsworthian fidelity to "common life" and the "language really used by men"; several came dangerously

[14] This letter, not included in *SL*, is printed in Elaine Barry, *Robert Frost on Writing* (New Brunswick, N.J.: Rutgers University Press, 1973), pp. 73-76.

near "the gaudiness and inane phraseology" against which the "Preface to the Second Edition of Lyrical Ballads" protests. Poe and Sill, though both Americans, looked to Tennyson as the greatest poet of their age, so that their presence does not alter the dominant British trend in Frost's early reading.

When another summary of Frost's literary background was prepared as part of a letter his wife wrote in 1935, for which he provided the information, Poe and the British Romantics were again dominant:

> He never read [all the way through] a book of any kind to himself before his 14th year. His mother read aloud constantly. Poe and Shakespeare, George McDonald [Macdonald]—old fashioned romances, like The Romance of Dollard. [A list of Frost's early prose reading follows: Romantic novelists and historians like Scott, Fenimore Cooper, Jules Verne, Jane Porter, and W. H. Prescott.] Read first poetry in 15th year. . . . In that year he read a little of Shelley and Keats in Christmas gift books. Almost learned all of Poe by heart. Keats and Arnold only other poets he ever found he knew as large a proportion of.[15]

Although Frost recollects his mother's role here, he does not associate it with nature poets like Wordsworth, Emerson, and Bryant. The details in the closing sentences suggest that his ability to recite "To a Waterfowl" from memory may be less significant than Thompson would have us believe. If the poetry he memorized in his youth is indicative of his earliest preferences, then surely we must conclude that what first excited his interest was the heady, impetuous power of Poe, Keats, and Arnold.[16]

[15] Mrs. Elinor Frost to Mrs. Edna Davis Romig, 4 Feb. 1935, EY, 500. This letter is not in SL. It is a valuable source of biographical information, and Thompson quotes extensively from it in the notes to EY (see "Romig" in Thompson's index).

[16] Frost demonstrated his knowledge of Poe, Keats, and Arnold throughout his life, often quoting apropos lines on the spur of the mo-

Thus it may be a mistake to assume, as Frost's critics have almost always done, that he started out as a nature poet, tranquilly recollecting emotions stimulated by the New England countryside. This view certainly would not prepare us for the poetic concerns we find in his early work: the conscious exploitation of techniques and philosophies of composition, the loading of every rift with poetic ore to evoke a beauty that—as Keats and Poe suggested, and as the Aesthetes insisted—could be an end unto itself. Mrs. Frost may not have intended to produce the results she did, but she seems to have stimulated imaginative tendencies in her son that led him away from rather than toward nature poets like Wordsworth, Bryant, and Emerson. Strangely, in the chapter that analyzes her literary relationship to her son, Thompson never mentions her deep admiration of one other Romantic poet, Robert Browning. Considerable evidence of this literary interest appears elsewhere in *Robert Frost: The Early Years*, and thus its neglect here seems to be yet another instance of the effectiveness of Frost's public image as a humble Yankee poet, even in the case of a biographer who sought to dispel the popular myths.

Although the letter to Lewis N. Chase proves that Frost read Browning while still quite young, the most obvious technical and formal influences did not appear until he wrote the dramatic pieces of *North of Boston* and later collections. A less obvious influence seems to have been conveyed indirectly, however, not through the poetry but through Mrs. Frost's Browningesque views of art and the artist. No devotee of Browning could read the major dramatic monologues in which painters, musicians, and poets are central figures without being impressed by the tensions between the artist and society at large.[17] And

---

ment. See *EY*, 115-116, 294; *YT*, 235, 288, 407-408, 662; and *SL*, 195, 212, 471.

[17] I assume that Mrs. Frost would have been familiar with the artists evoked in "Pictor Ignotus," "A Toccata of Galuppi's," "Old Pictures in Florence," "How it Strikes a Contemporary," "Fra Lippo Lippi," "Andrea del Sarto," and "Abt Vogler."

surely Mrs. Frost's devotion is manifest in the highly imitative dramatic monologue she published in 1884, "The Artist's Motive."[18]

To Wordsworth and Emerson, the poet was a representative man, a man speaking to men. Browning's flair for the dramatic, however, led him to construct utterances that were exotic and remote, sometimes even disturbingly grotesque. He "delighted," as Robert Langbaum has pointed out, "in making a case for the apparently immoral position." By giving so much attention to artists in his work, and by encouraging sympathy for their "extraordinary moral positions," he implied that the artist was, in a romantically alluring way, separate and different from the rest of mankind.[19] This assumption (fortified by Swedenborgian doctrine) underlies the Browningesque sentiments of Mrs. Frost's dramatic monologue.

"The Artist's Motive" centers on the discovery that worldly success cannot assuage the "heartsick soul" (l. 45). Casting aside human vanity and ambition, the painter-hero gives up a lucrative career and, in monastic solitude, learns to gaze "with faithful eye / Upon the face of nature" (ll. 58-59). For his sacrifice, he is rewarded in the climactic lines with a miraculous vision through which his painting suddenly becomes charged with "the spark divine" (l. 122). Although the moral suggests that the beatified painter can lead his fellow men to divine worship, Mrs. Frost's main concern is with the artist's ability to achieve his own personal salvation.

Orphaned as a child, widowed after an unhappy twelve-year marriage, and impoverished after her youthful glimpse of affluence and culture in Ohio, Isabelle Frost

[18] "The Artist's Motive" initially appeared a few days after Frost's tenth brithday in the paper his father worked for, the *San Francisco Daily Evening Post*, 29 Mar. 1884, p. 6, col. 1. Thompson reprints it, *EY*, 488-491.

[19] See Langbaum's argument that the power of Browning's dramatic monologues is attributable to "tension between sympathy and moral judgment": *The Poetry of Experience* (1957; rpt. New York: W. W. Norton and Company, 1963), pp. 85-92.

learned to find "consolation for the difficulties of her sor-
rowful life" through visionary experience (EY, xvi). Given
her unusual blend of religious conviction and artistic as-
piration, it is not surprising that her version of what
Thompson labels "the Romantic doctrine concerning the
sacred and prophetic function of the artist" (EY, 629)
should have been a late-Romantic version, emphasizing
the pain, the loneliness, and the self-sacrifice involved in
an artistic struggle against the ugliness of a scornful, ma-
terialistic world. And, given her dominant role in her
son's upbringing and schooling, it is not surprising that
he should have grown up thinking of the artist as part
romantic hero and part passionate martyr.[20]

His was not a happy childhood: its tensions and insecu-
rities interfered with his education (he became sick to his
stomach at the prospect of going to school) and kept him
sleeping in his mother's room until age eighteen. Against
such an unpleasant background, her literary interests and
her encouragement of his imaginative faculties must have
provided relief from the difficulties of *his* sorrowful life.
Urged to explore his fantasies and to listen for inner
voices, Frost used details from a dream to produce his first
composition even before he left San Francisco. It reveals
that his mother's Romantic attitudes, especially her belief
that the hero must be prepared for isolation and persecu-
tion, had made a deep impression on him. In the story
(summary, EY, 37-38), the hero runs away from home and
becomes lost in the mountains. He soon finds a charmed,
hidden valley and is "welcomed and honored as a hero by
a tribe of Indians" for whom the valley is a place of refuge
and a staging ground for intermittent sallies against
enemies in the outside world.

Surely the basic pattern of this youthful tale—our first
evidence of Frost's imaginative bent—is similar to that of

[20] Frost was taught by his mother at home in San Francisco (first
through third grades); he attended third grade briefly in Lawrence (fall
1885), then was a student in his mother's school in Salem Depot for
grades four through eight. See EY, 21-23, 58-59, 73.

his mother's poem: both heroes turn away from the world of men, and by bravely facing solitude they at last become magically ennobled. Hence, we should recognize that the young poet's tastes were not shaped solely by pure New England influences. Emerson may have been Mrs. Frost's favorite poet, but there is no reason to assume that this preference was transferred to her son. On the contrary, with regard to the poet's role and with regard to poetic style, he seems to have been most stimulated by some of the other poets she introduced to him. From what we can see, his early predisposition was toward the imaginative concerns of the poets he read avidly during his adolescence. Fleeing, escaping, seeking concealment; being lost, outcast, and outlawed; gaining mysterious, unexpected recognition as a hero; experiencing the abnormal and even the immoral—these elements were less appropriate to nature poetry than to the exotic, adventurous fantasies of Keats, Shelley, Poe, Arnold, and Browning.

The Wanderer Among Ideas

When Frost began to write poetry in the spring of 1890 (about the time of his sixteenth birthday), he relied on literary rather than regional or natural sources. Most of his initial compositions remained unpublished or uncollected until texts and pertinent scholarly information appeared in *Robert Frost: The Early Years* and Thompson and Lathem's *Robert Frost: Poetry and Prose*. There are still problems, of course, with the dating of some poems, but Thompson's diligent research at last establishes a workable basis for discussion.

Certainly, the record is now clear enough to substantiate that Frost's earliest work reflected the verse his mother had encouraged and prepared him to enjoy. Three of his first pieces—"La Noche Triste," "A Dream of Julius Caesar," and "Caesar's Lost Transport Ships"—use heroic, historical material and bespeak the young poet's affinity with many nineteenth-century Romantics who turned to traditional sources in their early verse.

"La Noche Triste" was probably Frost's first poem,[21] and its ornate, martial imagery and diction, along with the pounding ballad-stanza cadences (only three enjambed lines in twenty-five stanzas), show that the novice poet was struggling to adopt a voice suited to his heroic tale (the Spaniards' flight from Tenochtitlan, which he had read about in W. H. Prescott's *The Conquest of Mexico*). Archaisms abound: a war cry "soundeth," a mace "crasheth." Poetic contractions appear in almost every stanza. But perhaps the most obvious clue to the young writer's quest for heightened poetic language is his predilection for bombastic clichés: "The sound of ill portent"; "He died at duty's call"; "worked with might and main"; "all is lost"; "ages yet to come"; "His faithful charger"; "Pierced to the very heart"; "The deed is done." There may be parallels between this poem and the youthful extravagance of Keats's "Calidore," Poe's *Tamerlane*, and Arnold's "Alaric at Rome," but it is difficult to make comparisons favorable to Frost when we find such quatrains as these:

> For darkness of that murky night
> Hides deeds of brightest fame,
> Which in the ages yet to come,
> Would light the hero's name.
>
> .   .   .   .
>
> Upon the ground the dead men lie,
> Trampled midst gold and gore,
> The Aztec toward his temple goes,
> For now the fight is o'er.

Pyrotechnical poetic effects reminiscent of Keats and Poe are especially evident in "A Dream of Julius Caesar," with its exotic, luxurious diction and its mystical and fantastic vision of Caesar.[22] Written a year after "La Noche

---

[21] "La Noche Triste," Lawrence, Mass., *High School Bulletin* (1890); reprinted in *P&P*, 190-194. Thompson discusses composition but does not print the full text in *EY*, 93-94.

[22] "A Dream of Julius Caesar," Lawrence, Mass., *High School Bulletin* (1891); reprinted in *P&P*, 195-197.

Triste" and displaying more control and poise, it opens amid a conventionally idyllic landscape, replete with murmuring breezes, "sylvan shades," "fleecy clouds," and "a purling rill" (ll. 2, 3, 12). The speaker is a dreamer who finds himself charmed by nature's "circle of / Enchantment" and a "thrush's drowsy note" into a reverie of "flitting thoughts and dreams of bygone years" (ll. 5, 7-9). Soon, however, an approaching storm disrupts his idyll:

> a timely warning to the one
> Who, wandering far from shelter and from home,
> Forgets that space exists, that still he lives:—
> But wrapped in Nature's all entrancing shroud,
> Is lured to seek her wildest inmost realms.
>
> (17-21)

Beyond the threat of the storm, a greater danger seems to lie in the very act of contemplating nature. There are dark, mysterious connotations to the "entrancing shroud," and a nightmarish, deathly quality tinges the speaker's dream of being "lured" into "wildest inmost realms," realms in which no poet would be more at home than Edgar Allan Poe. As dark clouds advance, Frost exorcises his poem's idyllic spirit with a description of "woodland nymphs" in flight from the tempest, ascending shafts of sunlight that "stretch down / Upon each grove and mead" (ll. 29-34).

Just before the storm, Julius Caesar "glides down" one of the last sunbeams and confronts the speaker:

> With stately mien and noble wreathed brow,
> His toga streaming to the western wind,
> The restless fire still gleaming in those eyes. . . .
>
> (39-41)

Clearly, Caesar is the storm personified, with a billowing, cloudlike toga and lightning in his eyes. Frost even endows him with Jove's thunderbolt and a passion "to rule with storm and darkness o'er the world." The nightmare reaches its cataclysmic climax (ll. 61-64) as Caesar urges his "cohorts" to "spread terror in the air and vanquish

light." Although the imagery may be strained, Frost's jux-
taposition of the storm's force and Caesar's imperial
power is far from incompetent. Amid "the roar / Of chariot
wheels," the carnage begins. But the closing lines offer a
disturbing imagistic twist:

> blood in torrents falls around,
> Not crimson, but a lighter hue, such as
> The fairy hosts of silvery light might shed.

>   (65-67)

Using the blood of battle as a trope for torrential rain is
only a logical extension of the original formula, yet Frost
adds a brilliantly unexpected ingredient by linking the
victims of the slaughter, the "fairy hosts of silvery light,"
with the sunbeam-climbing "woodland nymphs" who
had seemed to climb to safety before the storm began.
Thus, with considerable sophistication for a seventeen-
year-old poet, he not only develops his extended meta-
phor, but also succeeds in undercutting the idyllic con-
ventions of the poem's first section. Through the initial
contemplation of nature, he creates certain expectations,
only to shatter them with the fantastic vision of storm and
terror—a vision so elaborately contrived that it seems less
a rendering of Caesar than a calculated exercise of the art-
ist's imaginative faculties.

This fledgling poet did not set out to write "descriptive
sketches" of the countryside as Wordsworth did, and
surely it is no New England scene we find in "A Dream of
Julius Caesar." Instead, Frost sought stunning, even
bizarre, effects such as he might have observed in an al-
legorical tour de force like Poe's "The Haunted Palace" or
in the phantasmagorical imagery of a poem by Keats. If his
language lacked the florid Spenserian intensity of the
young Keats or the imaginative brilliance of Poe, it was far
too gaudy for an aspiring Wordsworthian. And during
these years of experimentation, Frost was more concerned
with exploiting powerful poetic techniques than with tak-
ing a consistent point of view or establishing a literary

role for himself. Not the sensitive, philosophical, Words-worthian man speaking to men, he was closer to Keats's "camelion Poet" trying out some of his masks.

"Caesar's Lost Transport Ships" is another early poem on a classical subject that relies heavily on Romantic im-agery, in particular on the mystery and desolation of the sea evoked by Coleridge's "The Rime of the Ancient Mar-iner" and Poe's "MS. found in a Bottle."[23] A ship is seen in ominous silhouette, "full darkly figured on the sun / At sunset." Strange sounds are heard: "all night long a voice made wild lament." Finally, enigmatically, the vessel passes out of sight:

> With no sail set, deserted on the deck,
> And in the hull a tremor of low speech,
> And overhead the petrel wafted wide.

As he gained poetic maturity, Frost turned from classi-cal and historical material; but many of his poems of the 1890s are at least as derivative as those just discussed. Thompson points out that two teen-age efforts, "Clear and Colder—Boston Common" and "The Traitor,"[24] are exper-iments with the ballad stanza "he had been hearing since first his mother showed him her favorites in Scott's *Border Ballads* or in Percy's *Reliques*" (*EY*, 111). "The Traitor" apparently contains a direct allusion to Macpherson's *Ossian*, but its rich sonorities—the assonances, alitera-tion, strong rhyme (particularly the lugubrious "tomb-gloom" combination)—might as easily have been influ-enced by Poe as by the British antiquarians. Moreover, the name Lorna (repeated five times in the five stanzas) reso-nates well with names like Lenore and Eleonora. Frost's final stanza gives the flavor:

---

[23] "Caesar's Lost Transport Ships," *Independent* (1897); reprinted in *P&P*, 197.

[24] "Clear and Colder—Boston Common," never published by Frost, was probably written in 1891. "The Traitor" appeared in the *Phillips An-dover Mirror* (1892). Thompson reprints both poems in *EY*, 110-111, 508-509.

Sea-bird of the battle surf,
　　Lorna is dead,
Black on Colla's castled hill
　　Ruin is spread.
Royal seal upon the tomb
Where he sleeps in endless gloom.

Three other early compositions also seem indebted to Poe. "Song of the Wave," perhaps Frost's second poem, and "Sea Dream," a somewhat later piece, are explorations of an alien submarine world like that of Poe's "The City in the Sea."[25] Frost relies on pulsing rhythms and forceful rhymes (rhymed trochaic tetrameter tercets and lilting ballad stanzas) to capture the auditory richness of Poe's verse; furthermore, he strives for the grotesque and melancholy mood that distinguishes Poe's poems. In the earlier piece, the wave comes to a dark final catastrophe:

Lo! black cliffs above me loom,
Casting o'er me awful gloom,
And foretell my coming doom.

O! that I might reach the land,
Reach and lave the sunny sand
But these rocks on every hand—

Seem my joyous course to stay,
Rise and bar my happy way,
Shutting out the sun's bright ray.

Even more eerie and foreboding is "Sea Dream." Poe's shadowy turrets and towers, which "seem pendulous in air," might well be the source of the "leaning towers" in Frost's stanza:

I went in a great tide under the sea
　　And my robe streamed on before—

[25] "Song of the Wave," Lawrence, Mass., *High School Bulletin* (1890); reprinted in *P&P*, 194-195. Text and discussion of "Sea Dream" are in *EY*, 530-531.

> There were leaning towers as I passed by
> And shells on the dim sea floor.

Neither of Frost's poems develops the visionary power or the imagistic richness of Poe's strange, unforgettable city. But he was not afraid to try, not afraid to explore the unfamiliar—his own "wildest inmost realms."

Still another apprentice piece, "Parting. To — —,"[26] presents a tortured nightmare:

> I dreamed the setting sun would rise no more.
> My spirit fled; nor sought an aimless sun
> Whirled madly on through pathless space, and free
> Amid a world of worlds enthralled.

This distraught nocturnal flight recalls the weird journey—"By a route obscure and lonely / Haunted by ill angels only"—in Poe's "Dream-Land"; Thompson has also linked the poem to "Al Aaraaf" (EY, 115). But Frost falls short of Poe here by losing the incantatory quality that lends his other Poe-esque pieces a measure of *vraisemblance*.

As his youthful compositions indicate, Frost was a knowledgeable teen-ager when it came to poetry. During his teens and twenties, and even in his early thirties, as he struggled haphazardly to grasp the relationship between his individual talent and the poetic tradition, New England held no special meaning for his efforts to develop his artistic potential. Neither the honored Yankee writers nor the specific backcountry landscape stimulated his imagination.

Frost's two closest companions during the early period, Elinor White (his wife as of 1895) and Carl Burell, were deeply interested in literature. These three read and discussed poetry together frequently, and of the poets they "discovered" during the 1890s (they were "discoveries" to Frost in that his mother had not introduced them to

---

[26] "Parting. To — —," Lawrence, Mass., *High School Bulletin* (1891); reprinted in *EY*, 116.

THE POET IN THE MAKING **59**

him), the one who seems to have influenced Frost most immediately was one against whom he finally reacted: Percy Bysshe Shelley. Though two other "discoveries," Edward Rowland Sill and Emily Dickinson, remained of interest throughout his life, neither had much effect on his early development.[27] Shelley, however, deserves recognition as a major figure in Frost's literary adolescence. Representing the sort of Romanticism that Mrs. Frost distrusted, his grandiose vision of the artist was linked to religious skepticism and moral rebelliousness. It must have seemed a daring and exciting challenge to maternal authority.

Frost's friend Carl Burell was influential during this Shelleyan phase. Nearly ten years older than Frost, he had returned to high school after an absence of several years. His personal library impressed his young friend, and his interests ran not only to poetry, but also to evolutionary theory and controversy. He prided himself, needless to say, on his curiosity and open-mindedness. Mrs. Frost suspected him of "exerting a bad influence on her son."[28] Soon Shelleyan beliefs, especially with regard to personal and sexual freedom, were also part of Frost's relationship with his other close friend, Elinor White. Thompson de-

[27] The claim that Sill's "simplicities of . . . poetic diction" influenced Frost has been made in Horace Gregory and Marya Zaturenska, "The Horatian Serenity of Robert Frost," in *A History of American Poetry 1900-1940* (New York: Harcourt, Brace and Company, 1946), pp. 152-154. Yet such a theory hardly fits with the poetry Frost wrote in the 1890s. Sill's devotion to Tennyson has been documented by A. R. Ferguson in *Edward Rowland Sill: The Twilight Poet* (The Hague: Martinus Nijoff, 1955), and this is probably the source of Frost's interest. Certainly, as his admiring reference to Tennyson in the letter he wrote to Susan Hayes Ward on 22 April 1894 (*SL*, 20) shows, he had not at that time developed his opposition to Tennysonian diction. Similarly, while he may well have enjoyed Dickinson, as Thompson says, for "her terse, homely, gnomic, cryptic, witty qualities" (*EY*, 124), these qualities are not typical of his early work.

[28] I am indebted to Thompson's descriptions of Frost's relationship with Burell. See *EY*, 88-90, 94-95, 99-100, 119, 143-144, 156, 216-223, 263-278.

scribes the young couple's attachment to Shelley and their secret exchange of Shelleyan marriage vows in 1892 (EY, 136-137).

Making a Romantic commitment in the early 1890s to his art, his friends, and a style of life, Frost saw himself as one of a select band of open-minded freethinkers, the "wanderers among ideas," as he approvingly labeled them in an editorial he wrote for the Lawrence *High School Bulletin* (1892; rpt. *P&P*, 204). His high school valedictory speech, which Thompson terms a "Shelleyan defense of poetry," also paid homage to "the heroism of genius" that elevated great thinkers above mere "conventionalities."[29] To demonstrate his own disregard for the conventional, Frost took the gold medal awarded him for his outstanding high school career and sold it the day after graduation. The "wanderer among ideas" could be skeptical and intractable. He did not settle down to a college career or a steady job; he was willing to investigate and experiment; and he would not accommodate himself to orthodoxies. He had a lofty vision, one that he did not expect the world to understand. As Frost wrote in the gloss to *A Boy's Will*:

> The youth is persuaded that he will be rather more
>   than less himself for having forsworn the world.
> He is happy in society of his own choosing.
> He is in love with being misunderstood.
>
> (P, 529)

When first presenting himself to the literary world in 1894 (primarily to Susan Hayes Ward, literary editor of *The Independent* in New York), Frost played the arch-Romantic: the unappreciated, misunderstood, excruciatingly sensitive artist. He courted Miss Ward (who, as a fellow poet, might understand) with elaborately wrought confessions: "to betray myself utterly, such an one am I

---

[29] "A Monument to After-thought Unveiled"; text and commentary in *EY*, 128-132.

that even in my failures I find all the promise I require to justify the astonishing magnitude of my ambition." These exquisite phrases and lofty sentiments appear in Frost's first letter to Miss Ward—a clear attempt to demonstrate his qualifications as an aspiring member of the literary community. Though reading "a great deal" when well, he was often "irresponsibly iratable [sic] to the last degree" and thus unable to work. "It is due to my nerves," he explained, "they are susceptible to sound." In his good moments, however, he applied himself to the study of Greek and, "for relaxation," to French, to Romantic novels ("Scott and Stevenson inspire me"), and to poetry: "my favorites are and have been these: Keats' "Hyperion," Shelley's "Prometheus," Tenneson's [sic] "Morte D'Arthur," and Browning's "Saul"—all of them about the giants. Besides these I am fond of the whole collection of Palgrave's" (SL, 20-21).

"My Butterfly," Frost's first contribution to The Independent, displays an immature fascination with fullblown Romantic diction and with high sentiment. The years of apprenticeship enabled him to capture some of the richness of Keats, the strained, exotic imagery of Shelley, and the musical sonority of Tennyson:

> Thine emulous fond flowers are dead too,
> And the daft sun-assaulter, he
> That frighted thee so oft, is fled or dead. . . .

The poem is impressive, but the poet's hand is everywhere too evident. The imagery cloys. The "emulous fond flowers" and the "daft sun-assaulter," the "reckless zephyr" and the "dye-dusty wing" all have their power, and perhaps Keats or Shelley might have employed them effectively. But here they seem only pretentious echoes of a superannuated rhetoric.

Furthermore, there is too much decorative musicality in these lines for the poem's humble elegiac material. Frost later complimented himself on the second stanza, claiming that it "was when I first struck the note that was to be mine" (SL, 527). But despite his dexterity with rhyme and rhythm, assonance and alliteration, his evocation of the lost romance of summer does not succeed:

> The grey grass is scarce dappled with the snow,
> Its two banks have not shut upon the river,
>> But it is long ago,
> It seems forever,
> Since first I saw thee glance
> With all the dazzling other ones,
>> In airy dalliance.
>> Precipitate in love,
> Tossed up, tossed up, and tangling, above,
> Like a limp rose-wreath in a fairy dance.[30]

Some of these lines are splendid, especially the first two, which evoke the bleak, subdued autumnal setting. Frost picks up the vowel sound of the short a in "grass," "dappled," and "banks" and uses the assonance and rhymes of "glance," "dazzling," "dalliance," "tangling," and "dance" (along with the alliterative t's and d's) to give the stanza a kind of musical unity.

Regrettably, however, the remembered beauty of lepidopteral flirtation in the summer "long ago" lacks the force of Frost's best verse. The imprecise and unrhymed pronoun "ones" disrupts the flow of the stanza's three central lines: "I saw thee glance / With all the dazzling other ones, / In airy dalliance." The words "dalliance" and "precipitate" seem poorly matched. The former, with its Gallic flavor, its soft lateral and sibilant sound quality, and its sense of lazy relaxation, clashes with the latter, a crisp Latinate word full of explosive p's and t's and suggestive of speed, force, and finality. The contradictory connotations of the two words blur the stanza's central effect, and a succession of incongruous images ("tossed up, tangling, like a limp rose-wreath") leaves us without a

---

[30] I have used the 1894 manuscript version of the poem, which is printed in P&P, 208-209. The various printed texts in The Independent, A Boy's Will, and P differ slightly.

clear impression of the beauty the speaker seeks to elegize.

Among the other poems Frost wrote and published during the 1890s, few are as distinctive as "My Butterfly," and fewer still would distinguish their author as anything other than a struggling practitioner in the late-Romantic tradition. There are several sentimental love poems: four went into *Twilight*, the little book he had printed for himself and Elinor in 1894; two others, "Warning" and "The Birds do Thus," appeared in *The Independent*. A moralistic, biblical piece, "God's Garden," and an incidental poem, "Greece" (inspired by the Greco-Turkish War of 1896-1897), were published in the *Boston Evening Transcript*. But throughout the period, as Frost played the wanderer among ideas, attending two colleges and taking jobs sporadically as teacher, mill worker, and news reporter, he never thought of himself as a New England poet, and he certainly did not encourage anyone else to regard him that way.

Nevertheless, despite the thoroughness of Thompson's biography, scholars still perpetuate discredited notions about Frost's commitment to farming. One of the most recent studies, for instance, asserts that the Frosts were married "without any evident means of support except Frost's intention to be a farmer."[31] This not only distorts the poet's relationship with his wife, but it also misrepresents his basic outlook during the 1890s. In fact, he was working as a teacher at the time of his marriage, and Thompson indicates that the prospect of his continuing a career in education hastened Elinor's agreement to a wedding in 1895 (EY, 201-213). Furthermore, it was in pursuit of this career that Frost subsequently undertook two years of study at Harvard, hardly a training ground for prospective farmers. Even when he finally did begin raising chickens, there is no reliable evidence that he had a serious "intention to be a farmer."

[31] Poirier, *Robert Frost: The Work of Knowing* (New York: Oxford University Press, 1977), p. 102.

In truth, the young Frost was a much more dedicated littérateur than he liked to admit in later years. And this is no minor point. By ignoring it, observers have misconstrued the shape and dynamics of his development. He was, after all, over twenty-six when he moved to the Derry farm in 1900. He had been writing, reading, and thinking seriously about poetry for ten years, and his modest experiments had won him the attention of two editors, Miss Ward and Charles Hurd of the *Boston Evening Transcript*. Six poems were published in the 1890s; beyond these, he was accumulating a substantial pile of unpublished verse, from which several pieces were to appear in future collections of his work. In years afterward, the very existence of this material written *before* the Derry period constituted such a threat to Frost's Derry myth that he was reluctant to admit authorship of many youthful compositions. In 1928, for instance, when the Huntington Library acquired the files of *The Independent* and unearthed thirty-eight manuscripts Frost had sent to Miss Ward, his dissatisfaction was evident in the disingenuousness of his response (SL, 354-355). First, he disclaimed all but four of the poems, but then—revealingly—he inquired about suppressing the thirty-four he supposedly had not written!

Going Literally into the Wilderness

Prior to 1900, Frost's experience in rural New England was limited. He had always enjoyed visiting the country, of course, but during his first twenty-five years he generally went there—after the fashion of city people—on vacation. His longest trips north of Boston had been to Dartmouth in 1892 and to a rented cottage near Concord, New Hampshire, where he spent his honeymoon in 1896. Although he visited a farm owned by his uncle, Benjamin Messer, and another owned by one of the family's many landlords, Loren Bailey, he had only experienced real farm life once, and it had not excited his interest in agricultural work or rural poetry.

Ironically, when Frost, who was to become New Hampshire's twentieth-century "Rustic Bard," took a summer job as a farmhand in 1891, he happened to work on the very farm where New Hampshire's nineteenth-century "Rustic Bard," Robert Dinsmore (the original farmer poet extolled by Whittier), had cultivated his potatoes and poems more than sixty years before. It is indicative of Frost's early indifference to New England's rural literature that he never realized the significance of the Dinsmore farm. Furthermore, his distant relationship to the farm country is suggested by his inability to get along with the other hired hands or with Dinsmore's descendants. After only three weeks, he ran away—too discomfited to ask for his pay—and returned home with complaints about "the coarseness, the profanity" of rural folk.[32]

With this incident in mind, and with Frost's generally urban and sophisticated background taken into account, we should be able to appreciate—as many commentators have *not*—that the move to Derry was a departure into an alien world. Peter Davison and Archibald MacLeish are among the few critics who have noted the element of risk in Frost's frightening exploration into "foreign lands."[33] Like the couple in the poem "In the Home Stretch," the Frosts sensed that they were outsiders in the rural world, and they worried about exchanging their "lighted city streets . . . for country darkness" (P, 112).

One of the most frequently overlooked facts behind Frost's decision to take up farming is that it was not a reckless choice, as he often boasted, but a matter of medical advice. His physician, suspecting nervous fatigue or consumption, wanted to move the patient "out-of-doors and give him plenty of exercise" (EY, 251). Yet, contrary

[32] Thompson recounts Frost's unhappy experience at the Dinsmore farm, EY, 103-106. Neither he nor any of Frost's other biographers have noted that the John H. Dinsmore for whom Frost worked was the grandson of the "Rustic Bard."

[33] Peter Davison, "The Self-Realization of Robert Frost, 1911-1912," *New Republic*, 170 (30 Mar. 1974), 18. MacLeish's article is discussed in Chap. 1 above.

to the impression created by the Derry myth, Frost's involvement with farm work was often casual and haphazard. Although he liked to claim that he went to Derry alone, a "fugitive from the world" (SL, 158), his grandfather—far from telling him to "go out and die," as another favorite tale has it (see EY, 261, 547)—had taken the trouble to arrange for Carl Burell and *his* grandfather, Jonathan Eastman, to go with the Frosts and run all aspects of the farm save the poultry. So long as these two "helpers" remained, the enterprise was a success. But after the elder man died in 1902, Carl, at odds with Frost, left almost immediately, and the farm soon began to deteriorate. Frost was still unversed in such fundamental country arts as milking and stripping a cow. His awkwardness around livestock, his distaste for regular chores, his frail constitution, his fears of darkness, storms, and tramps, his difficulty in rising early in the morning, and his general inexperience with the basic elements of rustic husbandry all contributed to his unsuitability for farm life.[34]

Following his grandfather's death in 1901, Frost began to receive an annuity of $500 every July, which helped him to recognize that "it was time he stopped pretending he was a farm-poultryman" (EY, 315). He allowed his flock of chickens to dwindle and took up teaching at Pinkerton Academy in 1906. By the terms of his grandfather's will, however, he had to wait five more years, until 1911, before the farm was legally his to sell. Nevertheless, he moved his family to an apartment in Derry Village in 1909, leaving the farm "so badly neglected" that when he finally sold it he could only get about two-thirds of the initial purchase price (EY, 367).

Frost lived an isolated life in Derry. Like the professor in "A Hundred Collars" who visits country folk "he somehow can't get near," he was kept at arm's length by

[34] For the circumstances surrounding Carl Burell's departure from the farm and the evidence of Frost's difficulties as a farmer, see EY, 277-282.

locals who disliked his city-bred traits: his laxness in the management of his farm, his carelessness about debts and other obligations, his "independent" income, and his indulgence in lengthy vacations and an assortment of expensive, impractical sleighs and sulkies. By 1906 the wanderer among ideas was "on speaking terms with only a few people."[35]

Thus it seems regrettable that general readers are still exposed to persistent inanities like the fallacy that Frost "farmed for ten years among the well-wooded hills."[36] Since his two partners did most of the farming until 1902, and since he began teaching in 1906, his career as a serious farmer could have been no longer than four years; Thompson observes that even during these years Frost displayed "less interest in farming than in literary matters" (EY, 286). He maintained his correspondence with Miss Ward, and by and large he maintained his identity as a cosmopolitan, late-Romantic artist. In fact, he was extremely reticent about the farm activities that a few years later he began to describe proudly, even garrulously. Whatever references he did make to his rustication were apologetic and often accompanied by hints that this too would pass. "The great thing," he observed to Miss Ward in 1906, "is to get out where one can be read" (SL, 36).

Until he could "get out," Frost wanted Miss Ward to know that he was *au courant* with the latest developments in the arts. His correspondence reveals a consistent interest in the sophisticated literary world that Miss Ward represented and that he actually visited three times during the Derry period (in 1903, 1907, and 1911). In one letter he was coy enough to apologize for "our provincialism" even as he did his best to disprove it by encouraging her to see "a few selected operas at one house or the other" (SL, 38). The reference to two opera houses is especially

[35] *Ibid.*, 313. For instances of local antagonism toward Frost, see *ibid.*, 276, 285, 313-316.

[36] Robert Graves, "Introduction" to *Selected Poems of Robert Frost* (New York: Holt, Rinehart and Winston, 1963), pp. xi-xii.

esoteric: a cultivated New Yorker like Miss Ward would have appreciated this allusion to the "war" between the established Metropolitan Opera House and Oscar Hammerstein's gaudy upstart, the Manhattan Opera. "Sometime we intend to be nearer New York than we are," he wrote in 1907; but he feared that poetry would "be less likely to bring us there than prose" (SL, 40). While reluctantly suggesting that he might have to sacrifice his career as a poet, he did not mention, nor did he seem to regret, the contingent sacrifice of his life as a farmer.

Despite moments of doubt and despair, Frost kept writing poetry. It varied widely in form and quality, and he lacked the standards and the critical perspective to evaluate it. He failed to recognize which pieces showed the most promise, and he was uncertain about how to develop his art. In 1906 he vowed to Miss Ward: "I shall get the right tone yet, give me time." Five years later he was still apologizing that his "long deferred forward movement" would have to be delayed another year (SL, 37, 43). His problem was that he had not yet made the crucial decision about what the "right tone" would involve. As late as 1912, when he selected and arranged the material for A Boy's Will, he did not have a confident grasp of the tone that began to seem "right" for him just a few months later: the tone (or the blend of tones) exhibited in North of Boston. Prior to 1913 his failure to develop solid critical judgment resulted in inconsistencies of style and an uncertain control of theme and imagery. But a still more serious consequence of his irresolution was his inability to appreciate the advances he made during and even before the Derry period. We can see in retrospect that when he worked on poems like "The Tuft of Flowers" in the late 1890s, "Mowing" around 1901, or "The Death of the Hired Man" and "An Old Man's Winter Night" in 1905 or 1906,[37] he was moving away from Romantic habits—the

[37] Thompson discusses the composition of these poems in EY, 235, 274-275, 428, 550.

vaguely derivative effusions, the conventionally heightened and melodized diction—he had cultivated during the nineties. But he failed to capitalize on his progress. Each movement toward vigorous and original language, toward vividly imagined experiences and emotions, was followed by other poems that, despite flashes of brilliance, seem less than worthy of Frost at his best.

"The Tuft of Flowers" is generally recognized as the earliest of Frost's distinctive regional poems. With its end-stopped heroic couplets, its rather saccharine imagery and tidy moral, and its " 'wildered butterfly . . . on tremulous wing" (a bit too reminiscent of that earlier elegized butterfly),[38] it is less subtle and original than his most impressive work. Yet it has a pristine simplicity, a naive musicality, and an epigrammatic inevitability that he surpassed only in "Stopping by Woods on a Snowy Evening." Its central image, the "leaping tongue of bloom," gives eloquent expression to the reassuring "message from the dawn." The first mower's love of nature is appropriately and movingly communicated to the speaker (and to the reader) through this magnificent natural symbol.

In the context of Frost's poetic output during the 1890s, "The Tuft of Flowers" is especially noteworthy as an early experiment with regional material. At that time, however, his most extended rustic experience was the three-week fiasco on the Dinsmore farm six years earlier. Thus his speaker, though explicitly identified as a fieldworker, does not reflect a convincingly local sensitivity. The stilted, bookishly orotund language gives him away: "swift there passed me by"; "memories grown dim o'er-night"; "a spirit kindred to my own"; "held brotherly speech" (ll. 11, 13, 33, 37). Nevertheless, compared with Frost's earlier sentimental love poems like "Warning" (1895) and "The Birds Do Thus" (1896), "The Tuft of

---

[38] In early editions of *A Boy's Will* Frost used the poetic " 'wildered" to strengthen the iambic rhythm.

Flowers" represents a step forward. It is an initial attempt to confront a Wordsworthian situation "from common life," and it focuses—though somewhat distantly and uncertainly—on a common man, the farmworker.

A few other poems from the 1890s foreshadow the incipient regionalism of "The Tuft of Flowers." Lawrance Thompson has rightly called attention to the very early piece, "Now Close the Windows" (dating from Frost's semester at Dartmouth in 1892), as a "lyric symbol of Frost's moving out into his own for poetic gain."[39] But this first poetic exploration of the New England countryside does not establish the speaker's regional identity (as "The Tuft of Flowers" does); rather, it seems to be the utterance of a conventional poet, a figure distinguished only by his Romantically forlorn posture. Similarly, in "My Butterfly" and "Flower-Gathering," although Frost deals with the natural world, his speakers are not convincingly located in it. They might as easily be British as American. Instead of expressing their personal vision of a particular region, they evoke the generally familiar landscape of traditional nature poetry.

About 1901, several years after writing "The Tuft of Flowers," Frost returned to the one major innovation he had tried in it. In "Mowing" he captured the mower's voice much more effectively than he had in his first attempt. He threw off the showy mantle of the nineteenth-century poet to such good effect that he produced one of the finest sonnets of the modern period—the irregularly rhymed piece in which he first demonstrated mastery of his craft.

His greatest attainment in "Mowing" was the virtual elimination of distance between his speaker and the regional world of the poem. Instead of parading the "poetical" voice he had cultivated during his years of apprenticeship, he struck boldly at the unadorned poetic power

[39] Thompson, *Fire and Ice: The Art and Thought of Robert Frost* (New York: Henry Holt Co., 1942), p. 99.

of human speech, aiming not to describe or comment, but to dramatize the personal engagement of a regional character in specific, rustic activity. By moving closer to his regional material—in fact, by assimilating the mower's identity—he endowed "Mowing" with a depth and vibrancy that "The Tuft of Flowers," for all its charm, cannot approach. Although the persona in the earlier poem is supposed to be a fieldworker, we never observe him in the act of mowing. He is characterized not by concrete involvement with the local scene, but by his commentary and moral embroidery on it. The active regional figure, the man who had indeed mowed the field, is offstage. "Mowing" obliterates this separation: its vision is supported by the speaker's actual effort as a mower. When he refers to his "long scythe whispering to the ground" (l. 2) the full force of his experience is conveyed through imagery that has an organic centrality to the poem. As we read on, we appreciate that the meaning of the scythe's whisper is bound up with the labor of which it is a byproduct, and we share the speaker's exploration of this meaning.

By a strange coincidence, Frost also happened to use the same image (even the same six-word phrase) of the "long scythe whispering to the ground" in "The Tuft of Flowers" (l. 32). But there it is merely a graceful metaphorical way of alluding to the earlier mower's effort. The whispering sound, coming not from the speaker's own scythe, could only be posited speculatively. Since the speaker gives no consideration to the actual meaning of what was whispered, the image remains a conventional figure of speech. Compared with its vigorous resonance in "Mowing," its contribution to "The Tuft of Flowers" is little more than a measure of decorative rhetoric.

As this comparison suggests, Frost broke important new ground in "Mowing." In exploring regional experience more closely than he ever had, he began to stake out rich and invigorating linguistic territory. Unfortunately, throughout the Derry period he never fully appreciated or exploited his discoveries. It was not until a dozen years after writing this extraordinary sonnet that he recognized its significance. While writing a series of letters during the summer of 1913 to announce the theories on which his best work was founded, he at last realized that the "right tone" he had sought during the Derry years had actually been present all along in one of the first poems produced on the farm. While struggling to find his poetic voice, he had never paid much attention to "Mowing," but in 1913 he singled it out for praise. A letter to Thomas B. Mosher (17 July 1913) cites it as an approximation of his ideal: "I come so near what I long to get that I almost despair of coming nearer."[40] Precisely what it was that he had "come so near" he at last defined in a momentous letter to John Bartlett (4 July 1913) as the "vitality of our speech": "if one is to be a poet he must learn to get cadences by skillfully breaking the sounds of sense with all their irregularity of accent across the regular beat of the metre" (SL, 80).

Although less irregular and less intricately varied than some of Frost's mature poems, "Mowing" is a masterful example of irregular accents breaking across a regular beat. None of its lines contains five regular iambic feet. Only three lines (5, 11, and 12) are decasyllabic; in the rest, anapests are mixed with the predominant iambs (and occasional pyrrhic, spondaic, or trochaic feet) to produce seven lines with eleven syllables, three with twelve, and one with thirteen. Frost keeps control of the rhythm by consistently using irregular feet in the first part of each line (iambs appear less than half the time in the first three feet) and then reestablishing a solid iambic rhythm in the closing feet (the fourth foot is iambic in every line except the sixth and ninth, and the *only* irregular final foot is the anapest at the end of line 4).

[40] SL, 83. A letter to Sidney Cox (Dec. 1914) reaffirms the position: "I guess there is no doubt that ['Mowing'] is the best poem in Book I. We all think so over here" (SL, 141).

Frost's concentration on the sound of his speaker's voice in "Mowing" led him to adopt a subtle and sophisticated rhyme scheme in which the rhyming words are separated by at least two lines (even the one exception, the closing rhyme of *snake* and *make* in lines 12 and 14, is separated by line 13 to avoid the familiar poetic effect of the Shakespearian sonnet's final couplet). This subdued rhyme, together with the shifting rhythms, enables him to spin out contemplative sentences without letting poetic form obtrude. A rather loose, wandering, repetitive quality in the opening lines establishes the speaker's reflectiveness. The unemphatic verb "was" appears near the beginning of the opening line and is repeated early in the second, third, fourth, sixth, and seventh lines. The second and sixth lines begin with the same three words, "And that was. . . ." And there are numerous other repetitions: "sound" in lines 1 and 5, the root "whisper" in lines 2, 3, and 6, and the casual chiasmus of "Perhaps it was something . . . / Something perhaps" in lines 4 and 5. The speaker makes a relaxed effort at definition in these lines, shifting the ideas in his mind as he swings the scythe back and forth through the hay.

After this initial discursiveness, a single sentence dominates the central section of the sonnet, building gradually through six lines (ll. 7-12) toward the two decisive sentences (ll. 13 and 14) that provide a forceful, dignified closure:

It was no dream of the gift of idle hours,
Or easy gold at the hand of fay or elf:
Anything more than the truth would have seemed too
  weak
To the earnest love that laid the swale in rows,
Not without feeble-pointed spikes of flowers
(Pale orchises), and scared a bright green snake.
The fact is the sweetest dream that labor knows.
My long scythe whispered and left the hay to make.

(7-14)

The first two lines of the long central sentence (ll. 7-8) are negative definition. By indicating what the scythe did *not* whisper, the speaker moves forward from the vagueness of the opening lines to his first commitment to truth (l. 9) and love (l. 10), commitments that are finally subsumed in the climactic affirmation of line 13. But first, before that broad affirmation, he seems to digress, straining the syntax of an already lengthy sentence, to introduce the most vivid physical details in the poem: the decapitated orchises and the snake. A side effect of mowing is that flowers are reduced to stubble, and Frost uses a double interruption to dramatize his speaker's deep sensitivity to the natural world in which he works. First, the brilliant image in line 11 reveals concern for the orchid's pathetic death. Only someone who appreciates delicate floral textures and colors would give such emphasis to the distressingly cold, metallic futility of the truncated stalks, the "feeble-pointed spikes." Second, the parentheses in line 12 poignantly identify the flowers that no longer exist. So extended are these logical and syntactical disruptions that they threaten the connection between the verb "scared" in line 12 and its subject, "earnest love," in line 10. Nevertheless, Frost does not use the digression to indulge in mere rhetorical artifice. Instead, stressing observed details and evoking the speaker's response to them, he makes effective preparation for his moving tribute to "the fact" in the concluding lines. The poem gives vibrant animation to the rustic act of mowing; mowing is in turn an act of making—a figure of human creativity, of industry and art and love. Hence, what Frost pays tribute to is the "made" or "done" thing, subtly conveyed through the Latin background of the word "fact." The poem itself exemplifies its theme, and, like several of Frost's most profound works, it is in part an exploration in poetics.

Another piece deserving consideration as a forerunner of Frost's greatest regional work is an unpretentious and generally overlooked love poem, "Going for Water."[41]

---

[41] Frank Lentricchia has recently offered a perceptive interpretation of

New England's dry autumn weather provides background for a nocturnal quest that leads the lovers to a precious mystical moment. In moonlit woods, under a spell of romance, playfulness, and reverence, the couple discover a hidden spring, a valuable source in reserve, which Frost presents through images of music and lustrous treasure:

> A note as from a single place,
>   A slender tinkling fall that made
> Now drops that floated on the pool
>   Like pearls, and now a silver blade.

This may be slightly stilted, a bit too transparent and sentimental: under the white heat of objective criticism some dross will float to the surface. Yet Frost was working his way into a vein that would yield nuggets of indisputable purity and consequence. "The Pasture" (perhaps a contemporary piece), "West-Running Brook" (written some two decades later), and "Directive" (two decades later still) are three examples of what could result when he blended the themes of love and inspiration with regionally tinged imagery of the quest and the watering place.

Although a few other Derry poems, such as "Ghost House" and "Storm Fear," follow the lead of "Mowing" and present responses to specific regional settings and situations, their focus on regional "fact" lacks persuasive clarity. They do not achieve the skillful balance of form, imagery, and emotion found in that early sonnet and in the best poems of Frost's maturity. "Ghost House" is graced with touching, if not highly original, images: the raspberry-sprouting cellar hole, the "ruined fences" and resurgent woods, for instance. But the speaker strains too hard for nostalgia and an unmerited self-pity. His expression of his "strangely aching heart" is less convincing than the concretely inspired observations of "Mowing." His mood is suggested by his avowal that he "dwells in a lonely house . . . that vanished many a summer ago" (ll.

---

this poem in *Robert Frost: Modern Poetics and the Landscapes of Self* (Durham: Duke University Press, 1975), pp. 40-43.

1-2). But this is only a metaphorical dwelling, and his precise location in and relationship to the regional world remain undefined. Since we cannot determine what his experience actually is, we have no way of gauging the cause or basis of his heartache. Thus the mood—vaguely enunciated and rather familiar (insofar as we can perceive it)—makes no strong impression. "Storm Fear" is perhaps the most deeply felt poem in *A Boy's Will*, but its speaker's relationship to a hostile nature is not completely plausible; the reader must comprehend a fear for which the poem provides insufficient evidence. Frost's own fears may have made some of the images seem more powerful to him than they do to us. We feel desperation, but not as deeply as the persona does.

"The Vantage Point" and Other Uncertainties

Frost's perplexity about developing his art, even after several years on the Derry farm, is revealed by his failure to take good advantage of earlier and more forceful treatment of regional material in "The Tuft of Flowers" and "Mowing." This was the period of "Into My Own," "A Late Walk," "To the Thawing Wind," "Rose Pogonias," "In a Vale," "A Dream Pang," "The Vantage Point," "The Trial by Existence," "The Demiurge's Laugh." "A Line-Storm Song," "Reluctance"—poems that convey no regional perspective and no forceful concern with New England character or New England life, poems that make *A Boy's Will* an erratic and immature collection.

Indeed, Frost's lack of direction may have been the most important trait camouflaged by the Derry myth. Taken as a group, the poems of *A Boy's Will* indicate that prior to the trip to England he had no clear, stable vision of his role as poet. He had not yet become "one of the few artists"—as he would describe himself to John Bartlett in 1913—"who have a theory of their own upon which all their work down to the least accent is done" (*SL*, 88). As late as 1912, he thought of abandoning poetry so he could "write prose and earn an honest living" (*SL*, 60).

According to his myth, however, Frost found in the rural world at Derry a vantage point from which he was suddenly capable of producing great art—and without which he would never have developed his particular blend of talents, skills, and interests. Concealed behind the myth is the fact that by 1906 he had given up his ineffectual attempts to keep the farm going and turned to teaching at Pinkerton Academy. Thompson, noting Frost's financial reliance on the annuities of his grandfather's will during the Derry period, points out that by the time he took up teaching, "Everyone in the region knew he did very little farming, and not much with hens" (EY, 315). Paradoxically, a poem from this period, the sonnet titled "The Vantage Point," is frequently taken as support for the Derry myth, and many references to it in the critical literature reflect the poet's mythical self-image. But close examination will reveal that when Frost sent the poem to Miss Ward, after abandoning his life as a farmer, he had still *not* recognized either the techniques or the basic purposes that would ultimately characterize his mature work.

Despite some intriguing passages, "The Vantage Point" suffers from uncertainties of diction and an excessively Romantic evocation of its languishing speaker. The stylistic weaknesses of Frost's literary adolescence—the flowery phraseology, the faintly archaic or self-consciously literary language—are present in this sonnet, though less obtrusive here than in his unpublished verse and in other early poems like "In a Vale," "My Butterfly," "A Dream Pang," and "The Trial by Existence":

> If tired of trees I seek again mankind,
>> Well I know where to hie me—in the dawn,
>> To a slope where the cattle keep the lawn.
> There amid lolling juniper reclined,
> Myself unseen, I see in white defined
>> Far off the homes of men, and farther still
>> The graves of men on an opposing hill,
> Living or dead, whichever are to mind.

And if by noon I have too much of these,
 I have but to turn on my arm, and ló,
 The sunburned hillside sets my face aglow,
My breathing shakes the bluet like a breeze,
 I smell the earth, I smell the bruisèd plant,
 I look into the crater of the ant.

Although this attempt to define a vantage point was originally titled "Choice of Society" (in an early draft sent to Miss Ward on 6 August 1907), it does not evoke the Yankee voice that, after the dramatic experiments of *North of Boston*, Frost employed in "Christmas Trees," "New Hampshire," and numerous other regional pieces. There we would never find an obsolete, patently literary phrase like "hie me" (l. 2); nor would we be likely to see metrical accentuation of the sort placed on the normally elided syllable of "bruisèd." Additionally, the syntactical embellishments and extravagances of the second line, "Well I know where to hie me," the fourth, "There amid lolling juniper reclined," and the tenth, "I have but to turn on my arm, and ló," are hardly suited to a "plain New Hampshire farmer." The phrase "lolling juniper," for example, comes perilously close to the "shifted epithet," or hypallage, common in sentimental verse at the turn of the century. Lolling may describe the relaxed persona, but it is not appropriate to such a rugged, prickly shrub as juniper—for Frost, an uncharacteristically imprecise modifier.

More than specific vocabulary, it is Frost's arrangement of words and phrases that creates the slightly elevated and artificial tone, the faint rhetorical flourish of this sonnet. Both octave and sestet begin with parallel, formally balanced "if . . . and if . . ." constructions, and within each section highly complex sentences convey the speaker's vision of mankind (ll. 5-8) and nature (ll. 11-14). In the octave a single sentence stretches for five lines, creating an elaborate syntactical structure around the kernel "I see." Furthermore, we find unusual, poetic-sounding structures like "I see in white defined / Far off the homes of men" (modifying phrases separate verb and object). The sestet follows this long, convoluted clause with a series of six uncomplicated, but artfully constructed, independent clauses. In four of them (ll. 10, 11, 12, and 14) Frost shaped the clause structure to span precisely five iambic feet and thus produce neat, end-stopped lines. The other two clauses are even shorter and simpler. Paired in the poem's penultimate line, they combine the force of anaphora with a strong caesura and still another end-stop to intensify the formal and declamatory quality of the sonnet's closure.

Frost's prosodic skill is evident in "The Vantage Point," but what results is rather literary language. The inversions and syntactical elaborations evoke poetic convention, not a specific personality; hence they are far removed from the distinctive phrasing used to dramatize such speakers as the fieldworker of "Mowing," the contemplative speaker of "Mending Wall," or the shrewd, elliptical farmer of "Christmas Trees." By the time Frost wrote "Something there is that doesn't love a wall" and "Pasture they spring in, some in clumps too close / That lop each other of boughs," he had committed his poetic genius to "the speaking voice" (SL, 151, 159). His departure from common sentence patterns was not a literary affectation, but a calculated effort to establish his speaker's personality.

If "The Vantage Point" lacks the sound of Yankee sense and the subtle touch of New England sensibility that appear in Frost's mature poetry, what we hear instead is surprisingly close to the preciousness, the artfully expressed, self-imposed dejection, and the modish disdainfulness of fin de siècle literature. We hear the voice of a sensitive and perceptive individual, whose studied detachment is belied by his effort to be poetic. And while we may find a certain charm to his observations, we are likely to feel that he presumes too much on our sympathy with his solitary, misanthropic posture. He seems too sure of his own importance, too sure, as Denis Donoghue has observed in a perceptive discussion of the poem, "that he is worthy to adorn any landscape, fit to give it savor, just by being in it. So the world is his backdrop; he has but to pose in an engaging scene and his distinction will be revealed. It is all done with mirrors."[42]

The speaker's overwrought self-centeredness is what makes his hillside vantage point a mere poetic "backdrop." Frost was no Aesthete, and without doubt the differences between him and the Decadent poets of the late nineteenth century are much more significant than the similarities; yet there is an aesthetic quality in his approach to nature in "The Vantage Point," an aestheticism not found in his mature work. Behind his evident appreciation of his own sensibilities lies a preference for art—and an artistic perception of nature—over nature itself. The Aesthete is excessively concerned with the intensity of his response to the world around him; if "tired" of his surroundings, he ceremoniously turns to other things ("whichever are to mind") and probes his reactions to them. This self-concern is central to "The Vantage Point." As Frost strains to express the forlorn pleasure of his speaker's seclusion, the resulting bittersweet sentiments are not unlike those laid bare by such an arch-Decadent as Ernest Dowson, who also paid tribute (in his poem "Beata Solitudo") to the blessings of solitude in a "silent valley,"

> Where all the voices
>   Of humankind
> Are left behind.

> (8-10)

Just as Frost contemplates disengagement from mankind while relaxing "unseen" in the juniper, Dowson longed to be "hid out of sight" and rejoiced at the prospect

[42] Donoghue, "A Mode of Communication: Frost and the 'Middle' Style," *Yale Review*, 52 (Winter 1963), 205.

of leaving the "world forsaken," because he never doubted that nature would accommodate him. In his solitary refuge, he was sure he would "not find / The stars unkind" (ll. 15-20).

Stars will be kind and juniper will loll obligingly for poets who want them to do so. Although nature in Frost's sonnet, with its bluets and ant hills, may be less abstract than Dowson's, it is still only an accessory to the speaker's vantage point. Neither poem presents the meaningfully concrete setting needed for effective regional literature. Frost's secluded slope, like Dowson's silent valley, is not convincingly localized.[43]

In fact, the few memorable lines of Frost's sonnet (the closing portions of the octave and the sestet) do not deal primarily with the vantage point, but with the attitudes and emotions of the speaker—not with his *place* of observation, but with his *mode* of perception. They succeed by capturing the dramatic force of a personality in the process of reflection. Compared with the personae in Frost's mature lyric and dramatic verse, this personality is not especially interesting or convincing, nor are his reflections of great moment. Yet there is an undeniable power to his intricate phrasing, his ostentatiously detached reduction of humanity to a distant collection of vacuously white homes and graves (ll. 5-8). His unsettling vision of mankind, expressed in the dialectical polarities and intertwined contrasts of the second quatrain ("the homes of men . . . the graves of men," "Far off . . . farther still," "Living or dead"), ends with a surprising anticlimax. Having engaged our concern by developing a provocative tension between images of life and death, Frost suddenly undercuts it in line 8 with the premeditated equivocation of what seems to be an indifferent afterthought: "whichever are to mind."

---

[43] The Aesthetic element in "The Vantage Point" is also suggested in Richard Poirier's comparison of the poem with D. G. Rossetti's "The Woodspurge" (Robert Frost: The Work of Knowing, pp. 34-37).

The first five lines of the sestet do not sustain either the unpredictability or the verbal and intellectual complexity that distinguish the closing quatrain of the octave. We have seen too many poets turn to embrace nature. Sunny hillsides and quivering bluets are not now—and were not in 1907—fresh or stimulating images. Rather, they are conventional romantic gestures appealing to the tactile ("my face aglow") and olfactory ("my breathing . . . I smell . . . I smell") senses. Such suggestions of passive sensory receptivity may be appropriate, but they lend no vital or original impetus to the familiar man-versus-nature conflict inherent in the speaker's "choice of society." His unsatisfying relationship to humanity is conveyed in the strained, visually distanced images of the octave, and thus his "choice" of nature and the pleasant sensations it offers is all too foreseeable. Were it not for the final line, the sonnet's conclusion would be little more than an uninspired—and hence debased—reaffirmation of the Wordsworthian creed: "From nature doth emotion come" ("The Prelude," XIII, 1).

Fortunately, however, Frost achieves a masterful closing touch, one that, although it may not save the poem, shows a flash of the imagination that animates his most powerful verse. The sestet's last line revives the eccentric and intriguingly unpredictable sensibility displayed briefly at the conclusion of the octave. Frost shifts from the obvious passive pleasures of touch and smell back to the visual and actively analytical attitude of those earlier lines. He fashions an extraordinarily striking and suggestive image: "the crater of the ant." Through its bizarre, even oxymoronic, juxtaposition of the inhumanly large and inhumanly small, this image gives a disconcerting, incongruous quality to the sonnet's conclusion. Volcanoes have craters, the moon has them, bombarded battlefields have them; but they are not part of the stereotyped natural world the speaker has contemplated up to this point. Thus the line violates both the poetic decorum and the poetic diction supported by most of the sonnet.

Furthermore, since craters are not only huge and inhuman, but also barren, noxious, and (if actively volcanic) destructive, this single word shatters the sestet's idyllic mood of harmony with a benign nature. Frost's speaker does not merely "see" the ant hill, he actively *looks into* it; thus his disturbing image seems to be the result of analysis and reflection. It is subtle, but nonetheless effective, evidence of his recognition that he cannot simply will himself into harmonious union with nature. Turning from mankind to act out the poet's traditional "choice of society," he looks too closely into the natural world and suddenly senses that it too is alien to his sensibilities.

The sonnet's final line, with all the trappings of straightforward, climactic poetic closure, actually undermines the sestet it is supposed to conclude. It dramatizes the unconventional failure of a conventional late-Romantic figure to establish a vantage point from which he can indulge his aestheticism and sentimentality. The reason for his failure, of course, is that he cannot quite perform the role he has tried to adopt. Ironically, it is by failing—and by revealing uneasiness about his adopted role—that he achieves a measure of poetic depth and originality.

As a piece of historical evidence, "The Vantage Point" is probably more important for what it fails to do than for what it accomplishes. Despite its promising touches, Frost had evidently begun to recognize its liabilities by 1912.[44] It really does not portray a "choice of society," since it affirms neither of the alternatives under consideration; so he renamed it, perhaps thinking he could be more convincingly noncommittal about a vantage point than about a choice. In selected editions of 1923, 1928, and 1934, he further weakened the title from "The Vantage Point" (readopted from 1939 on) to "A Vantage Point."

[44] The narrative gloss in early editions of *A Boy's Will* refers apologetically to the poem's scornfulness (P, 530); furthermore, it was one of the poems that Frost in 1915 instructed W. S. Braithwaite not to read (SL, 158).

But insofar as the poem involves a vantage point, the speaker does not take his stand on it or *for* it with much verbal force. It surely provides no protection against the insipidity and overwrought preciousness of the first and third quatrains, nor does it contribute to the sonnet's successful moments. On the contrary, the poem succeeds best when the speaker reveals his uncertainty about the advantages of his vantage point: the self-consciously poetic isolation he has created for himself.

So far as this poem allows us to gauge Frost's artistic progress, it contradicts the myth that his years "in neglect" at Derry involved the discovery of a personally and poetically effective vantage point in rural New England. It shows further that his literary roots reached no more deeply into the native ground of that distinctive region than they did into the richly composted hothouse soil of nineteenth-century Romantic poetry. His late maturity resulted from uncertainties that are easily discernible in "The Vantage Point." Though well over thirty, he was still unsure of his purposes and his identity as a poet. And these uncertainties are attributable not to a Yankee farmer's secluded, unsophisticated background, but to an artist's awareness of and his struggles with the awesome complexity of the tradition he sought to join.

The writer who represented himself so frequently as fleeing, escaping, and hiding, but who never seemed to arrive anywhere in *A Boy's Will*,[45] could find no solid basis or consistent perspective from which to develop his art. To progress in the direction that "The Tuft of Flowers," "Mowing," "Going for Water," "The Death of the Hired Man," and "An Old Man's Winter Night" were leading, Frost had to gain the confidence and control needed to restrain his late-Romantic aestheticism and take advantage of his experience in rural New England. But

[45] Images of flight and concealment are most evident in "Into My Own," "Storm Fear," "Wind and Window Flower," "To the Thawing Wind," "A Dream Pang," "In Neglect," "The Vantage Point," "A Line-Storm Song," and "Reluctance."

when he arrived in England in the fall of 1912, the collection of poems he arranged for publication was firmly in the Romantic tradition. Submerging whatever identity he had acquired as a New Englander, he laboriously constructed a poetic narrative that recounted a sentimental education,[46] a portrait not of the Yankee or even of the American, but of the artist as a young man.[47] Had he died, disappeared, or otherwise ended his literary career in 1912, *A Boy's Will* would have earned him a place in the literary histories as a footnote to the "depressing list," as Roy Harvey Pearce terms it, of *fin de siècle* Romantics. Surely, Pearce's description of these poets, harsh as it is, touches on weaknesses that the young Frost did not escape: "Their poems are, in the bad sense, exercises in rhetoric, too-delicate evocations of the trivial or too-robust summonings-up of the 'sublime.' They feel like poets, but do not write like them—now over-excited, now playing it too safe, utterly at a loss to deal with live situations in live language. . . ."[48]

Although Frost had demonstrated that he could transcend these liabilities, he failed to sustain a mature or consistent poetic stance in *A Boy's Will*, especially in early editions that contained pretentious glosses and such mawkish (and later suppressed) pieces as "Asking for Roses," "In Equal Sacrifice," and "Spoils of the Dead." Strangely, it was his trip to England and his exposure to cosmopolitan literary trends that enabled him to discover the value of his experience in New Hampshire. Once he comprehended the full significance of his own unique vantage point "north of Boston," he soon produced a second collection that revealed his full powers.

[46] For analysis of the narrative elements in *A Boy's Will*, see Donald T. Haynes, "The Narrative Unity of *A Boy's Will*," *PMLA*, 87 (May 1972), 452-464.

[47] Richard Poirier has elucidated several similarities between Frost's and Joyce's versions of a "portrait of the artist as a young man": *Robert Frost: The Work of Knowing*, pp. 28-45.

[48] Pearce, *The Continuity of American Poetry* (Princeton: Princeton University Press, 1961), p. 256.

Three: The Poet from New England (1912-1915)

When he arrived in England in September 1912, Frost had not yet begun to think of himself as a Yankee farmer poet. His Shelleyan independence and intractability were still evident in a letter to Susan Hayes Ward (15 September 1912): "Perhaps I ought not to conceal from you, as one of the very few mortals I feel in any sense answerable to, that I am in the mood called aberrant" (SL, 52). Apparently, he regarded the trip to England as analogous to the earlier move to Derry. "My soul inclines to go apart by itself again and devise poetry," he confessed. He seemed to think he was not a New Englander, but a poet who had visited New England for a while, and who had now decided that a visit to Old England would benefit his artistic soul. He might perhaps move on to France in a year, and after that there was no telling where the Shelleyan wanderer might go. But New England held no more appeal than New York or the Pacific Northwest.[1]

At the close of his letter to Miss Ward, Frost gloated over his proximity to the sacred shrines "where Milton

---

[1] The trip to France was discussed in a letter (25 Oct. 1912) from Elinor Frost to Margaret Lynch (SL, 54). Frost's attraction to New York has already been mentioned, and his interest in moving to Vancouver Island is documented in Margaret B. Anderson, *Robert Frost and John Bartlett: The Record of a Friendship* (New York: Holt, Rinehart and Winston, 1963), pp. 28-32.

finished Paradise Lost . . . where Grey lies buried . . . where Chesterton tries truth. . . ." As he had in earlier years, he played the sophisticate for Miss Ward; but after paying tribute to the British landscape, he offhandedly denied the "virtue" of "Location," a denial that would have been heresy to a true regionalist:

> To London town what is it but a run? Indeed when I leave writing this and go into the front yard for a last look at earth and sky before I go to sleep, I shall be able to see the not very distinct lights of London flaring like a dreary dawn. If there is any virtue in Location—but I don't think I think there is. I know where the poetry must come from if it comes.

It mattered little where the "aberrant" poet went. When his soul needed to "go apart by itself," he was not partial, certainly not attached, to any special "Location." From Frost's point of view in 1912, New England had only been a setting for his sentimental education. Consequently, the product of this period, A Boy's Will, lacks the regional concern that characterizes the work of leading New England authors like Jewett, Robinson, Stowe, and Whittier. Even Longfellow's nostalgic poem, "My Lost Youth"— Frost's source for the title of A Boy's Will—gives much more attention to an identifiably regional setting (Portland, Maine) than does Frost's book.

During the year after his arrival in England, Frost evolved from the promising, yet inconsistent and immature, poet of A Boy's Will to the much more forceful and controlled artist of North of Boston. In the earlier collection, disguising himself here, parading himself there, he exhibited the familiar weaknesses of late Romanticism. A year later, however, no longer victimized by his Romantic background, he began to build on it, creating new and distinctive poetry. This advance involved an unprecedented synthesis of his lengthy apprenticeship to the tradition of nineteenth-century British poetry and his suddenly found appreciation for the literary potential of rural New England.

It was not a gain in poetic skill that enabled him to make such impressive development in a single year. He had long been an accomplished "lyrist," to use Emerson's term. What he had lacked, and what was painfully absent from *A Boy's Will*, was the "metre-making argument," the sense of purpose, the commanding point of view he finally acquired during his first year in England. This new perspective provided *North of Boston* with a depth and vigor often missing in regional literature, and it supplied a cohesive integrity found all too rarely in late-Romantic poetry.

The year from October 1912 to October 1913—the year that began with the submission and acceptance of *A Boy's Will* for publication by David Nutt and Company and ended with the completion of *North of Boston*—was such a crucial period in Frost's career that it ultimately threatened the credibility of the Derry myth. As Frost undertook his public relations campaign, he quickly realized that in order to validate Derry as the source of his artistic development, he would have to maintain that his poetry had never changed, that it was all of a piece. He would have to gloss over the changes and the growth that occurred in 1912 and 1913, and he would have to minimize the differences between *A Boy's Will* and *North of Boston*.

Frost's curious treatment of *A Boy's Will* after 1913 can only be explained in light of the campaign he waged to identify himself as the Yankee farmer poet. It was the only book to be altered for inclusion in collected editions of his poetry. As early as 1914 he had become dissatisfied with the glosses he had concocted in his final burst of Romantic self-revelation. He confessed in a letter to Sidney Cox that they were "a piece of fooling on my part. . . . not necessary and not very good" (SL, 141). Donald T. Haynes has observed that these glosses, by focusing attention on "the development of a youth," conflict with the mythical image Frost sought to project in the years after he gained public attention: "One hallmark of the myth is its static quality. A narrative cycle which emphasized the various stages through which he had passed clearly contradicted this. Only when the poet had obscured the narrative would he be able to reinterpret the individual poems and bring them into conformity with the complex myth."[2]

In order to do this, Frost suppressed the glosses and three immature poems ("Asking for Roses," "In Equal Sacrifice," and "Spoils of the Dead") from collected editions beginning in 1930. Furthermore, he sought to distract attention from the overwrought romanticism and contrived aestheticism of pieces like "Stars," "To the Thawing Wind," "Rose Pogonias," "Waiting," "The Vantage Point," "Pan With Us," and "A Line-Storm Song." In a letter of 22 March 1915, for instance, he informed W. S. Braithwaite (an influential critic who was preparing a review) that such poems should not be read "on any account" (SL, 158).

Seeking to conceal the pattern of growth implicit in *A Boy's Will*, Frost also did his best to obscure the contrast between the passionately self-conscious "youth" of that collection and the subdued but observant author implied by *North of Boston*. Nevertheless, there are several telling differences between the two works: the persona in the first book explores various sides of a single personality (his own), while in the second he treats a wide range of people and situations; and the responses of the implied observer of *North of Boston* are more vivid and imaginative than the personal outbursts of *A Boy's Will*.

Linked to these contrasts in scope and focus is the disparity between lyric and dramatic poetry. *A Boy's Will*, Frost's most unrelievedly lyric collection, gives us too much of the poet. On the other hand, *North of Boston*, a highly dramatic collection, is a "book of people" presenting a region and a perspective on that region (see the ded-

---

[2] Haynes, "The Narrative Unity of *A Boy's Will*," *PMLA*, 87 (May 1972), 452, 462.

icatory phrase, *P*, 534). Even the title suggests a shift away from the lyric introspection and self-absorption of *A Boy's Will*. It was the first of a series of geographical and regional titles (*Mountain Interval*, *New Hampshire*, *West-Running Brook*, etc.).

Frost's best work always involves at least a hint of the dramatic. The poems of *North of Boston* display an exceptional sensitivity to the tones, the rhythms, and the subtle inflections that give the human voice its suggestiveness and complexity, its emotional power and inherent poetic capacity. By studying the Yankee, and by paying attention to the voices and attitudes of rural characters, Frost developed the perspective that led to his rejection of Romantic lyricism and precipitated his realization that "the great fight of any poet is against the people who want him to write in a special language that has gradually separated from spoken language . . ." (*SL*, 141). With the publication of *North of Boston*, he became much more than a popular regional author. Like Twain and Howells, like Pound and William Carlos Williams, like Hemingway and Faulkner, like all the great movers and shakers of the American language, he had come to grips with the spoken word, devoting himself to the literary mission that T. S. Eliot enunciated in "Little Gidding" (with help from Mallarmé): "our concern was speech, and speech impelled us / To purify the dialect of the tribe." In Frost's own words (from a 1937 speech at Oberlin College), the goal was "to purify words until they meant again what they should mean" (*P&P*, 388).

To understand the remarkable transition from *A Boy's Will* to *North of Boston* we must consider how Frost's experiences in England in 1913 provided him with the confidence and self-assurance to adopt a new poetic identity. Even as late as January 1913—five months after leaving the United States—he presented himself as the scorned Shelleyan wanderer, the Romantic outcast, in a letter to a British poet he had just met, F. S. Flint. His deferential, apologetic allusions to poetry and poetics (Flint was the younger man by nearly a dozen years) bear witness to his sense of being misunderstood and unappreciated. He wished to assure Flint that he had been thrilled to participate in a British literary soirée: "I was only too childishly happy in being allowed to make one for a moment in a company in which I hadn't to be ashamed of having written verse. . . . I have lived for the most part in villages where it were better that a millstone were hanged about your neck than that you should own yourself a minor poet."[3]

The subservience about being "allowed" to rub elbows with the cosmopolitan British and the disparagement of New England villages are sufficient proof that the Yankee farmer poet had not yet come into his own. This is not the perspective of one who had learned to speak or see "New Englandly" (as Emily Dickinson had). In fact, the specific place hardly deserved mention; it might as well have been California or Virginia's Dismal Swamp. Frost would refer to it only as a vague "wilderness": "When the life of the streets perplexed me a long time ago I attempted to find an answer to it for myself by going literally into the wilderness, where I was so lost to friends and everyone that not five people crossed my threshold in as many years. I came back to do my days work in its day none the wiser."[4]

In these sentences, there are some echoes of, or developments on, the letter Frost had sent to Miss Ward a few months before, professing an "aberrant" mood and a soul inclined "to go apart by itself." But despite his claim to have returned "none the wiser" from the "wilderness," and despite his rejection (to Miss Ward) of the "virtue in Location," he had begun—even before writing the letter to Flint—to miss New England. In a letter written on

[3] Frost to Flint, 21 Jan. 1913. This letter is not in SL, but is printed in Elaine Barry, *Robert Frost on Writing* (New Brunswick, N.J.: Rutgers University Press, 1973), pp. 84-86.
[4] *Ibid.*

Christmas day 1912 he admitted, "I am homesick at times" (SL, 60). Although he was apparently surprised by it, his nostalgia increased during the winter.

Frost's chances of achieving recognition in the British literary world were enhanced by his meeting with Ezra Pound in March 1913. More important, his appreciation of the fundamental differences between himself and Pound must have helped to stimulate his sensitivity to his New England background. An unknown poet almost forty years old could hardly come before a well-established but much younger countryman (Pound was then in his late twenties) without some excuse for his obscurity, some rationale that might at once put his art in its best light *and* explain its unpopularity. Thus, on coming face to face with an American emigré who was well versed in the British tradition, Frost betrayed none of the lofty literary ambitions he had expounded to Miss Ward. Instead, he launched into what Thompson calls an "overdramatized and not too accurate" recounting of his personal life—a piteous tale that "was enough to arouse Pound's sympathy" (EY, 411).

Emphasizing the hardships and deprivations of farm life, Frost propagated the canard that his grandfather had disinherited and persecuted him (EY, 410-412). Consequently, Pound became the first—and perhaps the most influential—victim of the Derry myth. His review of *A Boy's Will* in 1913 did much to establish Frost as a simple rustic figure: "Mr. Frost's book is a little raw, and it has in it a number of infelicities; underneath them it has the tang of the New Hampshire woods, and it has just this utter simplicity."[5] By considering the book unsophisticated and appreciating it (somewhat condescendingly) for its innocence, Pound set the tone for a wide range of later reviews, virtually assuring the need for Reuben Brower's warning some fifty years afterward: "we must not suppose

[5] Pound, "A Boy's Will," *Poetry: A Magazine of Verse*, 2 (May 1913), 72.

because of Frost's Yankee manner (in part consciously acquired) that he *was* an innocent, or intellectually less sophisticated than contemporaries who went to England or the Continent."[6]

Pound could not consider even the more mature *North of Boston* an "accomplished work," and his review of that book stressed the author's "parochial talent."[7] Without doubt, Pound was *primus inter pares* among those who went to England and the Continent. Translator, scholar, poet, critic, reputedly well versed in European and classical literature, a close associate of William Butler Yeats, he knew much of the grand tradition and had been introduced to "old men with beautiful manners" like Henry James (whose misgivings about parochialism were renowned).[8] Hence he had special authority to define his countryman's place in the literary world, and his pronouncements are echoing yet through the mountains of Frost commentary.

The relationship that developed between Pound and Frost was significant mainly for its ironies and contrasts, and it did not last long. Despite Pound's energetic assistance, Frost's mistrust increased during the spring and summer, until in July he could no longer conceal his hostility for "that great intellect abloom in hair."[9] But surely the confrontation, with all its tensions and antipathies, contributed to his own recognition of his position as an American poet.

[6] Brower, "Parallel Lives," *Partisan Review*, 34 (Winter 1967), 116.

[7] Pound, "Modern Georgics," *Poetry: A Magazine of Verse*, 5 (Dec. 1914), 127, 130.

[8] Pound, "Moeurs Contemporaines," vii, "I Vecchii," in *Personae: The Collected Shorter Poems of Ezra Pound* (New York: New Directions, 1950), p. 181. It seems fitting that James and Pound, two of America's most notable expatriates, should have misapplied the same term to two of New England's most notable—and *least* parochial—authors, Frost and Thoreau. For James's animadversions on the latter, see his *Hawthorne* (New York: Harper and Brothers, 1879), p. 94.

[9] EY, 420. Thompson discusses Frost's "declaration of independence from Pound," pp. 419-423.

By the thirteenth of May 1913, within a few months of denouncing New England to F. S. Flint and about half a year after expressing his indifference to "Location," he was ready to write Miss Ward a second letter, radically different from the first. The moody Romantic poet, with his ornate, overwrought phraseology, had given way to a more direct, down-to-earth writer who was not afraid of seeming provincial or using simple sentences. Frost described the recent publication of *A Boy's Will* (a copy of which accompanied the letter), and he reported proudly on its popularity with readers like Yeats, Pound, and May Sinclair. But after summarizing his accomplishments in England with the whimsical comment, "I seem in a fair way to become an Englishman," he began a new and revealingly incongruous paragraph to conclude the letter:

> And yet we are very very homesick in this English mud. We can't hope to be happy long out of New England, I never knew how much of a Yankee I was till I had been out of New Hampshire a few months. I suppose the life in such towns as Plymouth and Derry and South Berwick [Miss Ward's summer residence] is the best on earth. (*SL*, 73-74)

The sudden shift in this closing paragraph set the pattern for many of Frost's letters during 1913.[10] Again and again, self-congratulatory allusions to his literary success in England led directly to confessions of homesickness and reflections on "how much of a Yankee" he was. After returning to America he observed, "I never saw *New* England as clearly as when I was in Old England" (*SL*, 160). Yet this change was less consequential than concurrent developments in his perception of his own identity as a New Englander. Strangely, publishing a book (*A Boy's Will* was released in April) and developing personal contacts in the British literary community (Flint in January,

---

[10] See, for instance, letters to John Bartlett (c. 16 June 1913, 7, 30 Aug. 1913), Wilbur Rowell (17 July 1913), and Ernest Silver (8 Dec. 1913), *SL*, 75, 84, 89, 91, 103.

Pound early in March, Yeats a few weeks later) gave him the confidence to see himself not as just a capable poet, but as an individual with an unusual past: a past that equipped him with certain attitudes and sensibilities, and one that—as he became more aware of it—could even make him feel homesick and nostalgic.

While developing a new sense of his relationship to the New England countryside, Frost also became aware of his affinities with the Georgian poets, a loosely connected group, rural in sympathy, who sought to write, as Edward Thomas noted in 1913, "in a natural voice and in the language of today."[11] But Frost's closest association with this movement did not begin until the fall of 1913,[12] by which time he had completed *North of Boston*. During the spring of that year, however, as he became familiar with the movement and as he first met Lascelles Abercrombie and Wilfred Gibson, he must have sensed that for these poets the contrived Romantic posture he had often assumed since the 1890s—the posture exhibited in *A Boy's Will*—would have little appeal.

Without influencing Frost's poetry directly, the Georgians contributed to a literary climate quite different from what he expected to find in England and highly conducive to his cultivation of a new role for himself: the Yankee farmer. While this identity contrasted sharply with his pose as sophisticated Romantic poet, he had actually begun experimenting with it before he left New England. During his year at Plymouth, New Hampshire (1911-1912), though "glad to be rid of the farm," he was, according to Thompson, "still perfecting the art of talking like a farmer" (EY, 371).

Despite his ambivalences about farming, Frost had gained enough confidence by May 1913 to adopt a new

[11] Thomas, review of *Georgian Poetry 1911-1912*, in *Poetry and Drama* 1 (Mar. 1913), 203.

[12] Frost met Edward Thomas in October 1913, and he moved to Gloucestershire in May 1914 to be near Lascelles Abercrombie and Wilfred Gibson.

identity and present it convincingly, especially when talking to critics and literary people who might spread his reputation. It would be a mistake to think that he consciously undertook a campaign of misrepresentation; he was apparently capable of convincing himself that he really *was* a rustic farmer. But occasionally, unguarded remarks to his closest friends betrayed an appreciation even in 1913 of the ambiguities of his position.[13]

Within a few days of writing to Miss Ward about discovering "how much of a Yankee" he was, Frost observed in a letter to John Bartlett (c. 10 May 1913) that he was "looked on as someone who has got the poetry of the farm" (SL, 73). This would seem to support Lawrance Thompson's theory that he "had been provided with a public image by the British reviewers": "He was a Yankee farmer who had made admirable poetry out of his farming experiences, and all he needed to do after that, to play the self-assigned part, was to 'become Yankier and Yankier' " (YT, 71).

The record indicates, however, that instead of being "provided with a public image" by the critics, Frost provided *them* with the image. In May 1913, only three significant reviews of *A Boy's Will* (released a month earlier) had appeared, and two of them made no references to "the poetry of the farm" or anything like it.[14] The third review was Pound's in the May number of *Poetry: A Magazine of Verse*, heavily influenced, of course, by Frost's mythical self-portrait. Since only a few poems in *A Boy's Will* were conspicuously agricultural ("Mowing," "Waiting," "The Tuft of Flowers"), it is unlikely that anyone would have looked on the collection as "poetry of the farm" had it not been for Frost's own efforts and those of "friends" like Pound. Even in the few months between his completion of the book and its publication, his attitude toward it

---

[13] See, for instance, the letter (5 Nov. 1913) facetiously chiding John Bartlett for getting away from farming: "Ain't working the land? Easier to write about it? Think I don't understand?" (SL, 99).

[14] Thompson quotes in full the notices from the *Athenaeum* of 5 April and the *Times Literary Supplement* of 10 April (EY, 414-415).

changed. In the fall of 1912 he still regarded it as a sentimental education of the artist as a young man: "a slender thing with a slender psychological interest. . . . a study in a certain kind of waywardness."[15] But by the spring and summer of 1913 it had become a "farm product"—a phrase that Frost liked well enough to use in letters written two months apart.[16] Accordingly, his comments on his reputation in May were not so much a reflection of critical opinion at that time as an indication of his hopes and intentions for the future.

Frost's ability to adopt the regionalist's role in public appearances, conversation, and correspondence was at least partially responsible for the enthusiasm with which he was initially received. Embarking on what Thompson calls a "very deliberate campaign of self-advancement" (EY, 587), he stressed the myth "that he was disinherited . . . reduced to poverty" (EY, 623) and suggested that he had been forced to farm for survival while at Derry. Curiously, in later years he tried to extend this myth by claiming that he had also been forced to turn to farming for sustenance while in England.[17] So well did Frost promulgate his "public image," spreading stories of his rustic seclusion at Derry, that reviewers were soon sighing over his life on a "lonely farm in a forest clearing,"[18] despite the absence of any such farm in A Boy's Will.

Turning the Mind to Run on Rusticity

During the early summer of 1913 Frost's growing sense of his regional identity resulted in an impressive burst of activity. After more than twenty years of experimentation,

[15] Frost to Ernest Silver, 25 Dec. 1912, SL, 60.

[16] Frost to John Bartlett, c. 10 May 1913, to Wilbur Rowell, 17 July 1913, SL, 73, 85.

[17] For discussion of Frost's use of myth to enhance his rustic reputation, see EY, 411-412, 587n, 603n, and the heading "Myth-Making" in the index, p. 623.

[18] Anonymous review of A Boy's Will, in Bookman (London), 44 (Aug. 1913), 189.

he suddenly brought to completion a well-matched set of seventeen poems—more than half of which critics of all persuasions have placed at or near the core of his most characteristic and distinguished work. When he wrote to Bartlett in May about being acclaimed for poetry of the farm, he had not actually published much verse concerned with the regional world he had observed in New England. Although "The Tuft of Flowers," "Going for Water," and "Mowing" are highly effective early pieces, their significance pales in comparison with the poems he gathered together in the three months following the letter to Bartlett, among them, "Mending Wall," "The Death of the Hired Man," "The Mountain," "A Hundred Collars," "Home Burial," "A Servant to Servants," "After Apple-Picking," "The Code," "The Fear," "The Wood-Pile," and one other oft-anthologized piece he finally decided to omit from *North of Boston*, "Birches." Drafts of three of these pieces, including "The Death of the Hired Man," may have been started as early as 1905 (*EY*, 594), but Frost's half year in the British literary community seems to have stimulated his commitment to a full poetic exploration of his experience in rural New England. This was no longer the poet who in 1907 had high hopes for poems like "The Vantage Point" and "A Dream Pang," while keeping "The Death of the Hired Man" hidden under a bushel of ill-fated manuscripts. Prior to his British adventure, he had neither the confidence nor the resolve to body forth his vision of a region and its people.

After the inspired productivity of May, June, and July, Frost wrote Bartlett again, rejoicing that "the next book begins to look large" and listing its prospective table of contents (*SL*, 88-89). His elation was in part attributable to his swift success at fulfilling the commitment—the unconscious prophecy—he had made in the spring. Without question he had mastered "the poetry of the farm." Noting that Bartlett had recently contributed articles to a farm journal, he made an observation that shows how conscious he had become of his new artistic identity: "without collusion we have simultaneously turned our minds to run on rusticity" (SL, 89). The verb "turned" is especially revealing here. It shows that several years *after* his departure from Derry Frost suddenly reached a new awareness of the poetic possibilities of rural New England. But in the process of running his mind on rusticity and mastering the "poetry of the farm," he also gained full control of his special poetic gift: his sensitivity to the speaking voice. He at long last firmly grasped that "right tone" he had been groping toward for a decade or more.

In July 1913, while at work on the poems of *North of Boston*, the "Yank from Yankville," as Frost now styled himself (EY, 415), began to conceptualize what his new literary identity was to be. The first of a series of brilliant letters developing his poetic theory was written on a marvelously symbolic date, the Fourth of July. Though there was probably more coincidence than sense of history involved, there can be no doubt that this was his declaration of independence from the British tradition.

Citing Swinburne and Tennyson by name, he condemned poetic "effects in assonation," effects that are also common in the work of many of his youthful favorites—Poe, Keats, Shelley, Arnold—and, let us not forget, in the verse of the young Robert Frost. In declaring independence, he stressed his role as an innovator. "To be frank with you I am one of the most notable craftsmen of my time," he told Bartlett with his tongue just enough in his cheek to avoid being pompous: "I am possibly the only person going who works on any but a worn out theory . . . of versification." The innovative poems he wrote at that time show the influence of his commitment:

I alone of English writers have consciously set myself to make music out of what I may call the sound of sense. . . . It is the abstract vitality of our speech. It is pure sound—pure form. . . . An ear and an appetite for these sounds of sense is the first qualification of a writer, be it of prose or verse. But if one is to be a poet he must learn to get cadences by skillfully breaking the sounds of sense with all their irregularity of accent across the regular beat of the metre. Verse in which there is nothing but the beat of the metre furnished by the accents of the pollysyllabic [sic] words we call doggerel. Verse is not that. Neither is it the sound of sense alone. It is a resultant from those two. (SL, 79-81)

Having sketched out this approach to poetics, Frost continued to work on it in other letters.[19] After his return to the United States, he elaborated it in correspondence, interviews, and lectures, and finally incorporated it in two of his most noteworthy essays: "The Figure a Poem Makes" (1939) and "The Constant Symbol" (1946).

In *Robert Frost on Writing*, Elaine Barry has suggested that Frost's critical theory "bears favorable comparison with the formalized criticism of Eliot or Pound." Despite her generally perceptive exposition of Frost's poetics, however, Barry fails to appreciate the complexity of his background. Denying that he ever had anything to do with "the musical assonance of most nineteenth-century poetry," Barry emphasizes the "colloquial tradition" in American poetry, the tradition of Emerson and Whitman, of "Emily Dickinson whose homely diction and frequent metrical irregularity give the impression of a speaking voice, and Edwin Arlington Robinson whose 'talking tones' Frost so much admired." Unfortunately, her conclusion that "Frost was heir" to this tradition, though plausible, adds little to the image he propagated for himself. What she misses is the unprecedented nature of his connection to the "colloquial tradition."[20]

Inheriting a tradition is different from *assimilating* it, and this difference has much to do with Frost's special

---

[19] See letters to Thomas Mosher (17 July 1913), John Bartlett (22 Feb. 1914), John Cournos (8, 27 July 1914), and Sidney Cox (Dec. 1914), SL, 83-84, 110-113, 128-130, 140-141.

[20] Barry, *Robert Frost on Writing*, pp. 33, 12.

distinction as a poet. We should not think of him simply as an inheritor when there is so much clear evidence that he regarded himself as an innovator, "one of the few who have a theory of their own" (SL, 88). Doubtless, he was familiar with the authors Barry cites, and he certainly moved closer to them in 1913; but what is important is that he brought to the "colloquial tradition" a rich experience in a highly dissimilar mode. It was this complexity, not merely his identification with a particular tradition, that enabled him to produce the original and powerful poetry of North of Boston.

This book, produced during a period of intellectual ferment and artistic growth, is frequently cited as Frost's best. Many critics feel that aside from containing more major poems than any of his other collections, it is his most effectively unified and sustained work. The source of all these strengths was the poet's newly developed sensitivity to his regional background. His concern with speech patterns and the sound of rural voices invests the book with great dramatic force. Additionally, his interest in the meaning of his own experience in the farm country of New England led him to unify the book not only by careful arrangement of its seventeen poems and skillful orchestration of its themes, conflicts, and images, but also by establishing a consistent point of view toward the region: the point of view of a sensitive, meditative observer.

Like A Boy's Will, North of Boston offers a faintly narrative evocation of its implied author. There are no glosses, of course, and no explicit references to the self-conscious "youth" of the earlier collection. But there is an overt link between the two books: a sentence on an unnumbered page between the table of contents and "Mending Wall" in early editions of North of Boston states that "Mending Wall takes up the theme where A Tuft of Flowers in A Boy's Will laid it down." By leaving "the theme" indefinite (it is not merely the theme of "A Tuft of Flowers," but a larger theme "laid down" there), Frost intimates that "Mending Wall"—and by implication, the remainder of the collection—is a continuation of the earlier volume. Even without this suggestion, however, *North of Boston* demands to be read, not as a haphazard collection of lyrics, dramatic monologues, dramatic narratives, and dialogues, but as a poetic study of rural New England. Pursuing his interest in natural speech, Frost shaped the voices of the individual poems into a larger dramatic form centered on his implied author, the observer whose discerning, refining, ordering mentality filters and unifies the diverse elements of the regional environment.

Many years later, in a letter to Whit Burnett (26 July 1942), Frost recollected arranging the contents of his first two collections to suggest a "larger design":

> looking backward over the accumulation of years to see how many poems I could find towards some one meaning it might seem absurd to have had in advance, but it would be all right to accept from fate after the fact. The interest, the pastime, was to learn if there had been any divinity shaping my ends and I had been building better than I knew. In other words could anything of larger design, even the roughest, any broken or dotted continuity, or any fragment of a figure be discerned among the apparently random lesser designs of the several poems? (SL, 501)

One reason for the effectiveness of *North of Boston*'s design is that the unusually small number of poems—only seventeen (Frost's eight other volumes contain from thirty to fifty pieces)—affords us an intriguing sense of pattern and relationship.

Frost had a gift for seeing designs of many sorts, and the elaborate notes, subtitles, and divisions in some of his collections (especially *New Hampshire* and *A Further Range*) testify to his intention of using the poet's eye not only in writing but also in gathering and arranging his poems. Generally, however, such efforts resulted in little more than meretricious contrivances; only in *North of Boston* do form and content combine effectively to produce a literary whole that seems greater than the sum of its parts. There are twelve lengthy "stories," as Frost once called them (SL, 89), ranging from about a hundred lines in length to well over two hundred, and they provide the dramatic and narrative force and the brilliant revelation of character for a portrait of rural New England that ranks with the very best produced by the prose local-colorists. Furthermore, for its pure, evocative language, for its compression and restraint, and for its fine sensitivity to character, situation, and theme, this book is virtually without peer in the regional tradition with which it has been linked.

As Frost developed his first extended treatment of New England, he did not attempt to write in the person of the Yankee farmer. He drew instead on his own experience as an outsider in Derry. *North of Boston* portrays rural life, but it also evokes a specific observer located in the regional setting, who seems to wonder whether he belongs there. Because of his role as observer, he stands somewhat apart from those he studies, and he finds himself susceptible to feelings of isolation and alienation. By conveying these feelings, Frost achieved an artistic depth and complexity often lacking in regional literature, and he transcended the predictability and chauvinism that afflict many New England authors.

Unlike most of the local-color writers, who settled for impressions that were all too monochromatic, Frost endowed his observer with an appreciation of many worlds north of Boston. There is an element of exploration in the book (epitomized in "The Mountain," "The Black Cottage," and "The Wood-Pile"), and instead of concentrating on a particular regional locale like Alice Brown's Tiverton or Robinson's Tilbury Town, the implied author roves through two states, New Hampshire and Vermont, discovering settings that range from desolate forest ("The Wood-Pile") and sparsely populated farm country ("Home Burial," "The Code," "The Fear") to rural villages ("The Mountain," "The Generations of Men") and mill towns or railroad junctions ("The Self-Seeker," "A Hundred Collars").

Even Frost's title, *North of Boston*, bespeaks an outsider's perspective. None of his other collections—as *Mountain Interval*, *New Hampshire*, and *West-Running Brook* suggest—place the country in relation to the city. Customarily, of course, New England writers have adopted the local point of view. In the regional novels of Mrs. Stowe, for instance, and in the fiction of Rose Terry Cooke and Mary Wilkins Freeman, there are many variations on the claim made most overtly by Alice Brown, that only "we who have walked in country ways" are qualified to write about the country.[21] Nevertheless, a precedent can be found in the New England tradition for *North of Boston*'s outside observer; significantly, it is in one of the most impressive pieces the tradition has to offer: Sarah Orne Jewett's *The Country of the Pointed Firs*. There is no evidence that Frost knew this little volume (though it was popular during the late 1890s when he was an avid reader); and even if he was familiar with it, there is no reason to believe that it influenced his handling of *North of Boston*. Still, both works provide exceptionally vivid portraits of New England by using observers who function as intermediaries between the reading audience and the rural world. They are not in any sense regional spokesmen, and their narrative concern is not only with local events, but also with their own explorations of the region. A special artistic sensibility results, involving subtle tensions between inner and outer, observer and observed.

Exploration North of Boston

Frost's first device to encourage his readers to consider *North of Boston* as a large poetic structure comprising seventeen interrelated dramatic units is the isolation of

[21] Brown, *Meadow-Grass: Tales of New England Life* (Boston: Houghton Mifflin Company, 1895), p. 15.

the short lyric, "The Pasture," on the page *before* the table of contents in the original edition of *North of Boston*. The poem is obviously an invitation to the reader ("You come too"). No less important, it is an introduction to the book's persona or implied author, the observing "I" who appears in a symmetrically arranged series of poems: the first two ("The Pasture" and "Mending Wall"), the last two ("The Wood-Pile" and "Good Hours"), the middle one ("A Servant to Servants"), and four others spread through the rest of the book ("The Mountain" and "The Black Cottage" in the first half; "After Apple-Picking" and "The Housekeeper" in the second half).

Although Frost extracted "The Pasture" from *North of Boston* and placed it at the beginning of his collected works in 1930, it fits well with *North of Boston*—and it fits in ways that commentators have overlooked because they have been charmed by its alluring idyllic surface. In particular, Leo Marx and John Lynen have made much of the poem as a pastoral invitation.[22] Yet, despite the presence of pastoral imagery (which Lynen emphasizes) and the motif of pastoral retreat (Marx's interest), Frost's speaker is a less convincing "swain" than Lynen would have us believe (p. 17), and the retreat he contemplates is not as idyllic as Marx indicates.

While "The Pasture" can be linked with the traditional invitation lyric found in the *Idylls* of Theocritus, the *Eclogues* of Virgil, and such Renaissance pastorals as Marlowe's "The Passionate Shepherd to his Love," Lynen and Marx neglect the voice of the speaker and thus miss some crucial undertones. The poem is not at all a simple invitation, and neither of their summaries does it justice:

the poet invites someone, perhaps a person he loves, perhaps just a friend, to come with him and see the

[22] Lynen uses "The Pasture" as his first illustration of "Frost's method as pastoral poet" in *The Pastoral Art of Robert Frost* (New Haven: Yale University Press, 1960), pp. 21-23. Marx also makes it his first example in "Pastoral Ideals and City Troubles," *Journal of General Education*, 20 (1969), 258-259.

glimpses of delicate beauty to be found in the pasture.
(Lynen, p. 22)

he invites us to leave the house of everyday life and
move out toward nature. Like most of Frost's work,
the poem may be taken in two ways, either in the
plainest sense, for the pleasure of reference, or for its
extended meaning. In this case we are also being in-
vited into a poetic world, an ideal pasture where the
writer will clear a channel to a hidden source of re-
newal and creativity. (Marx, p. 258)

"The Pasture" introduces a more complex speaker than
these summaries suggest. To be sure, he has the pastoral
inclinations Lynen and Marx ascribe to him; but the tex-
ture of his invitation is not without some faintly discord-
ant notes of uncertainty and self-consciousness:

I'm going out to clean the pasture spring;
I'll only stop to rake the leaves away
(And wait to watch the water clear, I may):
I shan't be gone long.—You come too.

I'm going out to fetch the little calf
That's standing by the mother. It's so young
It totters when she licks it with her tongue.
I shan't be gone long.—You come too.[23]

This persona is less self-assured and less forthright than
the speaker imagined by Lynen and Marx. He is sincere
and wants very much to be joined in his pastoral venture;
but his invitation is particularly poignant because of its
tentative, apologetic quality. After expressing his inten-
tion of going to clean the spring, he soon displays an
awareness that the outing may be suspect, at least by some
standards. The phrase "I'll only stop" in the second line
and the promise "I shan't be gone long" in the fourth

[23] Frost claimed in 1915 that there are no less than five different tones
in each stanza of "The Pasture." See his "Lecture to the Browne and
Nichols School," in Barry, Robert Frost on Writing, pp. 143-144.

create a tone of contrition, as if any prolongation of the trip or any expansion of the activities there would be reprehensible. His concern with time, the duration of his stay in the pasture, is evidence of apprehension about his pastoral longings. Having promised in line 2 not to pause or relax in the pastoral world but just to perform the simple task of removing leaves from the spring, he capriciously contradicts himself in line 3, disclosing new and far less productive motives for his trip. The parentheses and the mitigating equivocation "I may" show how diffident he is about revealing that his work as a spring cleaner is only an excuse for his indulgence in contemplative recreation.

Finally, after the speaker's hesitation and disingenuousness about what he wants to do (no invitation is made in the first three-and-a-half lines), there comes the abrupt, earnest, bashful "You come too." The smooth pentameter gives way to an irregular final line—prosodic testimony to his uneasiness. Of course, pastoral symbolism is important to the poem. But unlike the conventional swain, Frost's persona is unsure of his approach to the experience he contemplates. He is dubious about the propriety of his invitation, yet the disavowals and evasive ambiguities of his utterance show that he hopes to elicit not just an affirmative response, but an understanding and appreciative one.

Hints of defensiveness and indirection in "The Pasture" arise from the speaker's sensitivity to the disparities between what he assumes are widely accepted norms and his own values and desires. After introducing this conflict subtly in North of Boston's initial poem, Frost explores it more thoroughly in the rest of the collection. In an environment that encourages prudent impassivity and constructive action, his persona wants primarily to see, to contemplate, and to appreciate. Both stanzas of "The Pasture" make this clear. He cleans the spring because he wants to *watch* the water clear, and he fetches the calf because it *looks* so young and delicate to him. These motives are devoid of practical, agricultural purpose. The *pasture* spring, we should remember, does not provide water for the farmhouse; nor is there evidence that it needs cleaning. Such springs, after all, are for the live-stock, animals capable of brushing the leaves aside for themselves and hardly as concerned as some people might be about the water's clarity. Very faintly, from the speaker's hesitant tone, we may sense an undercurrent of guilt: perhaps, if pressed, he might confess that the pasture spring should be left to nature and the calf to its mother. At some point, nature worship becomes a viola-tion of nature.

Readers may interpret the pasture spring as symbolic of inspiration, purity, or regeneration, and the calf as sug-gestive of newness, fragility, innocence, or youth. But Frost's persona does not explain the significance of what he sees. The precise features of the moments of reverie and contemplation implied by "The Pasture" are left un-defined, and this adds to the poem's effectiveness as an in-troduction to *North of Boston*. The speaker invites us to join him in his study of the regional environment, but we must go on his terms. Rather than inviting us into a pastoral world, he asks us to share his exploration—a much more uncertain and ambiguous experience. "The Pasture" does not promise, nor does *North of Boston* pro-vide, the moral lessons and didactic social commentary of conventional regional literature. It would be a mistake to expect that the stone walls and woodpiles, the farms and mountains, the hired men and farm people will be inter-preted or explained to us. We must go, as Frost's speaker goes, to observe and reflect on rural New England.

"Mending Wall," the first poem in *North of Boston*'s table of contents, is linked to "The Tuft of Flowers" by the epigraph. Compared with the simple "men work to-gether" philosophy of the early poem, however, the speaker's attitude toward fellowship in *North of Boston* is speculative and irresolute, more in keeping with the tone of "The Pasture." The narrator of "The Tuft of Flowers" spoke with considerable authority about fellowship. Despite physical and temporal separation, he found a deep spiritual bond with the unseen but "kindred" reaper. The speaker in "Mending Wall" finds no such kindred spirit. Ironically, although he and his hidebound neighbor "work together" to repair the wall, the poem conveys a disquieting sense of incompatibility, of working "apart."

The conflict suggested in "The Pasture" develops in "Mending Wall" as Frost's persona reveals more of himself while offering his first portrait of a native Yankee. The prefatory poem offered hints of the speaker's incompatibility with hardheaded Yankees who might disapprove of pastoral outings and of time wasted in frivolous activities like waiting by a spring "to watch the water clear." In "Mending Wall," however, the tension between observer and observed assumes central importance, as a contemplative, whimsical speaker tries unsuccessfully to draw a taciturn Yankee out from behind his walls of habit and aphorism. The observer's attempt to analyze and comprehend his neighbor contrasts with the latter's complete satisfaction with his "father's saying."

As initial chapters or components of *North of Boston*, "The Pasture" and "Mending Wall" establish a raison d'être for the entire collection: they introduce the implied author, display his penchant for observation, and demonstrate his characteristic role as an outsider who is both disturbed and fascinated by an environment he can neither change nor fully accept. By letting the persona speak in the first person while presenting basic themes and conflicts in these two opening poems, Frost establishes a context for the objectively narrated piece that follows, "The Death of the Hired Man."

Despite the absence of connecting links (like the glosses in early editions of *A Boy's Will*), the first two poems in *North of Boston* imply an author who would be interested in characters like Silas, Mary, Warren, and Harold Wilson, although Frost never reveals the precise nature of his speaker's relationship with them. They may be neighbors, or they may be strangers he has met briefly or heard about in his travels across New England, which he describes in successive poems. But whoever they are, they conform to the broad patterns that the persona observes in the regional world. He has already confronted rustic obstinacy something like Warren's, and he has shown his own concern for impractical sensibilities like Mary's and a disdain for propriety like Silas's; hence he has reason to appreciate the relationships and conflicts dramatized in the poem.

Frost's masterful presentation of the voices in "The Death of the Hired Man" carries forward and builds on the dramatic tension implicit in "The Pasture" and "Mending Wall." On the one hand, Warren exemplifies the stern, pragmatic, down-to-earth confidence that comes from living in accordance with local customs and standards. He speaks with assurance, and his concern is with matters of economy, productivity, and usefulness. Although some traces of sympathy come out late in the poem, his primary interest in Silas is expressed by his sharp questions, "What good is he? Who else will harbor him / At his age for the little he can do?" (ll. 15-16).

Mary's voice, on the other hand, has much in common with the persona's in the preceding poems. She speaks defensively and apologetically, as if aware that her expression of sympathetic feelings for Silas violates (as indeed it does) widely accepted standards. Her imagination and her emotions distinguish her from her husband and add to the tension that invigorates their dialogue. With her sympathy for Silas, her willingness to spread her apron to the moonlight, her concern for "that small sailing cloud" that might "hit or miss the moon" (ll. 160-161), she seems too delicately sensitive for an environment in which a disgruntled farmer might feel justified in turning Silas out. Although Warren seems finally to accept her point of view, the poem makes clear that his conversion, like her sympathy, is a departure from local norms. By changing his mind and deciding to "have some pity on Silas" (l.

135), he proves himself worthy of being her husband, and simultaneously shows that he and Mary were the right people for Silas to come to.

To underscore the contrast of voices in the poem, Frost took pains to evoke the special qualities of Mary's speech:

> Part of a moon was falling down the west,
> Dragging the whole sky with it to the hills.
> Its light poured softly in her lap. She saw it
> And spread her apron to it. She put out her hand
> Among the harplike morning-glory strings,
> Taut with the dew from garden bed to eaves,
> As if she played unheard some tenderness
> That wrought on him beside her in the night.
>
> (103-110)

Inserted in the dialogue just prior to the climactic passage in which Mary's feminine sympathy begins to sway her husband (ll. 119-154), this description shows how Frost could capitalize on his youthful interest in British Romanticism to add force and depth to a stark New England drama. This is no traditional Yankee farmwife, with a strict sense of prudence and reserve. Instead, through rich Romantic imagery, Frost presents a vision of the enraptured singer, a vision characterized by that blend of music, moonlight, flowers, natural mysticism, and high passion that so appealed to English poets from Wordsworth and Coleridge on down to Tennyson and Swinburne. Mary's strumming of the "harplike morning-glory strings" (ll. 106-108) may in fact be an echo of Browning's treatment of the biblical harpist, David, in "Saul," a poem that Frost in 1894 called one of his "favorites" (SL, 20). Whether or not there is a conscious allusion here, the effect is similar to what Browning achieved through his description of David's harp, decorated with "lilies still living and blue / Just broken to twine around . . . [its] harp-strings" (ll. 12-13). In both passages a fusion of floral and musical imagery heightens our sense of the intensity and passion with which the speaker-singers (Mary

and David) attempt to soften the stern feelings of their au-
ditors (Warren and Saul).

If the twining of flowers and harp-strings with high
passion is a Romantic gesture, the emphasis on an unspo-
ken or nonverbal message is still more so. By suggesting
that Mary "played unheard some tenderness / That
wrought on him beside her," Frost revives the doctrine of
the ineffable sublime that received its most memorable
Romantic enunciation in the famous lines from Keats's
"Ode on a Grecian Urn": "Heard melodies are sweet, but
those unheard / Are sweeter." In this context, Mary's ren-
dition of "unheard tenderness" is all the more powerful
for its being figurative. The purpose of associating her
speech with music, moonlight, and flowers is to establish
that her plea to Warren addresses "the spirit"—to use
Keats's words—rather than "the sensual ear." And yet,
these undeniably Romantic lines are in no sense incon-
gruous. They are entirely necessary to the poem's care-
fully crafted dramatic structure; without them, the piece
would lose much of its distinctive force.

Along with Warren and Mary, the poem's other two
characters, Silas and Harold Wilson, establish a broad
range or spectrum of roles and relationships in the envi-
ronment north of Boston. They provide a commentary on
the book's implied author, a context in which his utter-
ances and his perspectives take on new significance. The
desires and attitudes, as well as the conflicting standards,
evoked in "The Pasture" and "Mending Wall" are mir-
rored and exaggerated in "The Death of the Hired Man."
Silas, the focal but "offstage" character, would not be one
to worry about the length of time he spent on an idle jaunt
to the pasture. Indeed, his promises to "ditch the
meadow" or "clear the upper pasture" (ll. 46, 52) are un-
reliable, as Warren knows all too well. Furthermore, he
seems unconcerned about his bad reputation. He does not
bother to maintain the customs and amenities of social in-
tercourse or to mend the personal fences implied and, de-
spite the persona's reluctance, preserved in "Mending
Wall."

Silas is, as even Mary must admit, "worthless" (l. 144), a man who can hardly get along in a world dominated by practical farmers like Warren and the neighbor of "Mending Wall." He conducts himself as if he can easily surmount the walls upheld by his neighbors; but he is, after all, only a hired man, and despite Mary's sympathy (and finally, Warren's), he is trapped by the disreputability he has brought on himself through his lack of respect for conventional barriers and restraints. His conflict with Warren, which Mary tries to arbitrate, pivots on the problem of neighborliness. Warren's statements support the dictum, "Good fences make good neighbors"; and fittingly, he chooses to stand on a simplistic aphorism: "Home is the place where . . . they have to take you in" (ll. 118-119). He attempts, unsuccessfully, to convince Mary that since Silas is not truly part of the family, he should be walled out and sent off to die with his relatives. Mary wins the argument, of course, and thus the poem—despite Silas's death—is one of the more optimistic and reassuring pieces in the collection. But the strength of the "good fences" thesis, and of the assumption that "all men" must "work apart," is demonstrated by the difficulty Warren has in accepting Silas's casual disregard for the social barriers between men, between families, and between employers and workers.

Frost's use of the dialogue as a poetic structure extends the ambivalence he attributes to his persona in the opening poems of *North of Boston* by developing a dual perspective (Mary's and Warren's) on Silas. Warren's apparent capitulation at the end of the poem is not a resolution so much as it is an indication that he too is capable of separating himself from regional standards that make it inappropriate to take "pity on Silas." But if Silas is something of a misfit in this world, and if Warren and Mary depart from accepted standards by befriending this shiftless, unreliable worker, the poem's fourth character, Harold Wilson, has a still more distant relationship to the environment evoked in the poem.

To be sure, Harold's role is minor, but his presence as a

complete outsider, a college student who once spent "vacations" doing farm work, constitutes a significant counterpoint to Silas's plight. The two men had worked together and apparently formed a bond of fellowship during one of Harold's summers on the farm. After that time, however, life closed in on Silas, while opening up for the younger man. There is a touching pathos in Silas's absurd hope that Harold, now a college professor, will join him again to "make a team for work" (l. 62) in the fields.

After such a somber, yet graceful and exquisitely crafted poem, Frost shifts effectively to one of *North of Boston*'s lightest and most understated pieces. In "The Mountain" he presents his persona in a new role, but one that the preceding poems have anticipated. Here he is clearly a tourist, and as he recounts his first visit to a rural town, we see his observer's sensitivity. He has an eye for the unfamiliar and notices that at night the mountain's "black body" obliterates certain "stars in the west" (ll. 3-4), stars that would of course not be missed by local folk. An eager sightseer, he rises early to scout around the base of the mountain in search of a path to the top. When a whimsical farmer he meets on the road tells him a tale about "a curious thing . . . almost like a fountain" (ll. 47, 64) on the peak, he is intrigued but also worried about the reliability of strangers' tales.

Unlike the neighbor in "Mending Wall," this farmer has a sense of humor, but the observer still finds himself baffled and frustrated by regional character. Garrulity, he learns, can be as impenetrable as taciturnity: the conflict is essentially unchanged. The local figure lacks the outsider's curiosity. He has no desire to climb the peak that dominates his world; nor does he need to see the miraculous mountaintop fountain or spring—any more than the neighbor of "Mending Wall" needed to know why good fences make good neighbors. We suspect, furthermore, that this droll Lunenburg farmer would be no more interested in the beauties of a pasture spring than he is in this one on a mountaintop. Believing that "all the fun's in how you say a thing" (l. 104), he has his fun at the observer's expense, describing the fountain enthusiastically and in detail (though he later confesses he has never seen it):

> One of the great sights going is to see
> It steam in winter like an ox's breath.
> Until the bushes all along its banks
> Are inch-deep with the frosty spines and bristles. . . .
> (50-53)

Frost's extraordinary versatility is evident in this section of the poem as he endows the farmer's speech with a slightly heightened poetic resonance (though without endangering its bantering tone). The tourist-persona, however, seems to think that how you *see* a thing is at least as important as how you *say* it. In response to the farmer's description, his voice takes on an even stronger touch of lofty musicality as he expresses his sudden, inspired vision (inspired by the scheming farmer):

> I saw through leafy screens
> Great granite terraces in sun and shadow,
> Shelves one could rest a knee on getting up—
> With depths behind him sheer a hundred feet. . . .
> (57-60)

Here we can see Frost's well-cultivated prosodic skills coming into play. He uses assonance (leafy screens, knee, sheer, feet) and alliteration (great granite; screens, terraces, sun; shadow, shelves, sheer) and builds toward the vertiginous climax in line 60 by gradually shifting from connotative to denotative imagery. He begins with "leafy screens," a suggestive, but indistinct, image. The "granite terraces," although still metaphorical, are more easily visualized. And in the next line the "shelves one could rest a knee on" may be slightly connotative, but what we feel with our knee is no metaphorical shelf. Finally, of course, the simple denotative impact of the word "depths" conveys the precariousness of the climber's position, especially in combination with the unusual stress acquired by the word "sheer" through its assonance, its unusual syntactical position, and the regularity of the line's iambic rhythm. The success of these lines has little to do with New England's "colloquial tradition." Contrary to what Barry and other critics have suggested, and what Frost himself often maintained, many vivid passages of this sort are indebted to "the musical assonance" of Romantic poetry.[24]

After showing how a voluble Yankee humorist had toyed with him, the implied author presents another comic poem, "A Hundred Collars," which also involves a regional character perpetrating a sort of tall tale on a gullible outsider. As in "The Death of the Hired Man," the persona leaves his own relationship to the poem's two characters undefined. However, since he has just presented himself as a traveler to a strange town in "The Mountain," and since "A Hundred Collars" is set in a hotel, the poem seems to reflect his direct or indirect experience north of Boston.

Although the professor, Dr. Magoon, is apparently the focal character, the garrulous traveling agent, Lafe, expresses the philosophy that underlies the poem: "I go nowhere on purpose: I happen by" (l. 154). He is an anomaly in the regional world: a misfit, as unreliable and unpredictable as Silas, but capable of avoiding the dangers and ill effects of flouting local standards. Much of the poem's humor arises from his attempt to give away his hundred collars. There is a metaphorical significance both to this freehanded gesture and to the collars themselves. The first clue is that as Lafe dons his shirt, his complaint has Carlylean overtones, asserting a symbolic relationship between the physical and the spiritual:

I'm moving into a size-larger shirt.
I've felt mean lately; mean's no name for it.
I just found what the matter was tonight:

[24] Barry, *Robert Frost on Writing*, p. 12.

I've been a-choking like a nursery tree
When it outgrows the wire band of its name tag.

(53-57)

If collars affect his personality, the process of outgrowing them is a manifestation of his increasing independence, for the poem indicates that he makes little of both physical and mental constraints. The timid doctor, by contrast, when asked about *his* collar size, clutches "his throat convulsively," strengthening the reader's suspicion that he is collared by much more than his shirt.

Like the farmer of "Mending Wall" and Warren in "The Death of the Hired Man," Magoon respects the walls between men. He dislikes sharing a hotel room, and his sense of propriety is violated by the thought of accepting such a personal item as a collar from another man. This "Professor Square-the-circle-till-you're-tired," as Lafe calls him (l. 44), will wear only his own collars, and it is his fastidiousness that cuts him off from the "old friends he somehow can't get near" (l. 7). Lafe, refusing to stand on ceremony, has no such problem. Happy to share his hotel room, his collars, his liquor, or his conversation, he can say, "I'm in with everybody, know 'em all" (l. 120).

Lafe resembles both the implied author of *North of Boston* and the characters in the book with whom the author seems most sympathetic. He is unusual because he is able—as many of the people in the book are *not*—to enjoy and appreciate the rural environment while maintaining his independence (keeping "his extrication," as Frost would phrase it later in "From Plane to Plane"). Significantly, in another of America's most renowned literary regions—William Faulkner's Yoknapatawpha County—the freest and happiest character is a traveling agent quite similar to Lafe, V. K. Ratcliff. Both authors seem to recognize the value of experiencing many aspects of country life and crossing the various social barriers that make the rural world so constricting and potentially frustrating for its inhabitants.

Having presented the lighter, carefree side of New England character in "A Hundred Collars" and "The Mountain," Frost turns back to the tragic and the pathetic in "Home Burial," one of his most unforgettable works. As in his best dramatic pieces, the characters are revealed not by what they say but how they say it. The husband in this poem seems to speak, as Warren did in "The Death of the Hired Man," with all the authority of local custom. Like Warren and like the farmer of "Mending Wall," he accepts things as they are and has little use for emotional responses to them. A dead child, a pasture spring or tottering calf, an old hired hand—these are facts of life in the rural world, and in accordance with the Yankee code he wastes no time in idle reflection on them. Along with many other characters north of Boston, he is most comfortable with platitudes and familiar precepts—what Randall Jarrell calls "rhetorical pronouncements."[25] He may well have mourned the loss of his child as much as his wife did, but he would not let his entire life become an expression of his grief. So he digs the child's grave with little sense of ceremony, talking all the while of "everyday concerns" and reiterating mindless (though imagistically appropriate) folk wisdom: "Three foggy mornings and one rainy day / Will rot the best birch fence a man can build" (ll. 92-93).

His words in "Home Burial" are "nearly always an offense" (l. 45) to his wife Amy because they are void of emotion; they are also a fence keeping her and her emotions from him, for he is another of North of Boston's partisans of "good fences." He maintains a wall of reserve between himself and his neighbors (including his wife and children), and thus he cannot fathom or accept his wife's grieving "so inconsolably" over what he pragmatically terms her "mother-loss of a first child" (l. 64). Amy, for

[25] Jarrell, "Robert Frost's 'Home Burial,' " in Don C. Allen, ed., The Moment of Poetry (Baltimore: Johns Hopkins University Press, 1962), p. 104.

her part, cannot tolerate his impassivity, his cold reference to "the child's mound" (l. 30), his sarcastic suggestion that she share her grief with him: "Tell me about it *if it's something human*" (l. 58; my emphasis). Along with many characters in Frost's book, she seeks escape—"I must get out of here, I must get air" (l. 37)—and her husband's attempt to talk, since it is the wrong kind of talk, only leads to her departure at the poem's end.

The characters in "Home Burial" are incapable of breaking down the walls between and around them. Amy's intense, but futile and destructive, emotions are reflected in contorted language that raises for the first time in *North of Boston* the hint of delusion and insanity. In the following poem, "The Black Cottage," this hint becomes stronger and continues to grow during the central portion of the book, creating an ominous specter of derangement as one tendency of New England character.

As he did in "The Mountain," the implied author plays a direct, though minor, role in "The Black Cottage." In a dozen lines or so he provides a narrative frame for the monologue of his traveling partner and guide, a local minister. His interest in the minister's story of the lady who had lived in the cottage fits with his established character as an inquisitive explorer. Once more, he explores conflict between regional figures who accept traditional beliefs unquestioningly and those who are less certain or openly doubtful. The attitude he expressed in "Mending Wall" toward the farmer who "will not go behind his father's saying" is vigorously contradicted here by the minister's climactic declaration: "For, dear me, why abandon a belief / Merely because it ceases to be true" (ll. 105-106).

Yet, in contrast to the farmer of "Mending Wall" and to the lady who had owned the black cottage, the minister in this poem is too sophisticated for "serene belief," though he is deeply attracted to it. Compared with the persona, he appears pretentious, even hypocritical, because he tries to retreat into the old world represented by the black cottage. He undertakes no exploration for the truth, preferring instead to remain inert, feasting on grandiose reveries:

> As I sit here, and oftentimes, I wish
> I could be monarch of a desert land
> I could devote and dedicate forever
> To the truths we keep coming back and back to.
>
> (111-114)

As the minister waxes bombastic, Frost pushes the poetry far beyond the limits of the "colloquial tradition." Through a series of stunningly exotic images he presents a utopia that seems increasingly strange, a mental cul-de-sac of eerie sterility and stagnation:

> Sand dunes held loosely in tamarisk
> Blown over and over themselves in idleness.
> Sand grains should sugar in the natal dew
> The babe born to the desert, the sandstorm
> Retard mid-waste my cowering caravans—
>
> (120-124)

Like the torpid caravans, the minister's fantasy bogs down, and the sudden loss of momentum (indicated by the aposiopesis at the end of the quoted passage) underscores the futility of the entire passage. Significantly, the minister imagines his dream world "walled / By mountain ranges" (ll. 115-116), and this desire to isolate himself links him with characters in *North of Boston* who admire "good fences" and are suspicious of wanderers.

"The Black Cottage" provides persuasive evidence of the difference between the immature, vaguely Romantic poet who struggled and generally failed to produce first-rate verse at Derry and the mature artist who succeeded with remarkable frequency in capturing the poetry, the foibles, and the unpredictable human spirit of New England's country life. Thompson gives the text of an early version of the poem (*EY*, 592-593), which shows the mannered, overblown style and the awkward sentimentality typical of many Derry poems. In it, we hear the voice of a conventional, undramatized persona who fondly describes the black cottage and "The solitary inmate there / Who bows her head with snowy hair." His saccharine treatment of the melancholy scene is perhaps best exemplified by this couplet: "Bestarred with fainting fireflies / The pallid meadow mists arise." In the later version, while some traces of this heightened, mellifluous rhetoric still appear in the minister's ramblings, they are objectified as a credible and truly intriguing element of his personality, a personality that is in turn effectively dramatized in the narrative frame presented by the even more detached and objective traveler-persona.

The intense power of "Home Burial" and the unusual dramatic language of "The Black Cottage" are followed by *North of Boston's* weakest poem, "Blueberries." With thumping anapestic tetrameter couplets, it seems immature; and despite a memorable simile or two, it simply lacks the drama and the vigor of its companion pieces. Nevertheless, it has a purpose to serve in the overall structure of Frost's study of rural New England. By reworking many of the collection's themes and conflicts, it functions as a recapitulation of the first and lighter half of the book. The tension between the two speakers involves the familiar conflict between practical productivity and indulgent observation or contemplation. The husband has been out in the pasture, and like the persona who went out to clean the spring but ended up waiting to "watch the water clear," he has indulged in aesthetic and unproductive observation of blueberries. The poem's other characters are not brilliantly portrayed, yet they help to fill out *North of Boston's* regional population. The wife represents down-to-earth practicality (somewhat like Warren in "The Death of the Hired Man"). The vagrant, hand-to-mouth farmer, Loren, is reminiscent of Lafe and Silas, except that he has a vagrant, hand-to-mouth family that roams the countryside with him. Finally, there is the generous neighbor, Patterson, not at all a believer in "good fences," who owns the land where the delectable blueberries grow and who "won't make the fact that they're rightfully his / An excuse for keeping . . . other folk out" (ll. 31-32). His open neighborliness contrasts with the reserve and isolation characteristic of most farmers north of Boston.

Profanation North of Boston

"A Servant to Servants," *North of Boston*'s central poem (seven poems precede it, and seven follow it in the original table of contents), is a pivotal piece in the book's development. In the first half of the collection Frost maintained a balance between the autonomy and independence of some characters (including his persona) and the restrictions and constraints imposed by others, that is, those who represent regional norms and expectations. After this crucial poem, however, the balance shifts, and the burden of restraint and confinement weighs more heavily—often *too* heavily—on the shoulders both of the persona and of the individuals he encounters in his travels.

In "A Servant to Servants," the implied author listens silently while the distraught speaker delivers her monologue. He hardly has a role in the poem, yet his character as a meditative, analytical explorer of the regional world is reinforced. As in "The Mountain" and "The Black Cottage," he is a tourist, apparently camping near Lake Willoughby in Vermont because he had read about the area "in a book about ferns." This easy mobility, an outsider's luxury, prompts the woman to remark, "You let things more like feathers regulate / Your going and coming" (ll. 36-37). True to his rover's instincts, he begins to edge toward the door before his interlocutor is ready to let him go (a motif repeated four poems later, at the end of "The Housekeeper," as the persona tries "to get away" from a similarly encumbering situation).

While the vacationer's tent symbolizes the persona's mobility, the central image of "A Servant to Servants" is the cage that dominates some forty lines in the middle of the poem. Highly successful as an objective correlative for the mood of repression and confinement with which Frost imbued *North of Boston*, this cage is also an effective metaphorical extension of the fences, collars, walls, and restraints of all sorts found earlier in the book. The crude pen of hickory poles had been used to incarcerate the woman's uncle, a man whose insanity resulted from emotional indulgence (grief at being "crossed in love," l. 108) similar in kind, though more extreme in degree, to the deviance portrayed in previous poems, most obviously in "Home Burial," where Amy's grief had become a derangement. There is no doubt, however, that the speaker's existence as "a servant to servants" is another "sort of cage" (l. 113). Her resemblance to her uncle is evinced both by her confession that she has "been away once" (l. 90) at the state asylum and by her recollection of, and disturbing identification with, his imprisonment:

I often think of the smooth hickory bars.
It got so I would say—you know, half fooling—
"It's time I took my turn upstairs in jail"—
Just as you will till it becomes a habit.

(144-147)

Throughout the monologue, she speaks with neurotic urgency, betraying a need for escape that she can neither gratify nor fully recognize. She is another of *North of Boston*'s restless, imprudent seekers. Her equivalent of the trip to "the pasture" is

To step outdoors and take the water dazzle
A sunny morning, or take the rising wind
About my face and body and through my wrapper.

(27-29)

For a moment, in the phrases "take the water dazzle" and "take the rising wind / About my face and body," we can hear the deep passion, the tantalizing hint of Romantic rhetoric and mysticism, which Frost quickly undercuts, first with the New England colloquialism "A sunny morning" (lacking the expected preposition "on"), and then with the discordantly mundane and anti-Romantic "through my wrapper."

Like her auditor, this woman came to the shores of Lake Willoughby hoping to find a pleasant environment. Unfortunately, the setting has been less than effective as a restorative:

> I looked to be happy, and I was,
> As I said, for a while—but I don't know!
> Somehow the change wore out like a prescription.
> And there's more to it than just window views
> And living by a lake. I'm past such help. . . .
>
> (152-156)

Indeed, her life is so confining and enervating that "window views"—momentary glimpses of the world outside—are no longer beneficial. Her disenchantment with what she sees out the window links her with Amy in "Home Burial," as does her frustration:

> I can't express my feelings, any more
> Than I can raise my voice or want to lift
> My hand. . . .
> It's got so I don't even know for sure
> Whether I *am* glad, sorry, or anything.
> There's nothing but a voice-like left inside
> That seems to tell me how I ought to feel,
> And would feel if I wasn't all gone wrong.
>
> (7-15)

As in earlier poems in *North of Boston*, the speaker's difficulties arise from an antagonism to conventional codes and standards. Following the pattern established in "The Death of the Hired Man" and "Home Burial," the wife's impulsiveness and impracticality conflict with her husband's rigid view of what is proper and expedient. And as before, the husband speaks with the authority of aphorism and traditional wisdom: "one steady pull more ought to do it, . . . the best way out is always through" (ll. 55-56). Sadly, in this case there is *no* way out. The servant to servants suffers a bondage from which there is no escape, except perhaps to the still more constricting cage of the state asylum. Her unrealistic desires, her emotionalism and imprudence in divulging so much to a stranger (and a seemingly unsympathetic one at that) are a profanation from which the tourist-persona seeks to turn away. He is not one to condemn violations of propriety, yet his inability to deal with her is implicit in the awkward tension of his departure and the futility of her final plea: "I'd *rather* you'd not go unless you must" (l. 177). His feelings of repulsion seem prophetic: when she can no longer be dealt with (and we sense that such a condition is not far off), she will have to be put "away." Although she herself suggests (in words that echo "The Death of the Hired Man") that "it does seem more human" to keep the insane "at home" (l. 96), she knows full well that "it's not so: the place is the asylum" (l. 97). And thus the vicious circle north of Boston is complete. Confinement breeds insanity; insanity leads to more confinement. The farmer's precept from "Mending Wall" is here carried to its appalling extreme: "Good cages make good neighbors."

The abject desperation of "A Servant to Servants" becomes the dominant tone in the rest of the collection. Although anticipated in preceding pieces, it was offset by the lighter, more genial tone in "The Pasture," "The Mountain," "A Hundred Collars," "The Black Cottage," and "Blueberries." Even Amy, by far the most distressed speaker in the first part of the book (and the most similar to the wife of "A Servant to Servants"), was able to assert her independence by leaving her husband and taking her grief "to someone else" ("Home Burial," l. 57). But such options are rarely available to those most in need of them in the last half of *North of Boston*.

After "A Servant to Servants," even Frost's persona seems subdued as he contemplates the burdens and limitations of life in "After Apple-Picking." This poem moves away from the inquisitive exploratory mood of "The Pasture," "Mending Wall," "The Mountain," and "The Black Cottage." Where the first half of the collection implies a relatively carefree figure rambling about the countryside, we now find him "drowsing off." His repose involves both physical fatigue and the satisfaction of fulfillment, but it is also a meditation—and a revelation— that transcends the poem's concrete autumnal setting. Through his frosty looking glass—the sheet of ice skimmed from the drinking trough—he enters (and the musicality and compressed imagery of his utterance allow the reader to enter) a world of the imagination in which the elements of his harvest experience symbolize human effort and human desire: the ambitions and struggles, the joys and pains, the failures and accomplishments of life's myriad harvests.

"After Apple-Picking," perhaps more than any of Frost's other poems, maintains that exquisite tension between the lofty power of Romantic vision and the flat, hard reality of New England life, a tension that this poet was uniquely capable of achieving. From the colloquial, yet marvelously vivid and suggestive first line, "My long two-pointed ladder's sticking through a tree," Frost fleshes out a very human persona and a palpable harvest-time experience. We are impressed by the many concrete images—ladder, tree, barrel, drinking trough, cellar bin, cider-apple heap—and we are won over by the relaxed sincerity of the language, with its contractions ("ladder's," "there's," "didn't," "it's"), colloquial phrasing ("Sticking through," "drowsing off," "ten thousand thousand," "its coming on"), and conversational vagueness ("a tree," "some bough," "whatever sleep it is," "just some human sleep").

Yet, while Frost preserves the sound of sense throughout, there is as much of Keats and Shelley in this piece as there was in "My Butterfly" some twenty years before. Several lines approach the limits of direct, natural speech or idiomatic discourse:

fruit to touch,
Cherish in hand, lift down and not let fall,
For all that struck the earth
No matter if not bruised or spiked with stubble,
went surely to the cider-apple heap. . . .

(30-35)

Such phrases and images are faintly reminiscent of
Keats's "To Autumn," but Frost's central concern with
the mysteries of sleep and dream, death and spiritual
transcendence, creates an even stronger bond between his
great ode and those of Keats and Shelley. Indeed, when
we finish "After Apple-Picking" we face the same ques-
tion Keats poses at the end of his "Ode to a Nightingale":
"Was it a vision, or a waking dream?" Our inability to an-
swer springs partially from Frost's mastery of the vi-
sionary Romantic tradition, partially from his discovery of
local fact and specific experience worthy of visionary
treatment (experience lacking in "My Butterfly"), and par-
tially from his ability to make us see and believe both the
experience *and* the vision. For these strengths, the poem
is arguably one of the great triumphs of twentieth-century
verse.

In the "larger design" of *North of Boston*, "After
Apple-Picking" reaffirms the persona's deep sensitivity to
his surroundings and thus strengthens the cogency of the
entire collection as a record of his experience. The emo-
tional and imaginative pattern of this poem encourages
us, as we read the rest of the book, to reflect on the impact
of the region, with its particular scenes and characters, on
an observer so susceptible to suggestion, to dream, and to
fantasy. Indeed, we *can* "see what will trouble" his sleep,
for as the book draws to its close, we are reminded that his
is not a world of orchards and pastures only. There is a
social world, too, composed of men and women who
struggle unsuccessfully to live and work together.

In "The Code," "The Housekeeper," "The Fear," and
"The Self-Seeker," the men and women north of Boston

are defeated by the social roles they attempt to play. "The Code" dramatizes an outsider's awareness of the frighteningly rigid conventions and shibboleths that suffocate both those who conform and those who do not. Because of his outsider's role, we are likely to associate the "town-bred farmer" of this poem (l. 9) with the implied author of *North of Boston*. He is another questioner and auditor, and although he escapes harsh treatment, he learns that the punishment for even slight infractions against regional codes can be severe.

The following poem, "The Generations of Men," heightens the contrast between outsiders and insiders by emphasizing the relaxed idleness and independence of the vacationing Stark cousins. Their sophisticated objectivity and their sensitivity to the irony and ambiguity of their situation clash with "The Code's" focus on single-minded inflexibility and stubbornness. By dealing with a family reunion, Frost takes up a favorite motif of the local-color writers. But the conventional family reunion story, as recommended by Whittier and exemplified in the fiction of New England authors like Rose Terry Cooke and Sarah Orne Jewett,[26] takes place in splendid weather and focuses on large family gatherings characterized by deep kinship between the generations. Frost effectively subverts the convention by concentrating on an isolated couple and emphasizing their separation from their rustic progenitors. The old homestead is nothing but a cellar hole, and inclement weather keeps apart a family that has evidently *grown* apart (the young cousins have never met). Frost also undercuts the restrained courtship by following the poem with "The Housekeeper" and "The Fear," two macabre studies of the inability of men and

[26] For Whittier's endorsement of family reunions—along with Thanksgivings, apple-bees, huskings, berry pickings, sleigh rides, and courtships—see his essay "Robert Dinsmore," in *The Complete Writings of John Greenleaf Whittier*, vi (Boston: Houghton Mifflin, 1894), 248. Good examples of the family reunion story are Cooke's "Hopson's Choice," in *Huckleberries Gathered from New England Hills*, and Jewett's "The Bowden Reunion," in *The Country of the Pointed Firs*.

women to get along with one another. These dialogues are closely linked in theme and imagery to "Home Burial" and "A Servant to Servants." By portraying female characters who are emotionally crippled and confined, Frost anticipates the crippled hiker in "The Self-Seeker," the naturalist whose love of ferns, flowers, and trips to the pasture has been nightmarishly frustrated by a sawmill accident. He is the last character observed by the implied author of *North of Boston*, and his plight carries the collection toward its conclusion in a mood of deprivation, delimitation, and despair.

Although Frost wrote "The Wood-Pile" and "Good Hours" during the winter of 1911-1912 while he was still in New Hampshire,[27] the two poems function successfully as concluding pieces for *North of Boston*. They convey his awareness—half a year before he went to London—that the New England chapter of his life was drawing to its close. Appropriately, they do not focus on the trip *out* to the pasture, rural village, or mountain. Instead, they give attention to the return, the journey's end, and both have a subdued, apologetic tone that surely undercuts whatever pastoral affirmation might have been achieved at the beginning of the collection in "The Pasture." In the first half of "The Wood-Pile" the persona stresses his capriciousness as an outsider and explorer. He mentions his indecision about going on or turning back, and the imagery and disjointed syntax evoke a faint sense of transgression:

> The hard snow held me, save where now and then
> One foot went through. The view was all in lines
> Straight up and down of tall slim trees
> Too much alike to mark or name a place by
> So as to say for certain I was here
> Or somewhere else. . . .
>
> (4-9)

He is also confused about his motives and about whether he was or was *not* following a small bird through the

[27] Thompson dates these two poems, *EY*, 433.

woods. Thus he prepares the reader for his strange concern with the abandoned woodpile. What interests him is its ambiguity, and with much irony he attributes a metaphysical purpose to it, whimsically suggesting that the unknown woodcutter had left it "To warm the frozen swamp as best it could / With the slow smokeless burning of decay" (ll. 39-40).

Since the speaker has portrayed himself as a self-consciously unproductive hiker (aligning himself with the independent characters in *North of Boston* who, like Lafe, "go nowhere on purpose"), it is fitting that he should appreciate impractical, unproductive, and even unintended "purposes" for the woodpile's existence. By regional standards, of course, the woodcutter's efforts have been wasted. The hardheaded Yankee farmers depicted in "Mending Wall," "The Death of the Hired Man," "The Mountain," "Home Burial," and "The Code" would not be likely to make such a mistake. "The hand that knows his business," as "The Code" demonstrates (l. 22), wastes no time, and only a wasteful man would let himself be carried away by an inexpedient plan for a woodpile "far from a useful fireplace" (l. 38). But the persona's failure to censure this imprudence, and his proposal of the still more fatuous purpose of warming up the uninhabited swamp, establishes his extreme incongruity in the region that his book has studied.

His choice of the phrase "useful fireplace" shows his sensitivity to the difference between Yankee attitudes toward usefulness and his own. The woodpile interests him precisely because it is *not* useful. Frost's speaker, with his taste for the anomalous, resembles the woodsman whose existence the poem presupposes. And the woodpile itself, standing near the end of *North of Boston*, is in a position to function as a metaphor for the whole collection. Having strayed from regular pursuits, the persona leaves a record of his observations, a gathering of poems. He fears that it is no more "useful" than the abandoned pile of logs—the woodcutter's "handiwork on which / He spent himself" (l.

37). He seems, in fact, to doubt that the explorations on which he has spent himself have enabled him to accomplish even so trivial a purpose as the warming of a "frozen swamp."

The apologetic and contrite tone of "The Wood-Pile" carries over into "Good Hours," *North of Boston's* epilogue or envoy. A little-known piece, it nevertheless deserves attention as an indication of the state of Frost's mind in 1913, when he decided not only to use it as the final poem for his collection, but also to italicize it and set it apart from the other poems on an unnumbered page (thus linking it explicitly with "The Pasture"). As in "The Wood-Pile," the persona describes a solitary winter walk that takes him away from the community of his fellows. This pattern at the close of a "book of people" is highly significant. The observer seems finally to be drawing *away* from people; his ramblings lead him beyond the pale and force him to consider his analytical efforts a profanation (l. 15) of the rural environment he had originally set out to study. He travels alone—"No one at all with whom to talk" (l. 2)—and although he sees the "cottages in a row" (l. 3) where people live, he is uncertain of his relationship with the inhabitants. He describes even the "good hours" of his trip tentatively: "I *thought* I had the folk within" (l. 5; my emphasis). (Frost uses the verb "think" to undercut his persona in both of his concluding poems.)

Ultimately, the persona comes to the critical issue faced in "The Wood-Pile." He enjoyed the "good hours" (l. 9) of his walk as long as he was "outward bound"; but once he got away, once he arrived where "there were no cottages found," he had to decide whether to "turn back" or "go on further." The poem invests the end of the collection with a mood of confession, apology, and repentance, repudiating the venturousness of the preceding piece and of the numerous explorations that the book records. Unlike the implied author of the opening poems, and unlike Lafe, the carefree traveler of "A Hundred Collars," the speaker here seems not to have benefited from his explorations. Like the woman in "A Servant to Servants," who realizes that she is "all gone wrong," he must make a despondent confession. In the closing stanzas he laments both the loss of the "good hours" going out and the wretchedness of the trip back:

> I turned and repented, but coming back
> I saw no window but that was black.
>
> Over the snow my creaking feet
> Disturbed the slumbering village street
> Like profanation, by your leave,
> At ten o'clock of a winter eve.

On this dejected note Frost concluded his portrait of rural New England. Surely a poet of his sensitivity to linguistic overtones could not have failed to recognize that, coming on the book's final page, the apology for "creaking feet" (l. 13) would be a double-entendre extending the signification of the speaker's penitence for disturbing and profaning the "village street." The implied author of North of Boston seems to regret the creaking iambic feet through which. he conveyed his profanation of the rural world. And in this context, the phrase "by your leave" in the penultimate line can be taken not only as a direct apology, but also as a subtle message of gratitude to those unconventional readers who might have stayed up late, defying the curfews of orthodoxy, to finish the book and accompany the vagrant poet in his meditative, increasingly irreverent exploration.

We can see in retrospect that by turning his attention to his Yankee background and running his mind on rusticity during the spring and summer of 1913, Frost came up with material for a book that displays his full powers and, indeed, bears the stamp of genius. Creating a strikingly unorthodox and strikingly vivid dramatization of an independent observer's experience with local "fact" (both social and natural), Frost was able to probe deeply into the good and bad of rural life, its joys and satisfactions, its fears and limitations. In this way, he revealed much of human nature, as well as a wide range of local character. But at the same time, as he selected and arranged the material in the fall of that crucial year, he was not completely satisfied with his role as an observer of New England. Accordingly, his decision in 1914 to return to the farm country and work in earnest (which he had never done before), not as a farmer but as the Yankee farmer poet, was of great importance. He found, as we shall see, a more comfortable and reassuring role than the one displayed in *North of Boston*.

Four: The Poet of New England

Although Frost can be said to have reached his artistic maturity in the summer of 1913 when he completed the regional poetry that made *North of Boston* a significant contribution to American literature, he soon discovered how difficult it was to combine his new role as Yankee poet with his ambition to be "one of the most notable craftsmen" of the age. By December of that crucial year, the struggle to select, revise, and organize his poetry into an effective structure left him "clean shucked out,"[1] and, as the conclusion to *North of Boston* indicates, somewhat distraught and discouraged.

In the ensuing years, he sought a more reassuring regional identity, a different approach to the "poetry of the farm." Instead of presenting himself as an observer, analyst, and explorer north of Boston, he often posed as a spokesman for the region and an embodiment of its virtues. Although less faithful to his personality and background, this pose was gratifying in several ways. The more he played the true rustic, the more favorably his audiences and commentators seemed to respond. It was also easier to forget or overlook fears and uncertainties about his relationship to New England than to confront them as he had in his second collection.

His decision to place "The Wood-Pile" and "Good Hours" at the end of *North of Boston* is the most obvious

[1] Frost to Ernest Silver, 8 Dec. 1913, *SL*, 103.

evidence of his unsettled frame of mind late in 1913. Although written earlier, the two pieces seemed to present a judgment on his recent work, implying that the brilliantly dramatized regional studies were a "profanation" of New England, an unworthy artistic endeavor.

The precarious state of Frost's artistic development is also suggested by another conclusion he reached while struggling with the "larger design" of *North of Boston*: his decision to exclude from the volume a poem referred to as "Swinging Birches" in his letter of 7 August to John Bartlett. Strangely, among the twelve "New England Eclogues" described to Bartlett as destined for the "next book," only "Birches" was later found unworthy to appear in the final version.

How are we to explain this change of heart? Possibly, Frost failed to reach a satisfactory revision of "Swinging Birches" until after *North of Boston* had gone to press. It seems more likely, however, that if he had the piece well enough along to mention it to Bartlett in August, he *could* have completed it, had he been committed to it, by November, when he gave the collection to his publishers. His apparent lack of early commitment is particularly significant, given his tendency in later years to single out the poem as one of his most characteristic pieces.[2] But his decision was the right one: "Birches" is not well suited to *North of Boston*. On the contrary, it is important as a transitional piece, prefiguring much of the post-1913 poetry.

Although not comparable to the twelve overtly dramatic poems in *North of Boston*, "Birches" is broadly similar in form to the three meditative lyrics, "Mending Wall," "After Apple-Picking," and "The Wood-Pile"; thus Frost could not have omitted it on generic grounds alone. Yet he evidently knew that he had done something different in it, something not quite appropriate to the tone

[2] Reginald Cook notes that when Frost "reads 'Birches' in public, he sometimes says, 'this is one I am very fond of,' or, 'I lean on that,' as much as to say, 'Well I haven't done it better.' " Cook, *The Dimensions of Robert Frost* (New York: Rinehart and Company, Inc., 1958), p. 109.

and dramatic impetus of the other poems. Its speaker is a much more confident, affirmative, and dominating figure in the poem than are the other speakers. They face conflicts that leave them perplexed and uncertain, whereas the swinger of birches, surmounting all doubts and difficult questions, is given to pronouncements that have an oracular finality about them, despite their casual tone: "Earth's the right place for love. . . . One could do worse than be a swinger of birches" (ll. 52, 59).

It is noteworthy that two scholarly detractors of "Birches," Cleanth Brooks and Radcliffe Squires, though not concerned with its relationship to *North of Boston*, have nevertheless elected to contrast it with "After Apple-Picking," one of the 1913 meditative lyrics that *does* belong in that collection. The contrast between these poems is important because Frost shifted his focus subtly when he wrote "Birches," moving away from vivid evocation of experience (as in "Mending Wall," "After Apple-Picking," "The Wood-Pile," and the other poems in *North of Boston*) and toward ardent expression of philosophy. The speaker proclaims a Yankee identity with unprecedented confidence, coming "downstage," as Brooks phrases it, "to philosophize explicitly." His tone and the stance he takes in the poem are entirely different from what we saw in *North of Boston*, where the persona tends to be unsure of himself, a bit uncomfortable, and occasionally apologetic.[3]

The philosophy articulated in "Birches" poses no threat to popular values or beliefs, and it is so appealingly affirmative that many readers have treasured the poem as a masterpiece. Among Frost's most celebrated works, perhaps only "Stopping by Woods on a Snowy Evening" ranks ahead of it. Yet to critics like Brooks and Squires, the persona's philosophical stance in "Birches" is a seri-

[3] See Brooks, "Frost, MacLeish, and Auden," in Brooks, *Modern Poetry and the Tradition* (Chapel Hill: University of North Carolina Press, 1939), pp. 112-114, and Squires, *The Major Themes of Robert Frost* (Ann Arbor: University of Michigan Press, 1963), pp. 55-59.

ous weakness. And another perceptive commentator, Randall Jarrell, has complained that so much popularity makes it almost impossible for us to approach Frost without "the taste of 'Birches' in our mouth—a taste a little brassy, a little sugary."[4] Associating such an undesirable flavor with the "Yankee Editorialist side of Frost," Jarrell proposes, as a major objective for his essay "To the Laodiceans," to cleanse away this all-too-persistent pungency.

It is not the purpose of the present study to arbitrate the dispute over "Birches." No easy compromises are likely, owing to sharply conflicting tastes among Frost's readers. The didactic and philosophical element that some critics have attacked strikes others as the very core of Frost's virtue. The poet's friend Sidney Cox dedicated an entire book to expounding the philosophy of the "Swinger of Birches," with exempla from the poems and from the conversation of the master.[5] Indeed, the brassy, sugary taste that offended Randall Jarrell may appeal to many other readers precisely because of its reassuring strength in an age of anxiety and uncertainty.

Perhaps impartial observers can accept the notion that "Birches" is neither as bad as its harshest opponents suggest nor as good as its most adoring advocates claim. There must be some poetry in a work that remains so delightful and touching, so vivid and quotable after half a century in the spotlight. Yet, how can we consider it a true masterpiece when a significant group of intelligent, expertly qualified, independent readers—undoubtedly a minority, but still a group to be reckoned with—has raised serious and thoughtful objections to it? What needs to be recognized is that it is a controversial piece, and that we can find nothing quite like it in Frost's work up through the Beaconsfield period. The intense debate it has aroused should also help us to realize that the poem is an anomaly

[4] Jarrell, "To the Laodiceans," in Jarrell, *Poetry and the Age* (New York: Random House, 1953), p. 37.

[5] Cox, *A Swinger of Birches: A Portrait of Robert Frost* (1957; rpt. New York: Collier Books, 1961).

deserving close study as an initial and highly consequential experiment with a new approach to New England poetry.

Robert Langbaum's *The Poetry of Experience* provides a theoretical basis that helps to explain the difference between "Birches" and Frost's other meditative lyrics of 1913. Langbaum has demonstrated the importance of what he calls the "extraordinary perspective" as a device "to keep the poem located—to keep the dramatic situation from turning into a rhetorical device and the landscape from turning into a metaphor for an abstract idea."[6] Extraordinary perspectives dominate "Mending Wall," first in the speaker's perception of a mysterious "something . . . that doesn't love a wall," then in his quirky glimpses of fence mending as game, ritual, even tragedy, and finally in his climactic vision of the neighbor as an "old-stone savage." In "After Apple-Picking," the pervasive "strangeness" (l. 9) of looking through a thin sheet of ice leads to chimerical dreams and recollections of the harvest effort. And "The Wood-Pile" presents extraordinary perspectives not only on the "slow smokeless burning of decay" and the remarkable "small bird" who seemed to take things "as personal to himself," but also on the entire setting, where "the view was all in lines" and the speaker could not say "for certain" whether he was "here / Or somewhere else."

"Birches," on the other hand, contains three fairly lengthy descriptions that do not involve unusual perspectives. In fact, the most original and distinctive vision in the poem—the passage treating the ice on the trees (ll. 5-14)—is undercut both by the self-consciousness of its final line ("You'd think the inner dome of heaven had fallen") and by the two much more conventionally perceived environments that follow it: the rural boyhood of the swinger of birches (ll. 23-40) and the "pathless wood," which represents life's "considerations" (ll. 44-47). As a

---

[6] Langbaum, *The Poetry of Experience* (1957; rpt. New York: W. W. Norton and Company, Inc., 1963), p. 47.

result, the poem's ardent concluding lines—its closing pronouncements on life, death, and human aspiration—do not arise from a particular experience. Instead, they are presented as doctrines that we must accept or reject on the basis of our credence in the speaker as a wise countryman whose familiarity with birch trees, ice storms, and pathless woods gives him authority as a philosopher.

Since in "Birches" the natural object—tree, ice crystal, pathless wood, etc.—functions as proof of the speaker's rusticity, Frost has no need for extraordinary perspectives, and therefore the poem does little to convince us that an "experience," to use Langbaum's wording, "is really taking place, that the object is seen and not merely remembered from a public or abstract view of it" (p. 47). This is not to deny that the poem contains some brilliant descriptive passages (especially memorable are the clicking, cracking, shattering ice crystals in lines 7-11 and the boy's painstaking climb and sudden, exhilarating descent in lines 35-40), and without doubt, the closing lines offer an engaging exegesis of swinging birches as a way of life. But though we learn a great deal about this speaker's beliefs and preferences, we find at last that he has not revealed himself as profoundly as does the speaker in "After Apple-Picking." It is remarkable that the verb "to like," which does not appear in Frost's nondramatic poetry prior to "Birches," is used three times in this poem: "I like to think" (l. 3); "I'd like to get away" (l. 48); and "I'd like to go" (l. 54). The speaker also tells us what he would "prefer" (l. 23), "dream of" (l. 42), and "wish" (l. 51). But while his preferences are generally appealing, and while they seem intellectually justified, they are not *poetically* justified in the sense that Langbaum suggests when he discusses the "extraordinary perspective" as a "sign that the experience is really taking place": "The experience has validity just because it is dramatized as an event which we must accept as having taken place, rather than formulated as an idea with which we must agree or disagree" (p. 43).

"Mending Wall," "After Apple-Picking," and "The

Wood-Pile" are centered on specific events that involve the speaker in dramatic conflicts and lead him to extraordinary perspectives. The act of repairing the wall and trying to reason with the crusty farmer, the termination of the harvest and the preparation for a winter's rest, the vagrant woodland ramble and the discovery of the perplexing woodpile—all these are events that we indeed "accept as having taken place."

Unlike the meditative lyrics Frost selected for *North of Boston*, however, "Birches" does not present a central dramatized event as a stimulus for the speaker's utterance. Although the conclusion seems sincere, and although Frost created a persuasive metaphorical context for it, the final sentiments do not grow dramatically out of the experiences alluded to. Yes, the speaker has observed ice storms that bend the birches "down to stay" (l. 4); he has "learned all there is / To learn" about swinging birches (ll. 32-33); and he has struggled through the "considerations" of life's "pathless wood" (ll. 43-44). But the relationship of these experiences to his present utterance—the poem—is left unclear. We would be more willing to accept what Squires calls a "contradictory jumble" of images and ideas if we were convinced (as Eliot and Pound often convince us) that the diverse materials had coalesced in the speaker's mind. Frost's confession that the poem was "two fragments soldered together" is revealing;[7] the overt, affected capriciousness of the transitions between major sections of the poem (ll. 4-5, 21-22, and 41-42) indicates that instead of striving to establish the dynamics of dramatized experience, he felt he could rely on the force of his speaker's personality and rural background. In early editions, a parenthetical question, "(Now am I free to be poetical?)," followed line 22, making the transition between the ice storm and the country youth even more arbitrary.

---

[7] See Cleanth Brooks and Robert Penn Warren, *Understanding Poetry*, rev. ed. (New York: Henry Holt, 1950), pp. 603-604.

By comparing "Birches" with Frost's other work in 1913 we can see that even before completing *North of Boston* he had begun to explore a different way of exploiting his new sense of identity as a New Englander. The confidence he gained while fashioning his "book of people" encouraged him to don his Yankee mask more aggressively than he had in poems like "Mending Wall" and "After Apple-Picking." Less than a year after denying to Miss Ward the "virtue in Location" (SL, 52), he produced a poem that relies on a fundamental association of his poetic self—"So was I once myself" (l. 41)—with the rustic lad who tended cows and lived "too far from town to learn baseball" (ll. 24-25). The poem's philosophy presupposes a philosopher who was once himself just such a rustic lad—a role that Frost was more than willing to play, even though *his* boyhood had been one of basepaths rather than cowpaths, and town sandlots rather than country pastures. (His biographer attests that he knew more about stealing bases when he was fourteen than he did about milking cows at twice that age.)[8]

It may seem arbitrary to press too hard the issue of honesty in this poem. Art, after all, relies on fantasy and deception. Yet there are different types of fantasy and many motives for deception. If we are confident that an artist has kept faith with some personal vision or inner self, we can accept falsification of many things. When Frost presents himself as a farm worker, for instance—a mower wielding his scythe or apple picker resting his weary body—the fantasy seems sincere and convincing. When we consider Frost's career and personal history, however, we may wonder about his motives in falsifying the character of his childhood. The resulting images lack originality and inspiration. Surely "Birches" contains some vivid and forceful passages, but when a line or phrase gives us too strong a sense of the poet's calculated effort to validate

[8] On Frost's early enthusiasm for baseball, see *EY*, 58-59, 74-75; on his difficulty in learning to milk and care for his cow in Derry, *EY*, 277-278.

his speaker's rusticity, the spell of the poem, its incantatory charm and imaginative vision, is threatened. Fortunately, in "Birches" this threat is hardly noticeable, certainly not overwhelming or repellent, unless we want it to be.

"Birches," of course, is not an extreme instance of the Yankee farmer as poetic persona. But after writing for more than twenty years, Frost had never—not in his two early experiments with a regional speaker ("The Tuft of Flowers" and "Mowing") and surely not in North of Boston—come so close to producing advertisements for himself as a Yankee poet. Thus this poem in 1913 was a significant step toward more blatant exhibitions soon to come. He had not been in England a year when he began to speculate about how his "New England impressions" might be jeopardized by too much exposure to alien settings (SL, 91). Soon the planned trip to France was called off, and shortly after North of Boston went to press, he started to entertain a "dream" that, having gained a name for himself in London, he could "do the rest of it from a farm in New England where I could live cheap and get Yankier and Yankier" (SL, 103).

The Yankee Poet and Other Misconceptions

On returning to New England in 1915, Frost wasted no time in locating himself (or rather his family, since he spent much of his time traveling to promote his literary career) farther north of Boston than he had ever lived before. The White Mountains, where the Frosts had occasionally vacationed during the Derry years, were about 150 miles from Boston, while Derry was just across the Massachusetts border. The many differences between this new and much more "strategic" retreat in 1915 and the move to Derry fifteen years before were consistently overlooked—both by the reading public, who knew no better, and by Frost himself, who did. "Christmas Trees," the first full exploitation of the Yankee farmer persona, was his way of giving notice in 1915 that he had assumed his rightful position in the farm country. Let the city slicker beware, he seemed to say, of trying to outsmart this shrewd Yankee by undervaluing his rustic wares. For his "friends . . . in cities," on the other hand, the farmer poet might have occasional gifts: he might even wish to send a Christmas tree, but since he "couldn't lay one in a letter," perhaps a poem could be as lovely as a tree—if it came fresh from the farm.

While writing "Christmas Trees" and enjoying his first White Mountain snows in December 1915, Frost may also have been at work on another wintry poem, one that placed him even more decisively within the tradition of New England regional literature: "Brown's Descent or, the Willy-Nilly Slide." This comic piece in nineteen rollicking iambic tetrameter quatrains was completed in time for use on the poet's first reading tour in January 1916. The initial twelve stanzas are an enjoyable description of Brown's marvelously stylized, almost balletic, slide from his "lofty farm" (l. 1) down a two-mile, ice-coated hill.

As Reuben Brower has demonstrated in detail, Frost marshals his prosodic skills in these opening quatrains to produce not only a genuinely witty narrative, but also "a piece of sophisticated and intricate art metrically and 'vocally.' "[9] Through shifting rhythms and unexpected enjambments, through a touch of the mock-heroic, and through carefully phrased, often parallel or balanced sentences, he demonstrates his ability to transcend the conventions and expectations of regional literature. Brower even discerns the prosodic sophistication of Dryden and Pope in these two stanzas:

> Sometimes he came with arms outspread
>   Like wings, revolving in the scene
> Upon his longer axis, and
>   With no small dignity of mien.

[9] Brower, The Poetry of Robert Frost: Constellations of Intention (New York: Oxford University Press, 1963), p. 13.

> Faster or slower as he chanced,
>   Sitting or standing as he chose,
> According as he feared to risk
>   His neck, or thought to spare his clothes.

(21-28)

Once Brown reaches the bottom of the hill, however, the poet-narrator suddenly indulges in a lengthy digression, coming downstage to philosophize about Yankee character for six stanzas, until a final quatrain recounts Brown's undaunted but roundabout walk home.

Like "Christmas Trees," and somewhat like "Birches," "Browns's Descent" is a significant failure—significant as an indication of the dangerous tendencies Frost's regional pose seemed to encourage. By forcing the homiletic Yankee sage into the poem, by insisting too much on his "authority" (l. 49) as a regional figure, he undermined what might have been an effectively sustained tour de force— not a major work, of course, since the subject is trivial, but a creditable minor piece. A skilled poet, Frost was capable of treating his regional material with verve and originality. Yet he was not satisfied to work within the framework established by the narrative stanzas (ll. 1-48, 73-76). Going well beyond the sort of character study appropriate to a "book of people," he inserted the philosophical reflections of a rustic persona, reflections that devitalize the poem's comic spirit and weigh down its light, whimsical tone.

"Sometimes as an authority / On motorcars," declares the speaker as he begins his digression in the thirteenth quatrain, "I'm asked if I / Should say our stock was petered out" (ll. 49-51). Of course, he is *not* an "authority" about cars; the simile is just a device to establish that he is generally regarded—and hence *deserves* to be regarded —as an expert on what he sweepingly calls "our stock" (ll. 51, 62): Yankees. Sadly, his conclusions, like many expert opinions, involve more platitude than insight— and hardly touch the poetic at all:

Yankees are what they always were.
   Don't think Brown ever gave up hope
Of getting home again because
   He couldn't climb that slippery slope;

Or even thought of standing there
   Until the January thaw
Should take the polish off the crust.
   He bowed with grace to natural law,

And then went round it on his feet,
   After the manner of our stock;
Not much concerned for those to whom,
   At that particular time o'clock,

It must have looked as if the course
   He steered was really straight away
From that which he was headed for. . . .

                       (53-67)

The poem loses its momentum in these stanzas. Frost gives up his portrait of a particular "Farmer Brown" and starts to generalize about the type. The vigor and spirit of the opening quatrains gradually dissipate in labored excogitation, insipid, almost clichéd language ("gave up hope," "bowed with grace," "the course / He steered"), and occasional vapid, awkward lines ("At that particular time o'clock," "From that which he was headed for"). The poem's delicate thread of anecdote stretches and finally breaks.

Even Frost recognized that the moralistic digression in stanzas 13-18 was an artistic liability: after omitting the eighteenth quatrain in his 1923 *Selected Poems*, he went on to delete three (16-18) from what he called his "final version" in 1945.[10] Although at least one scholar has found this text effective,[11] Frost inexplicably reverted to

[10] See David McCord's anthology, *What Cheer* (New York: Coward-McCann, Inc., 1945), pp. 5-7, 398n.

[11] Walter Gierasch, "Frost's 'Brown's Descent,' " *Explicator*, 11 (June 1953), 60.

the original for the 1946 Modern Library edition of his poetry, the version followed in all subsequent collections. One of the many ironies of his reputation as the poet of New England is that this conspicuously regional piece quickly became a literary albatross. Within a few years of its completion, Frost realized that it was "not a good poem," yet it was so popular with the audiences at his public appearances that throughout the rest of his career he could not escape the unpleasantness of being "often asked to read 'Brown's Descent' " (SL, 75).

Two lines in the digressive passage of the poem seem especially important in the larger context of Frost's literary development. The first, the aphoristic dictum that "Yankees are what they always were," may remind us of maxims like "Good fences make good neighbors" and "the best way out is always through" from such sententious characters as the neighbor in "Mending Wall," Len in "A Servant to Servants," Warren in "The Death of the Hired Man," and the husband in "Home Burial." What is important, however, is that while the implied author in *North of Boston* seemed unsympathetic to these simplistic pronouncements, Frost's more intensely regional speaker in 1915 takes the opposite stand and affirms the virtue of hardheaded Yankee practicality.

Another line, "He bowed with grace to natural law," echoes the imagery of a still earlier work: the melancholy Romantic lyric "Reluctance" from *A Boy's Will*. But there the younger Frost had taken a very different position. Instead of praising a pragmatic submissiveness to natural law, he had asked:

Ah, when to the heart of man
  Was it ever less than a treason
To go with the drift of things,
  To yield with a grace to reason,
And bow and accept the end
  Of a love or a season?

                                                              (19-24)

The contrast between these attitudes toward bowing gracefully before the inevitable is instructive about the tension between Frost the poet and Frost the regionalist. The former loved to challenge "natural law." Bowing, yielding, and accepting were not among his virtues. He may have thought of his contentiousness as "a lover's quarrel with the world," yet he often regarded his poetry as "a figure of the will braving alien entanglements."[12] As a self-conscious regional spokesman on the other hand, Frost was much less daring and combative. He was neither an explorer nor an experimenter; instead of probing and questioning life's difficulties, he presented answers and solutions. Where his instinct as a poet might have led him to dramatize a conflict (Brown's comic struggle against gravity and the icy hill), his tendency as a regionalist was to draw conclusions, to formulate advice and moral lessons (doctrines about the hardy, level-headed reliability of "our stock").

Charmed by his own Yankee mask, Frost was susceptible to delusions of rustic grandeur; yet he donned the mask most often and most vigorously not in his writing but in his public appearances, appearances that had an unmerited and misleading influence on his reputation. Even before leaving England, he had done much to assure that he would be recognized—if and when recognition came—as a New England poet. Aware that impressing the reviewers was "all sorts of a game" (SL, 88), he regaled his literary acquaintances with tales of life on the farm.

He also took steps to strengthen the validity of his claim as a Yankee spokesman. In July 1913, for instance, he first expressed a rather ambivalent interest in making contact with one of New England's leading poets, Edwin Arlington Robinson. "I wish sometime if you know Robinson," he wrote Thomas Mosher (a publisher and leading literary figure in Portland, Maine), "you could put me in

---

[12] Quotations from "The Lesson for Today" (P, 355) and Frost's essay, "The Constant Symbol" (1946; rpt. in P&P, 401).

the way of knowing him too—*sometime*, if it comes right"
(*SL*, 84). His sudden interest in this acquaintanceship—
after having put the Atlantic ocean between himself and
Robinson—was evidently another of the ironic effects of
his contact with Ezra Pound. For when Pound entertained
the unheralded author of *A Boy's Will* in March 1913,
"the first poet . . . talked about was Edwin Arlington
Robinson," according to Frost's own recollection.[13]
Clearly, this was a poet with whom an aspiring New Eng-
land writer would do well to associate himself.

Not content to let the British reviewers shape his repu-
tation, Frost mounted a campaign in the summer and fall
of 1913 to establish his identity as Yankee farmer poet in
the region from which this identity was supposedly
drawn. He wrote a series of letters coaxing his friend John
Bartlett, a journalist, to write an article for American cir-
culation on the success of *A Boy's Will*. In addition to
supplying copies of reviews as material for the essay,
moreover, he explained how they were to be treated:

> No one of the articles but should be used with some
> judgment. This Bookman piece for instance makes
> me out as able to earn a living on a farm with both
> hands in my Norfolk-jacket pocket. Rats. I should
> rather you would eliminate that. The word "stark" in
> it will do well enough, though it is wide enough of
> the mark. As things go here in criticism it passes for a
> term of praise. . . . On the whole I think the Bookman
> article needs manipulation as little as any. (*SL*, 88)

The goal of this manipulation is clear. The line in the
Bookman review that Frost wanted to excise—and which
Bartlett obligingly and discreetly (that is, without disclos-
ing the ellipsis) deleted from his article[14]—was the in-
nocuous statement that Frost "was nothing much of a

[13] Frost, "Introduction" to *King Jasper* (1935; rpt. in *P&P*, 350).

[14] Bartlett's essay is reprinted in Margaret Anderson, *Robert Frost and
John Bartlett: The Record of a Friendship* (New York: Holt, Rinehart and
Winston, 1963), pp. 67-72.

farmer, but contrived to make enough of it for the needs of himself and his family."[15] While trying to establish himself as countryman, he could not tolerate even this faintly irreverent estimate of his farming career, no matter that it was a patently generous account. For in truth, farming had not provided "for the needs of himself and his family." On the contrary, in just six years at Derry he had spent $3,000 in inheritance (from his grandfather's estate), borrowed an additional $750 by mortgaging the farm, and begun earning a salary as a teacher at Pinkerton. Later, once his reputation was secure, he could confide to a trusted friend like Untermeyer: "Let's be truthful about the farming: it didn't earn me a living" (*RF/LU*, 122). But in 1913 he preferred the admittedly imprecise adjective "stark" to anything that might hint at the true nature of his life as a farmer.

Frost's return to New Hampshire in 1915 and his assumption of the Yankee farmer's role could hardly have been better timed. Benjamin T. Spencer has identified a resurgence in American regionalism from about 1912 into the 1920s, noting that localism was especially dominant in American poetry from 1915 to 1925.[16] At this time, American literature seemed to focus on regional environments: Ellen Glasgow's Dinwiddie, Virginia; Robinson's Tilbury Town; Carl Sandburg's Chicago; Willa Cather's Black Hawk, Nebraska; Edgar Lee Masters's Spoon River; Sherwood Anderson's Winesburg, Ohio; and Sinclair Lewis's Gopher Prairie, Minnesota. Thus it is entirely understandable that Frost's residence on a White Mountain farm—together with his pose as the Yankee farmer poet and his promulgation of the Derry myth—had a profound effect on the literary community. *North of Boston*, released in New York just prior to his return from

[15] Anonymous review of *A Boy's Will*, *Bookman* (London), 44 (Aug. 1913), 189.

[16] Spencer, "Regionalism in American Literature," in Merrill Jensen, ed., *Regionalism in America* (Madison: University of Wisconsin Press, 1951), p. 244.

England in February 1915, went on the best-seller list and into its fourth printing during the summer before the poet was completely settled on his new farm (YT, 56). So adept was Frost at performing his rustic role, however, that during the spring of 1915, well before moving to the farm, he had beguiled interviewers, critics, and urban acquaintances into thinking that he was already engaged in agricultural work.[17]

With considerable fanfare, magazines and newspapers hailed Frost as "New England's New Poet," the "Poet of the Hills," "Poet of New England," "The Farmer Poet," "The Poet of New England's Hill-men." To Amy Lowell he was an "uncompromising New Englander," to Harriet Monroe, a spokesman for "Puritan New England." William Dean Howells found his verse "very genuinely and unaffectedly expressive of rustic New England," while Jessie B. Rittenhouse informed *New York Times* readers that he was "a farmer in New Hampshire" who had "tilled his acres before he converted them into poetry."[18] The myths that the literary world was so ready to believe in 1915 ultimately became the source of fundamental and

[17] Although Frost did not move to the Franconia farm until June 1915, *Atlantic* editor Ellery Sedgwick wrote that on 6 May 1915 Frost "had once again returned from his farm . . . to see me" (SL, 176). Frost is also portrayed as an active New Hampshire farmer in Sylvester Baxter, "Talk of the Town," *Boston Herald*, 9 Mar. 1915, p. 9.

[18] Sylvester Baxter, "New England's New Poet," *American Review of Reviews*, 51 (April 1915), 432-434; "A New Poet of the Hills," *Brooklyn Daily Eagle*, 24 April 1915, sec. 2, p. 5; W. S. Braithwaite, "A Poet of New England: Robert Frost a New Exponent of Life," *Boston Evening Transcript*, 28 April 1915, pt. 3, p. 4; Joseph Anthony, "Robert Frost: The Farmer Poet," *Farm and Fireside*, 45 (June 1921), 4; John Farrar, "The Poet of New England's Hill-men," *Literary Digest International Book Review*, 1 (Nov. 1923), 25; Amy Lowell, "North of Boston," *New Republic*, 2 (20 Feb. 1915), 81; Harriet Monroe, "Frost and Masters," *Poetry: A Magazine of Verse*, 9 (Jan. 1917), 202-207; William Dean Howells, "The Editor's Easy Chair," *Harper's Monthly Magazine*, 131 (Sept. 1915), 165; Jessie B. Rittenhouse, "North of Boston," *New York Times Book Review*, 16 May 1915, p. 189. These reviews and many others pertinent to Frost's regionalism are listed chronologically in the appendix.

enduring misconceptions about Frost's regionalism. Thus, although much of the praise was based on faulty premises, he was often saluted not merely as a regional author, but as America's *most* regional author—the most sensitive and faithful representative of his region.

Curiously, however, the most influential testimonials to his Yankee fidelity came from critics who followed Ezra Pound's lead, stressing the New Englander's simplicity and parochialism, even to the point of condescension. Their patronage was too obviously patronizing. Amy Lowell, herself a prominent New Englander, insisted that Frost was "saturated with New England" and linked him directly with Whittier and Alice Brown. But her imperious early review of *North of Boston*, in the *New Republic* of 20 February 1915 manages to suggest that there are standards—"subtler senses"—by which New England literature in general, and *North of Boston* in particular, can be found lacking:

> not only is his work New England in subject, it is so in technique. No hint of European forms has crept into it. It is certainly the most American volume of poetry that has appeared for some time. I use the word American . . . to mean work of a color so local as to be almost photographic. Mr. Frost's book is American in the sense that Whittier is American, and not at all in that subtler sense in which Poe ranks as the greatest American poet. (p. 81)

Evidently, to the celebrated Imagist and sophisticated interpreter of French poets and John Keats, New England regionalists were, for all their "photographic" local-color skills, a limited group. Whittier and Alice Brown, after all, hardly deserved comparison with Edgar Allan Poe, the American grandfather (once removed) of *le symbolisme* and a putative great-grandfather of Imagism. This is not an unreasonable opinion; but what Lowell and a host of later critics failed to consider is the crucial difference between Frost and the local-colorists. She was wrong indeed if she thought of him as a simple countryman who would fail to see her backhanded compliment for what it was.[19] And she was still more wrong to suggest that such poems as "Mending Wall," "The Mountain," "The Death of the Hired Man," "A Servant to Servants," "After Apple-Picking," and "The Wood-Pile" succeed only as photographic representations of New England. The region is there, of course, and Frost was surely as accurate with his verbal photography as any New England writer. But the idea that he was New England "in technique" is a simplistic misjudgment of his poetry. Lowell did not know that he had considered the title "New England Eclogues" for *North of Boston*, nor was she aware that he had achieved an outstanding record as a classics scholar at Harvard,[20] so she had no reason to suspect how much depth and breadth there was to his literary background. Nevertheless, *North of Boston*'s reliance on dramatic forms—forms pioneered by Tennyson and Browning—should have been sufficient evidence that this was not a poet who restricted himself to regional techniques.

Ultimately, by endorsing the assumption that Frost's greatest virtue lay in his fidelity to the region,[21] Lowell's review of *North of Boston* not only misrepresented the book but also strengthened the biographical tendencies

[19] Although gratified to receive attention from such a consequential figure as Miss Lowell, Frost took umbrage at her subtle deprecations. When an extended version of her review appeared in her *Tendencies in Modern American Poetry* (New York: Macmillan Co., 1917), pp. 79-136, he revealed his resentment to Untermeyer. See *SL*, 221-224, 249-250.

[20] For Frost's discussion of alternate titles for *North of Boston*, see *SL*, 89; for his classical background, see *EY*, 79-88, 100-101, 230-236, and *SL*, 30, 401-402.

[21] This was the assumption made by such critics in England as Ezra Pound, Richard Aldington, Wilfred Gibson, Lascelles Abercrombie, and F. S. Flint. Pound's opinions had appeared in *Poetry: A Magazine of Verse*, of course, and another American, Alice Corbin Henderson, had reviewed Frost in *The Dial*, 57 (1 Oct. 1914), 254; but Lowell was the first prominent member of the American literary community (and, more important, the *New England* literary community) to give Frost critical recognition.

that, with occasional support from Frost's "myth-making" performances, have persistently plagued criticism of his poetry. Emphasizing that his photographic "pictures" and "characters" were "produced directly from life," she slighted the exceptional artistic vision and the immense craftsmanship that distinguish *North of Boston* from countless local-color sketches that are "produced directly from life," yet lack inspiration and artistry. Frost's specific skills as a poet could not have been of much concern to a critic so taken with his personal identity as a regional figure:

> He is not writing of people whom he has met in summer vacations, who strike him as interesting, and whose life he thinks worthy of perpetuation. . . . He is as racial as his own puppets. One of the great interests of the book is the uncompromising New Englander it reveals. That he could have written half so valuable a book had such not been the case I very much doubt. (p. 82)

This estimate disregards the import of the vacationer or tourist in "The Mountain," "A Hundred Collars," "The Black Cottage," "A Servant to Servants," and "The Generations of Men," though surely the references to camping, tents, and rental cottages in "A Servant to Servants" (ll. 2, 41, 168) indicate that the auditor is indeed on a summer vacation.[22] The persona's tents, in fact (as suggested in Chapter Three), provide an effective imagistic contrast to the cage in "A Servant to Servants" that symbolizes the local speaker's life of frustration and constraint.

If Lowell goes too far in denying Frost his vacations, her insistence that he is "as racial as his puppets," seems an even more serious distortion of a book that gives so much attention to a broad spectrum of regional and nonregional

---

[22] For evidence that "A Servant to Servants" is a summer vacation poem, see accounts of the Frosts' tenting trips to Lake Willoughby, Vt., in *EY*, 350-353. Note also that Mount Hor and Lunenburg ("The Mountain," ll. 19, 91) are near the Lake Willoughby resort area.

characters—locals and tourists, insiders and outsiders.[23] She is right that "one of the great interests of the book" is the speaker or implied author it reveals; but this figure is not intensely "racial" (by which she presumably means deeply imbued with regional traits), nor is he an "uncompromising New Englander." The neighbor in "Mending Wall" *is* uncompromising. Uncompromising, too, are characters in "The Death of the Hired Man," "Home Burial," "A Servant to Servants," and "The Code." But the speaker in the nondramatic poems (especially in "Mending Wall" and "The Wood-Pile"), and the observer implied in many of the dramatic poems, is not at all the hard, unyielding, determined Yankee. On the contrary, he is tentative and irresolute, prone to vacillation and capriciousness, susceptible to doubts and perplexities. Rather than ingrained racial traits, he displays great sensitivity to the differences and tensions between himself and those he observes; as we see him in his encounters with local farmers in such poems as "Mending Wall" and "The Mountain," he is nothing if not a compromiser.

Despite her misjudgments of *North of Boston*, Amy Lowell could hardly have done Frost and his regional reputation greater disservice than to suggest that, as a faithful representative of New England, he could succeed or accomplish all that he was capable of without bringing into play two of poetry's most sacred requisites, imagination and music: "As there is no rare and vivid imaginative force playing over his subjects, so there is no exotic music pulsing through his verse" (p. 82). Not only do *North of Boston's* three great dramatic lyrics—"Mending Wall," "After Apple-Picking," and "The Wood-Pile"—contain

---

[23] Seven of *North of Boston's* seventeen poems make use of tensions between insiders and outsiders: speaker and farmer in "Mending Wall"; Silas and Harold Wilson in "The Death of the Hired Man"; tourist and local inhabitant in "The Mountain"; Lafe and Magoon in "A Hundred Collars"; speaker and auditor in "A Servant to Servants"; experienced workers and "town-bred farmer" (l. 9) in "The Code"; and city lawyer and rural sawmill worker in "The Self-Seeker."

passages of unforgettable imagination and musicality (the most obvious example being the brilliantly assonant and echoic "magnified apples" passage in "After Apple-Picking" [ll. 18-26]), but even the relatively prosaic, rural speakers in dramatic pieces like "The Mountain," "The Black Cottage," "Home Burial," "Blueberries," and "A Servant to Servants" have their moments of lyric intensity. In addition to the examples cited in Chapter Three, there are rhapsodic and melodically resonant utterances throughout the collection that often threaten and occasionally violate Frost's supposed photographic fidelity to regional character. An alliterative tour de force in "Home Burial," for instance, lends great power to the wife's description of her husband digging the child's grave:

Making the gravel leap and leap in air,
Leap up, like that, like that and land so lightly
And roll back down the mound beside the hole.

(75-77)

A passage of this sort is much more than photographically faithful to New England. Horror and overwhelming grief are not exclusively regional emotions, nor are they established here merely by a regional technique. The strange interplay of alliteration, repetition, and iambic stress (léap and léap in aír, / Leap úp, like thát, like thát and lánd so líghtly) evokes both the husband's jerky digging motion and the wife's convulsive emotional response. Furthermore, the oppressive iambic rhythm, accentuated by commas and repeated words, seems to build up and up like the mound of dirt, until the feminine ending of "lightly" at the end of line 76 constitutes a final superfluity (the eleventh syllable in the line, the ninth *l* in a span of eight feet) providing just enough excess weight to precipitate the miniature landslide of gravel back down the mound. Moreover, this passage lends a vital symbolism to the poem. The gravel rolling back toward the hole from which it came demonstrates the cyclical ashes-to-ashes, dust-to-dust pattern of existence—a pattern the wife cannot accept, though its inevitability is reinforced through the symmetrical sonorities of line 77 (*roll* and *hole* at the beginning and end of the line, *down* and *mound* in the middle). Despite Amy Lowell's animadversions, Frost's control of rhythm and sound in these supposedly prosaic lines might have impressed even such a consummately musical poet as Edgar Allan Poe. Moreover, we can see that for his combination of imaginative force and subtly disciplined sophistication Frost deserves to be seen not as opponent or apostate to the nineteenth-century masters, but as a successor—when he wanted to be—capable of rivaling their achievement.

As Frost's reputation took hold during the teens and twenties, he performed the role of Yankee spokesman so well that his critics never realized how important his non-regional background was in making his regional poetry truly distinctive.[24] On his many visits to the city (New York or Boston) and on his reading tours, he conveyed the impression that he was just coming from or going back to some important agricultural responsibilities; but as Thompson demonstrates in some detail, he enjoyed this work chiefly "because so much of it could be neglected" (*YT*, 48). The farm was in reality a retreat—a retreat with definite public relations value—to which he could repair for short spells of rest and composition before sallying out again to discomfit his enemies and sell the chief marketable produce the countryside yielded him: his poetry and his appeal as a performer.

He did not hesitate on his return from England to make

[24] Only one essay in the early period managed to steer clear of Frost's regional posing and to subject the poems themselves to perceptive scrutiny: Edward Garnett's "A New American Poet," *Atlantic Monthly*, 116 (Aug. 1915), 214-221. Garnett alone confronted the question that most of Frost's readers and reviewers never thought or dared to ask: "Is his talent a pure product of the New England soil?" (p. 215). His answer—that Frost exhibited a "subtle blend" of English and American influences, much as Cooper, Poe, Hawthorne, and Melville had before him—was ignored by an American literary community that apparently (*vide* Amy Lowell) liked its regionalism pure.

contact with two leading New England authors of the day: Alice Brown, whose regional fiction Amy Lowell had praised while reviewing *North of Boston*, and E. A. Robinson. But neither of these contacts ever developed into a close association. Indeed, Frost's frequent references to Robinson and Brown reveal that while he was glad to have them as supporters and allies in the literary world, he had no deep affinities with either of them.[25] His relationship to rural New England was significantly different from theirs, and that difference probably inhibited any chance for real friendship.

After spending his childhood in San Francisco and Massachusetts with his Scottish-born, Ohio-raised mother, Frost had moved to the countryside and become—or tried to become—a Yankee. Thus he often played the role with something of the convert's zeal. Brown and Robinson, on the other hand, much more typical regionalists, had moved in the opposite direction. Coming from rural New England towns, they had used their verbal talents to gain entrance to the sophisticated literary communities of Boston and New York. Needless to say, they did not present themselves as rustics, but as writers, and they located themselves not in the countryside, but in apartments and townhouses in Cambridge, Boston, and New York.

Readers of early twentieth-century periodicals and newspapers often found photographs of Alice Brown at social functions, literary events, and testimonial dinners for celebrities like Twain and Howells. Robinson, though a loner who cared little for social and literary affairs, also had friends in high places.[26] But even more decisively

[25] In several letters written shortly after his return to the United States, Frost referred to Alice Brown as a friend (SL, 167, 171, 174). His more complex relationship with Robinson, which involved jealousy and suspicion (chiefly on his part) as well as respect, is discussed at length by Thompson (YT, 43-46, 254-256, 380-381, 489-491, 529-532, 605-606, 667-668).

[26] Though Theodore Roosevelt was his most renowned admirer, Robinson's friend Josephine Preston Peabody carried a bigger stick in Boston's literary world. Edwin S. Fussell has noted, however, that he

than Brown, he had turned away from his rural background, informing Josephine Preston Peabody as early as 1902 that "What little of New England was ever in me has been pretty much extirpated. . . ."[27] He wrote his Tilbury Town pieces early in his career and then committed his last two or three decades to nonregional work: his plays, Arthurian poems, and long narratives. Even in his first and most regional collection, *The Children of the Night* (1897), he interspersed poetry on classical and literary subjects among the Tilbury Town pieces. With poems like "Horace to Leuconoë," "The Chorus of Old Men from 'Aegeus,' " and the sonnets on Verlaine, Zola, and Crabbe, the book lacks the concentrated, rather self-conscious regional focus of collections like *North of Boston*, *Mountain Interval*, and *New Hampshire*.

Perhaps, having examined the peculiarities of Frost's background, we can understand why this poet who had *become* a New Englander should have sought to wrest the regional mantle from Robinson, who was or at least *had been*, a truly home-grown Yankee.[28] Yet the tendency has been to assume, as Lowell did, that Frost triumphed simply by being the most regional regionalist. This assumption underlies R.P.T. Coffin's book-length study of Frost and Robinson, for instance; even Louise Bogan's less regionally oriented *Achievement in American Poetry* contrasts the two poets by calling Frost "closer to the soil than his fellow New Englander." Stress is laid on his proximity to the "actual New England country dweller," whom he is able "not only to describe in his work, but to exemplify, in part, in his life and person."[29]

"was part of no group, participated in no movement" (Fussell, *Edwin Arlington Robinson: The Literary Background of a Traditional Poet* [Berkeley: University of California Press, 1954], p. 51).

[27] Robinson to Miss Peabody, 14 Aug. 1902, *Selected Letters of Edwin Arlington Robinson* (New York: Macmillan Co., 1940), p. 52.

[28] While discussing Robinson, Frost is said to have made a Hemingwayesque observation to Mark Van Doren: "There can only be one heavyweight champion at a time." During the teens, he evidently felt he was the challenger (*YT*, 531).

[29] Coffin, *New Poetry of New England: Frost and Robinson* (Baltimore:

Of course neither Robinson nor Frost deserves to be taken as an example of the "actual country-dweller." But where Frost came to rural New England with a fresh and imaginative receptivity, Robinson's attitudes toward the region were deeply ingrained. He was incapable of separating his perception of the rural world from feelings that had evolved through long exposure to what Yvor Winters calls "the influence of a place and a culture upon his mind and character."[30] Thus his regionalism might be characterized as deductive. The Tilbury Town poems were not a response to specific situations and settings but an evocation of his dominant mood, his general feeling about New England. In this light, Frost might be called an inductive regionalist, working from particulars toward a broad statement. He locates his poems precisely and concretely, and his speakers react to their environments in varied, unpredictable ways. They observe regional phenomena both analytically and contemplatively. But though they struggle for comprehension, their observations often remain indecisive and ambivalent, likely to change within a few lines or phrases. The poems often build toward aphorism, epigrams, and overtly didactic closing passages,[31] yet such conclusions are apt to be undercut by a subtle or not-so-subtle irony. The desired "momentary stay against confusion" is sometimes more ephemeral than it seems at first glance.

Frost's inductive, exploratory approach to New England allowed him to use a variety of masks or personae, and this is one reason why *North of Boston* is such a stimulating collection of poems. Each speaker enunciates

---

Johns Hopkins University Press, 1938); Bogan, *Achievement in American Poetry: 1900-1950* (Chicago: Henry Regnery Company, 1951), pp. 48, 22.

[30] Winters, *Edwin Arlington Robinson*, rev. ed. (New York: New Directions, 1971), p. 18.

[31] Obvious examples would be "The Tuft of Flowers," "Hyla Brook," "The Gum-Gatherer," "The Star-Splitter," "Maple," "Wild Grapes," "Two Tramps in Mud Time," "Departmental," "A Considerable Speck," "Haec Fabula Docet," and "How Hard It Is to Keep from Being King When It's in You and in the Situation."

a unique, deeply felt, and poignantly expressed response to his (or her) situation. At his best, Frost seemed to create an entirely new persona in each poem (some of his best poems, of course, contain two well-individuated personae). Thus, although he had written excellent short pieces ("Mowing," "The Pasture," "The Oven Bird," "Hyla Brook," and "The Road Not Taken") by 1915, his greatest achievement up to that time lay in his longer dramatic work—not only the monologues and dialogues, pieces of a hundred lines or more, but also the medium-length dramatic lyrics, meditative lyrics, and dramatic narratives like "Mending Wall," "After Apple-Picking," "The Wood-Pile," "An Old Man's Winter Night," "Birches," and " 'Out, Out—.' " Such relatively long forms gave him sufficient scope to unravel the attitudes, psychological tendencies, and personal vision of his speakers. As we read these poems, the persona is created, or creates himself, through the compelling power of a voice and a sensibility engaged in the quest for order, for meaning, for that elusive "momentary stay."

Robinson's regional poetry, by contrast, is most suitably and effectively conveyed in short forms. Working deductively from his awareness of the anguish, the frustration, and the isolation of rural life, he created characters to fit his mood and outlook. John Evereldown, Charles Carville, Reuben Bright, Richard Cory, Miniver Cheevy, Aaron Stark, Cliff Klingenhagen, Bewick Finzer, and the rest are instances of a single basic proposition: life is a trial, and generally a disappointing one at that. They all have their own stories, but it is Robinson's attitude *toward* the story that counts. Instead of presenting the personal voice and vision of the regional characters he writes about, he offers his own essentially unchanged and unchanging point of view. For this reason, though his regional pieces are characterized by a depth of feeling and a profound moral concern, they are limited in scope. They are magnificent miniatures, but miniatures nevertheless. Development or elaboration would destroy their subtle irony and disturb their refinement and unity of effect.

To succeed, Robinson's New England poems must be crystallized and condensed; hence the poet's control is more evident than it is in Frost's verse. The tight forms and carefully sculpted prosody of the Tilbury Town poems do not allow for the indecisive equivocations and digressions found in Frost's poems. The great tragedy of Robinson's career is that he failed to see how the impetus for a brilliant sonnet or short poem could lead to oppressive and maudlin poetry if pushed too far or dragged out too long. (This is why the massive, overwrought poems he wrote in the latter half of his career—truly impressive failures—sometimes seem to be sonnets masquerading as psychological novels.) His point of view, since it does not change or develop, is difficult to sustain for more than twenty or thirty lines. Indeed, it is significant that his one early attempt at a long regional poem ("Captain Craig") was not a success, despite its brilliant passages, because it lacked dramatic and narrative cohesiveness.

Having considered Frost's and Robinson's poetic use of New England, we can see how the relationship of these two regional poets has been misrepresented.[32] Frost was able to capture an impressive array of Yankee voices and viewpoints, not because he was "saturated with New England" or "closer to the soil" than Robinson, but because, as an outsider, he benefited from a flexibility, an independence, and a complex awareness of regional character that Robinson never acquired.

Conversely, Robinson's experience of growing up in the state of Maine was so intense and pervasive that, to him, Tilbury Town was not so much a place as a state of mind. He evoked this state of mind in trenchant, regional poetry; but since the mind was always his, the poems offered only one perspective on the region. Unlike Frost, whose inter-

[32] One thoughtful study of Frost's and Robinson's relationship to New England is Barton L. St. Armand, "The Power of Sympathy in the Poetry of Robinson and Frost: The 'Inside' vs. the 'Outside' Narrative," *American Quarterly*, 19 (Fall 1967), 564-574. St. Armand is one of the few scholars to recognize that Robinson is much closer to the New England tradition of Jewett and Freeman than Frost is.

est in diverse voices led to a preponderance of first-person poems, Robinson tended to use the third person. Even his few first-person poems were "still somehow in the third," as Roy Harvey Pearce has noted, pointing out that such works "are not really expressive of the psyches of their protagonists; rather they are expressive of the poet's, and putatively the reader's, mode of understanding them."[33] Thus Robinson's contribution to New England literature lacks the variety, the multiformity, and the broad scope of Frost's, though it surely has as much vividness and artistry, and perhaps somewhat more cohesiveness.

It is a regrettable fact of Frost's literary development that as he gained confidence in his identity as the Yankee farmer poet, he learned to exploit it more and more deviously. And as he became more sophisticated and knowledgeable about the literary world and his position in it, he recognized the desirability of disclaiming his sophistication and presenting himself as a simple, old-fashioned New Englander. The sudden forward thrust of modern poetry in the teens and twenties—the innovative and experimental work of poets like Pound, Eliot, Cummings, and Williams—heightened his sense of responsibility. But by committing himself to his role as the poet of New England, he gave up much of the analytical and exploratory concern that animate *North of Boston*, and he lost sight of the tensions and dramatic conflicts unleashed in that collection. In so doing, he abandoned elements that had contributed largely to the originality and the extraordinary imaginative power of his regional art.

The first collection to show the debilitating influence of his regional commitment is *Mountain Interval* (1916). As in his first two volumes, he arranged the contents to suggest an underlying narrative. In *A Boy's Will* he had traced "the development of a youth from initial withdrawal to final return to society,"[34] and through an epi-

[33] Pearce, *The Continuity of American Poetry* (Princeton: Princeton University Press, 1961), p. 260.

[34] Donald Haynes, "The Narrative Unity of *A Boy's Will*," *PMLA*, 87 (May 1972), 452-464.

grammatic link he implied that *North of Boston* reflects the romantic youth's exploration of rural New England. At last, in *Mountain Interval*, the youth (now much less youthful and romantic) has evidently given up his aberrancy (which had left him with a feeling of "profanation" at the end of *North of Boston*) and settled down once and for all on a farm in a mountain valley that a Yankee farmer might call an "interval."[35] Here the story apparently ends. The youth, now Yankee, can live happily ever after, having found his secret valley. We are not apt to take him very seriously when he threatens (in "The Sound of Trees," the book's concluding poem) to "make the reckless choice" and "set forth for somewhere." The collection is not the work of a reckless poet.

Like "The Pasture" in *North of Boston*, "The Road Not Taken" is italicized and set apart from the rest of the poems in *Mountain Interval* as an introductory piece. It was originally intended as an ironic "gentle joke" on Edward Thomas. But Frost's decision to use it as an introductory poem, and to follow it with the overtly regional "Christmas Trees," is perhaps best explained as an attempt to link his new book with *North of Boston*. The hiker in "The Wood-Pile" and "Good Hours" was uncertain about where he was headed and why. In "The Road Not Taken" he apparently decides—or, more accurately, he tries to convince himself—that by taking a "less traveled" road, he has provided his life with a direction "that has made all the difference" (ll. 19-20). That direction, the structure of *Mountain Interval* suggests, is toward the countryside, toward the rustic self-reliance and the Yankee shrewdness displayed, even flaunted, in "Christmas Trees." Indeed, the first two lines of this poem take on a special significance at the start of such a regionally oriented collection. They evoke a rural world free of per-

---

[35] When questioned about the term "interval," Frost responded officiously, insisting that he followed "the inherited speech" of New England's "oldest inhabitants." Frost to George H. Browne, 18 Aug. 1916, in Elaine Barry, *Robert Frost on Writing* (New Brunswick, N.J.: Rutgers University Press, 1973), pp. 71-72.

nicious urban influences: "The city had withdrawn into itself / And left at last the country to the country."

This Yankee voice dominates the rest of *Mountain Interval*, particularly those poems written after Frost's crucial decision to return to the New Hampshire farm country and "get Yankier and Yankier."[36] We no longer find an implied author who rambles about the New England countryside, investigating mountains and butterflies around Lunenburg, Vermont, or peering into hotels and family reunions in Woodsville Junction and Bow, New Hampshire. Instead, Frost's new speaker is located very concretely on his own farm. We see him first, of course, in "Christmas Trees," confronting the intruder from the city, bartering with him, and showing off his trees in "hope of hearing good of what was mine" (l. 28). The element of self-display is evident in the repeated use of first-person possessives: "*our* yard," "*my* Christmas trees; / *My* woods," "*my* trees," "what was *mine*" (ll. 5, 12-13, 21, 28; my emphasis). The responsibilities of rural proprietorship so evident in "Christmas Trees" are reinforced by a sense of agricultural domesticity in "The Exposed Nest," as the farmer poet, accompanied by his child, exhibits nesting instincts while working in his hayfield. Subsequent poems, such as "In the Home Stretch," "Birches," "Pea Brush," and "Putting in the Seed," extend the image of the farmer on the farm: a confident, affirmative figure in harmony with a natural world he has no trouble comprehending or expressing.

Almost precisely in the center of *Mountain Interval*, Frost placed "A Time to Talk," a piece of no particular

---

[36] *Mountain Interval* is an interesting mixture of about a dozen poems written (or begun) before Frost went to England, seven or eight composed in England, and roughly a dozen more produced after he returned to the United States. Among this last group are the most emphatic evocations of a regional persona: "Christmas Trees," "The Exposed Nest," "A Time to Talk," "The Bonfire," "A Girl's Garden," "Brown's Descent," and "The Gum-Gatherer." Thompson supplies dates (some of them speculative) for all but three of *Mountain Interval*'s poems (YT, 540-542).

distinction except that it seems to represent in miniature the regional dynamics of the entire collection. On the one hand, as Reuben Brower has observed in *The Poetry of Robert Frost*, it displays the voice "most readers expect to find in Frost," maintaining and deftly controlling "the tug between rigidity of meter and laxness of speech" in order to capture "the odd arrest and flow of American country speech": "Frost meets the demands of syntax, drama, and meter so quietly that it is hard to say whether speech is striking across meter or meter striking across speech."[37] But on the other hand, it is sad to note that a poem singled out as an example of Frost's most characteristically rural voice has so little to say.

Adopting his regional pose in poems like "A Time to Talk," Frost produced finely crafted work that is both technically impressive and pleasant to read. But in tailoring himself to this role, he left much of his personal, deeply felt response to New England out of the poem. What remains lacks force and originality. The familiar Yankee farmer hoeing his field has the familiar Yankee's pragmatic awareness that time spent conversing with a neighbor is time lost from work; yet he also has the familiar Yankee's knowledge of rustic convention, and when he sees a friend slowing "his horse to a meaning walk," he appreciates and accepts the tacit invitation to come talk, and thus shows himself in harmony with local customs. The decisive, self-satisfied tone ("I don't stand still and look around. . . . No, not as there is a time to talk") bespeaks the farmer poet's assurance that his affirmation of this rustic harmony is, in some important way, virtuous and commendable. This regional persona knows and does the right thing. He refuses to sell his Christmas trees at an unworthy price, he tries to repair the exposed nest, and he keeps his social fences mended. He seems unacquainted with guilt, uncertainty, and fear. And it is these limitations that make the Yankee persona a liability for Frost: he

[37] Brower, *Poetry of Robert Frost*, pp. 9-10.

evinces no susceptibility to deep emotions or to flights of the imagination. Both the intensity and the eccentric sensitivity of the best poems in *North of Boston* are unsuited to the speaker who dominates *Mountain Interval*. For this secure regional figure, a problem is not something to regret or worry about; rather, it is something to defy and to take pride in having combatted.

In the six collections that followed *Mountain Interval* we often find a persona much like the one in "A Time to Talk." Though gifted with exceptional charm, he is likely to disappoint us as we reread or think more deeply about what he has to say. We hear him in many poems of the 1920s, from long ones like "New Hampshire" and "Wild Grapes" to short ones like "Blue-Butterfly Day," "The Cocoon," and "The Times Table." His voice is still characteristic during the thirties and forties, especially in verse like "The White-Tailed Hornet," "A Roadside Stand," "Afterflakes," "To a Young Wretch," "A Young Birch," and "To the Right Person." We can hear him even in later work from the fifties and early sixties, perhaps most obviously in "Peril of Hope," "Questioning Faces," "The Objection to Being Stepped On," and "In Winter in the Woods."

Though not the only New England voice Frost knew, it was in itself a remarkable literary accomplishment. Nimble, graceful, and adroit, it provided the impression of a robust, comfortably relaxed relationship between poet and audience, and Frost's reliance on it is therefore understandable. But if there is something impressive about a voice that never hits a false note, there is also something regrettable about its limitation to a well-rehearsed and safely restricted range. No hesitations, no uncertainties, no unresolved tensions threaten this speaker's composure. When we finish reading, a subtle undertone lingers on. We sense that despite its droll, unassuming surface, this is the voice of a sage whose basic purpose in speaking is to answer the great questions and solve the great problems of life.

Though never expressed overtly, this reassuring message is implicit in the confident, sensible voice of the speaker who dominates Frost's regional work after the return to New England in 1915. Yet we may not always be able or willing to see things his way. We cannot ignore the opinion of such critics as Yvor Winters, George B. Nitchie, and Radcliffe Squires, who maintain that what seems to be the voice of wisdom is actually rather inconsistent and illogical. Furthermore, a reading of Frost's letters or Thompson's and Winnick's biography raises doubts about the integrity of the characteristically Frostean voice exemplified in "A Time to Talk": the serene, good-humored confidence it expresses bears so little relationship to the poet's personal experience.

As *Mountain Interval* draws to its close, the poet of New Hampshire remains confident, even overbearing, especially in "The Bonfire," "Brown's Descent," and "The Gum-Gatherer." The last of these poems provides the clearest contrast with Frost's poetic stance in *North of Boston*. Its situation is the same as that in "The Mountain": the speaker and a local character share a perambulatory conversation. Yet where the earlier poem shows the speaker's failure to extract useful information and advice from a wry, inscrutable Yankee, the later composition is dominated *not* by the gum gatherer but by the persona, who offers information and advice both to his rustic companion and the reader. Unfortunately, the philosophizing and moralizing about gum gathering make ineffective poetry. Like the Yankee sage's other philosophies of birch swinging, bonfire playing, and taking the long way home after a calamitous fall ("Brown's Descent"), the philosophy of solitary gum gathering is not justified either logically or poetically in the narrative and descriptive poem that precedes the didactic tag (ll. 34-39). Furthermore, although gum gathering is obviously a metaphor for writing poetry, the analogy is not convincing. Writing poetry is (or *should* be) a much more complex and creative act than simply "reaching up with a little knife, / To loose the resin and take it down / And bring it to market when you please" (ll. 37-39). We may be justified in suspecting, however, that Frost's infatuation with his regional role led him to imagine that a Yankee poet *could* lead the gum gatherer's "pleasant life" (l. 34). In his rustic seclusion, with hardly any effort and without the difficulties of contact with humanity, the farmer poet could harvest his verbal crop of marketable material.

Although a regional persona dominates *Mountain Interval*, and dominates it detrimentally, a few excellent poems are scattered through the collection, poems in which the regional concern is legitimate and not forced by the speaker. Three magnificent sonnets (or near-sonnets)—"Hyla Brook," "The Oven Bird," and "Putting in the Seed"—and two medium-length narratives—"An Old Man's Winter Night" and " 'Out, Out—' "—rank with Frost's best regional work (see further discussion in Chapter Five). Of somewhat less distinction, yet still of definite interest, are the unusual series of linked short poems titled "The Hill Wife" and the two extended dialogues, "In the Home Stretch" and "Snow," which carry on the dramatic impetus of *North of Boston*. Regrettably, "The Hill Wife" is somewhat fragmented and uncertain in its point of view, and the two long pieces are not only longer but also windier and considerably more bland than the best poems in the earlier collection. They fail to capture the full resonance of the powerful themes and conflicts treated in "The Death of the Hired Man," "Home Burial," "A Servant to Servants," and "The Fear."

Taking Both Roads

Mountain Interval, released in December 1916, was in many ways the first major disappointment in Frost's career. It was not the commercial success that *North of Boston* had been, and since the critics had praised the earlier book so enthusiastically in 1915, many of them did not feel called upon to say something new in 1917. From an artistic point of view, this collection demonstrated that while Frost's pose as a Yankee farmer had a great deal of popular appeal, it was a distinct liablility to his full development as a poet. He was too content with the gratifying but limited achievement of such poems as "Christmas Trees," "A Time to Talk," "Brown's Descent," and "The Gum-Gatherer." Although he structured the collection so that these recently composed pieces would seem dominant, their underlying pretentiousness is clearly seen in comparison with the integrity and genuine inspiration of pieces like "An Old Man's Winter Night," "Hyla Brook," "The Oven Bird," and "Putting in the Seed"—all of which date from 1906 or 1907. In fact, of the poems written after the publication of *North of Boston*, only " 'Out, Out—' " truly seems to rival the best of the pre-1914 poetry. Significantly, in that one poem Frost set aside his Yankee mask and resorted to the contemplative, somewhat troubled and uncertain persona he had used in *North of Boston*.

Conclusive proof that his regional identity was more useful in public performances than in writing poetry can be found by comparing his busy schedule of readings, lectures, and other appearances with his paltry output of poems in the years following his reinstallation in New Hampshire. Under pressure from his publishers, who, according to Thompson, "begged hard for a third volume of poetry," he had "somewhat resentfully" churned out perhaps a dozen poems in 1915 and 1916 to add to those already in hand for *Mountain Interval*.[38] But in the four years following that publication, he had only four new poems printed (YT, 565n).

What he was doing during these years, of course, was pioneering the dual role of public performer and academic poet-in-residence that ultimately sustained him for the rest of his life. In this effort, his regional identity was highly beneficial. From 1915 until his last years in the early 1960s he beguiled editors, critics, academics, liter-

---

[38] Thompson's comments on Frost's overindulgence in "noncreative activities" and his difficulties in completing *Mountain Interval* are in SL, 154.

ary figures, news reporters, politicians, celebrities, and general audiences with his rustic, Yankee charm. Needless to say, he would not have been willing or able to exhibit that charm at Dartmouth or Harvard in the 1890s, or in Lawrence or Derry during the years preceding his departure for England. Among American writers, perhaps only Mark Twain was a more effective performer, and even in Twain's case, the stage persona was perhaps less effective than Frost's as a support (or seeming support) for the literary oeuvre.

Thompson and Winnick have documented Frost's many campaigns in great detail,[39] but what made the regional role so important in the latter part of Frost's career is that he seems to have regarded it as a means of simultaneously distinguishing himself from and ingratiating himself with the sophisticated urban and academic audiences he catered to. This was a key to his public success, and by strengthening the illusion of his close association with rural New England and his separation from cosmopolitan and "literary" society, it contributed to the failure of many readers and commentators to understand his peculiar position as a regional artist.

John Gould Fletcher, one of the few writers to comprehend the powerful influence of Frost's regional identity on the literary community, has attributed Amy Lowell's admiration for the poet of New England to her impression that he represented not merely a regional world, but a fascinatingly alien and unapproachable one: "Frost stood in her mind for unfamiliar New England, not the New England of the cultivated and the affluent, among whom she had always lived, but the remote, shy, hermit-like New England of . . . the backwoods farmer. . . . "[40]

[39] See YT, Chaps. 2, 5, 6, 11, 15, 22, 25, 27, 31, 33, and LY, Chaps. 3, 4, 14-17. Also consult indices for "Campaigner," "Farmer," "Myth-Maker," "Talks," and "Teacher," in the former volume, and in the latter, "Ambition," "Competitor," "Restlessness," "Satisfactions," "Success," and "Teacher."

[40] Fletcher, *Life is My Song* (New York: Farrar and Rinehart, Inc., 1937), p. 204.

The poet who in 1912 had doubted that "there is any virtue in Location" had evidently realized by 1915 that if presented forcefully, his Yankee location could have considerable virtue, at least in winning him an audience. Thus his instinct, or his *habit*, was to adopt his regional identity whenever he felt he was on display. Elizabeth Shepley Sergeant reports that he enjoyed conversing with fellow travelers on trains, hoping to be asked about his livelihood so he could answer with the claim, "I am a farmer."[41] Although this may seem a whimsical game for a prize-winning poet to play, he often made similar claims to those he wanted to impress.

Literary people were favorite targets. Having honed his skills in England, he was well prepared to captivate the critics, interviewers, reporters, and editors he encountered back in the United States. An interesting example of the effect of his posing appeared in the *Philadelphia Public Ledger* of 4 April 1916, a few days after he had given a reading at the University of Pennsylvania. Under the eye-catching headline, "Poetry of Axe Handles Urged by Robert Frost," was an enthusiastic article full of flattery for this "Yankee of Yankees" who had come to Philadelphia—much like a carton of eggs or crate of apples— "fresh from his farm on Sugar Hill" (p. 11). City folk always like their farm produce "fresh," and Frost was a genius at giving his audience that earthy tang first praised by Ezra Pound. But why the Yankee farmer was in Philadelphia, rather than in New Hampshire preparing his fields for spring planting, the article did not explain. Nor did it mention that trips to the University of Pennsylvania and similar institutions were a primary source of income for the farmer poet.

One of Frost's most exaggerated performances in his regional role led to his curious connection with *Farm and Fireside* magazine in 1921. He contributed three poems to this publication: "The Grindstone," "The Gold Hes-

[41] Sergeant, *Robert Frost: The Trial by Existence* (New York: Holt, Rinehart and Winston, 1960), p. 337.

peridee," and "On a Tree Fallen Across the Road" appeared respectively in the June, September, and October issues. Furthermore, in the June issue he was the subject of an article and a short editorial comment, both of which sought to recommend him to an audience of farmers. The editorial, titled "Do You Like Poetry?" asked readers to help disprove the myth that "farming people don't like poetry" by sending in comments on "the poems Robert Frost is writing for you." Frost's address was provided, and he was said to be interested in hearing from farm readers. The accompanying article, "Robert Frost: The Farmer Poet," hailed "the farmer's own poet from coast to coast" and asserted that "for a good many years of his life Robert Frost has been a farmer to get a living out of the soil." Finally, country readers were assured that when the farmer poet went to New York "on one of his rare trips," it was "better than a circus to see him with some serious 'literary man' with tortoise shell glasses and a project for remaking the world."[42]

Frost was not always as partisan about farming as this article suggests. Readers of the various editions of his letters know that his correspondence was not with farmers but with literary and academic people. His favorite correspondent, Louis Untermeyer, might well have been described as a "literary man" from New York "with tortoise shell glasses and a project for remaking the world." Yet farming was never far from Frost's mind. When he retired from Amherst in 1920, he could consider it an excuse: "I needed to get back to my farming." Then, when he moved from Franconia to Vermont, it constituted a motive: "We seek a better place to farm and especially grow apples" (SL, 250, 254).

After moving to Vermont, the poet of New Hampshire quickly associated himself with such Vermont authors as Dorothy Canfield Fisher and Sarah Cleghorn, earning the

---

[42] Joseph Anthony, "Robert Frost: The Farmer Poet," *Farm and Fireside*, 45 (June 1921), 4.

right to be called a "Green Mountain" writer as early as 1927. By 1936, we find him proudly employing the phrase "We in Vermont" in his introduction to Sarah Cleghorn's autobiography, *Threescore.*[43]

It might seem that Frost's extended activity in the academic world would have weakened his commitment to the Yankee-poet role, but just the opposite was the case. He taught, was poet-in-residence, or held some official position at Amherst (1917-1920, 1923-1926, 1926-1938, 1949-1963), the University of Michigan (1921-1923, 1925-1926), Harvard (1939-1943), and Dartmouth (1943-1949), and was also associated with the Bread Loaf School of English during summers from 1921 on. In this pedagogical capacity, however, he apparently regarded himself as a beleaguered spokesman for old-fashioned, down-to-earth values. Especially in his first college position at Amherst in 1917, he found himself in conflict with ardent liberals and sophisticated intellectuals like President Alexander Meiklejohn and Professors Raymond Gettell, John Erskine, and Stark Young. His strategy as an adversary was to make the most of his authority as an experienced, pragmatic working man and to imply that his opponents were flighty and unreliable dreamers who knew little of the real world. George F. Whicher recollects that there was a shrewd self-consciousness behind the rustic conversational posture: "Frost was dead set not to appear either academic or literary. He was all farmer. . . . we spent an animated ten minutes discussing the healthful properties of horse-manure."[44]

Nevertheless, Frost had to struggle to convince people that he was primarily a farmer and to keep them from realizing how much of his time was spent and how much

[43] John Farrar, "Robert Frost and Other Green Mountain Writers," *English Journal,* 16 (Oct. 1927), 581-587; Cleghorn, *Threescore* (New York: Smith and Hass, 1936), pp. ix-xii.

[44] Whicher, "Sage from North of Boston," in Whicher, *Mornings at 8:50: Brief Evocations of the Past for a College Audience* (Northampton, Mass.: Hampshire Book Shop, 1950), p. 35.

of his income earned on college campuses. Typical of the distortions he helped to propagate is a description of his academic duties that appeared in the introduction to a British collection of his verse: "Really his job is that of resident poet; what is required of him is not a minimum set of lectures; but that he should be on the spot *when the farmer's seasons permit.*"[45] Of course, Frost did obtain some highly flexible arrangements as a poet-in-residence, but this description misrepresents his priorities in order to make him appear more rustic. It conveys the false impression that his primary concern was the management of his farm and that his activities in the academic world were subordinate—minor interests fitted in around raising crops and tending livestock.

Unfortunately, early readers and critics have not been the only ones deceived by myths about the Yankee poet who "lived much of his life as a farmer in New Hampshire and Vermont" and "came out of a folk who lived close to the soil."[46] Even Lawrance Thompson's first book on Frost, *Fire and Ice*, made much of the poet's origin as "a New Hampshire farmer himself in the early years" and presented the poetry as an embodiment of "that inner strength and satisfaction which comes from living close to the soil."[47] Another influential book-length study, also by a well-qualified scholar and personal acquaintance of the poet, opens with a lengthy discussion of the poet's supposedly rustic "race" and "traits," alludes to his "confederate's knowledge of husbandry and tillage," and suggests that "the device on his poetic coat-of-arms could well be (after Abraham Cowley) 'The plough in a field arable.' "[48]

[45] Preface to *The Augustan Books of Poetry: Robert Frost* (London: Ernest Benn Ltd., 1932), p. iii (my emphasis).

[46] Carl and Mark Van Doren, *American and British Literature Since 1890* (New York: Century Company, 1925), p. 21, and Alfred Kreymborg, "The Fire and Ice of Robert Frost," in Kreymborg, *Our Singing Strength: An Outline of American Poetry 1620-1930* (New York: Coward-McCann, Inc., 1929), p. 317.

[47] Thompson, *Fire and Ice: The Art and Thought of Robert Frost* (New York: Henry Holt Co., 1942), p. 112.

[48] Cook, *Dimensions of Robert Frost*, pp. 3-40.

Such estimates provide the basis for the image of Frost still perpetuated in literary histories and widely marketed paperbound editions of the poems. Especially misleading in this regard are prefatory and editorial comments in *Selected Poems of Robert Frost*, edited by Robert Graves, and in *A Pocket Book of Robert Frost's Poems*, edited by Louis Untermeyer.[49]

In the years since 1966, when Thompson published the first volume of his biography, *Robert Frost: The Early Years*, only a few commentators have seen the need to re-evaluate the poet's relationship to the farm country. C. P. Snow noted the importance of Thompson's research in *Variety of Men*. Reuben Brower, always one of the closest and most insightful analysts of the verse, warned against inferences based on Frost's rusticity in a *Partisan Review* essay, while James Dickey analyzed the mythical Frost (as revealed by Thompson) in an article for the *Atlantic*.[50] But by and large, recent scholarly publications make assumptions about the Yankee poet that, in light of Thompson's research, are surprising—and also indicative of the strength of the myths that must be overcome if Frost's early development is to be understood. Certainly, readers will fail to appreciate his literary background, his artistic ambitions, and the complexity of his poetry if they pay too much attention to studies in the last few years that approach him as a nineteenth-century New England villager and a poet "who lives physically in the mountain land of New England 'North of Boston.' " Nor does it help to imagine that the "country poet" in Frost can be separated from the "cosmopolitan poet," as has been suggested by a leading scholar and long-time Frost acquaintance.[51]

[49] *Selected Poems of Robert Frost*, ed. Graves (New York: Holt, Rinehart and Winston, 1963), and *A Pocket Book of Robert Frost's Poems*, ed. Untermeyer (New York: Washington Square Press, 1946).

[50] Snow, "Robert Frost," in Snow, *Variety of Men* (New York: Charles Scribner's Sons, 1967); Brower, "Parallel Lives," *Partisan Review*, 34 (Winter 1967), 116-124; and Dickey, "Robert Frost: Man and Myth," *Atlantic*, 218 (Nov. 1966), 53-56.

[51] The three studies referred to are: Arthur M. Sampley, "The Myth and the Quest: The Stature of Robert Frost," *South Atlantic Quarterly*, 70

The present sway of these persistent myths and misconceptions is nowhere more evident than in the hefty commemorative volume, *Frost: Centennial Essays*. Here we find discussion of "Frost's devotion to the old New England of subsistence farming," and we learn that the poet's great achievement was to capture "the very essence of the late Puritan spirit that lingered on in the desolate and half-deserted New England countryside"; yet we are also told that Frost was a descendant of Emerson and Thoreau, a transcendentalist, skeptic, and relativist.[52] Even more revealing are some suggestions made by James Dickey in an interview with Donald Greiner. In this piece and in his earlier essay for *Atlantic*, Dickey shows full awareness that the mythical image of Frost falsifies the depth and sophistication of the poetry. Nevertheless, his conversation seems often to revive the simple rustic farmer, "the plain-speaking guy," whose work Dickey recommends to students and young writers not for its subtle craftsmanship but for "the plainness and simpleness of the language."[53]

In the years after 1915, as Frost settled into his regional identity, the liabilities exhibited in *Mountain Interval* frequently threatened his poetry. He never outgrew his attraction toward the smug rustic sage who teased and delighted lecture audiences with witticisms and facile philosophy, although this sort of performance was much better suited to the stage than to the page. Even in his eighties, as a consultant to the Library of Congress, he put

---

(Summer 1971), 287-298; Richard Foster, "Leaves Compared with Flowers: A Reading in Robert Frost's Poems," *New England Quarterly*, 46 (Sept. 1973), 403-423; and Theodore Morrison, "Frost: Country Poet and Cosmopolitan Poet," *Yale Review*, 59 (Dec. 1969), 179-196.

[52] George W. Nitchie, "Robert Frost: The Imperfect Guru," Perry D. Westbrook, "Robert Frost's New England," and James M. Cox, "Robert Frost and the End of the New England Line," in Jac L. Tharpe, ed., *Frost: Centennial Essays* (Jackson: University Press of Mississippi, 1974), pp. 42-50, 239-255, 545-561.

[53] Greiner, " 'That Plain-Speaking Guy': A Conversation with James Dickey on Robert Frost," in Tharpe, ed., *Frost: Centennial Essays*, p. 51.

on such performances for reporters, celebrities, and politicians that some observers were upset.[54]

The final two volumes of the official biography, *Robert Frost: The Years of Triumph* and *Robert Frost: The Later Years*, make clear that the last part of the poet's life was hectic, exhausting, and harrowing. Only a man of extraordinary stamina and spirit could have maintained the pace Frost did through such a whirl of travel and upheaval, politicking and literary squabbling, personal tensions and family tragedy, courting of friends and chastising of foes, and, above all, laborious promotion of the popular "Yankee poet" image. That poetry continued to come out of such a career seems miraculous. But reading through this later verse, we can see that there were significant changes in Frost's art, changes that involved attenuation and fragmentation of the regional concern that characterized the collections from *North of Boston* in 1914 to *New Hampshire* in 1923. Beginning with the poems gathered in the fifth collection, *West-Running Brook* (1928), we find that Frost's mind was increasingly engaged by topics and situations unrelated to New England. Of course he churned out his quota of recognizably regional poems, but with only a few exceptions these lack the resonant diction, the striking imagery, the emotional range and force, and the sheer imaginative power of the masterpieces that appear in the first four volumes.

After the mid-1920s two related patterns are discernible in Frost's work. While New England poems truly deserving comparison with the best of his earlier verse crop up less frequently, his most compelling poetry often appears in distinctly nonregional pieces: "Once by the Pacific," "Acquainted with the Night," "The Lovely Shall Be Choosers," "Departmental," "Neither Out Far nor In Deep," "Provide, Provide," "The Silken Tent," "All Reve-

[54] See Dwight MacDonald, "Masscult and Midcult," *Partisan Review*, 27 (Spring 1960), 203-233, and Roy P. Basler, "Yankee Vergil—Robert Frost in Washington," in Basler, *The Muse and the Librarian* (Westport, Conn.: Greenwood Press, 1974), pp. 56-77.

lation," "Never Again Would Birds' Song Be the Same," "The Gift Outright," and "Escapist—Never."

In fact, dropping the Yankee pose was crucial to many of Frost's most effective later poems. These succeed not by offering a particular point of view, but by gathering provocatively incongruous snatches of vivid imagery, concrete detail, abstract philosophy, and common wisdom and blending them in a wide range of poetic styles, from demotic doggerel to Augustan wit and epic loftiness, from puns and bons mots to ironically inappropriate clichés and figures of speech. The background material provided by Thompson and Winnick enables us to see how the nonregional triumphs of Frost's late period sprang from important incidents and personal relationships. The two extraordinary sonnets inspired by his devotion to Kathleen Morrison, "The Silken Tent" and "Never Again Would Birds' Song Be the Same," are excellent examples (see *LY*, 23, 304), demonstrating the immense capabilities he still possessed when his imagination went to work on something *he* cared about instead of something he thought *others* might find impressive.

Another significant development in Frost's work during the 1920s was a shift toward shorter forms. Only three of the distinguished late pieces exceed sonnet length; the longest, "The Lovely Shall Be Choosers," is, at fifty-three lines, less than half the length of the major narratives and dramatic poems in the first four collections. During his last four decades Frost devoted considerable energy to producing clever, epigrammatic miniatures like "Devotion," "Hannibal," "Ten Mills," "On Our Sympathy with the Under Dog," "The Secret Sits," "Iota Subscript," "A Wish to Comply," "Beyond Words," and "From Iron." Thirty-seven of these witty couplet- or stanza-length pieces appear in the last five collections: three in *West-Running Brook* (1928), ten in *A Further Range* (1936), eight in *A Witness Tree* (1942), eight in *Steeple Bush* (1947), and eight in *In the Clearing* (1962). On the whole, they are not distinctly regional poems. Their didacticism and distilled philosophy can nonetheless be considered a sort of ultimate excrescence, a pure, disembodied wisdom toward which Frost's sapient regional persona had been moving even in such manifestly regional poems as "Birches," "Christmas Trees," "Brown's Descent," "A Time to Talk," "New Hampshire," and "A Roadside Stand." The late collections often seem to be predicated on the assumption that the poet's authority as a Yankee sage is beyond question.

If Frost's regional identity strengthened a tendency toward miniaturization and fragmentation in his art, this diminution of power and scope seems in turn to have undermined his success with long poems. As mentioned above, "In the Home Stretch" and "Snow" in *Mountain Interval* fall short of *North of Boston*'s best pieces. The next collection, *New Hampshire*, contains several lengthy dramatic poems, but only one, "The Witch of Coös," is truly memorable. In the other long pieces, particularly "New Hampshire," "Maple," "Wild Grapes," and "A Fountain, a Bottle, a Donkey's Ears, and Some Books," Frost's self-conscious mixture of cleverness and sentimentality bespeaks a fundamental lack of seriousness that makes us prize all the more highly the excellent short lyrics in the collection.

After completing *New Hampshire*, Frost apparently recognized that he had lost his command of the extended narrative and dramatic forms. Though notable as a dialogue, "West-Running Brook," from the late 1920s, is more philosophical and dialectical than dramatic, and its seventy-five lines do not provide scope for the kind of development found in *North of Boston* and "The Witch of Coös." (The shortest of Frost's best dramatic poems is "The Fear" at ninety-three lines; all the rest are over one hundred lines, many of them two or three times that length.) The Masques and the few long poems written after 1930 are graced with pleasant comic touches and many well-turned phrases; yet, on the whole, there is too much prosy glibness, too little dramatic conviction. The cleverness often seems forced or trivial, and the wisdom pompous or gratuitous. (The major cases in point are "Build Soil," "The Discovery of the Madeiras," "The Literate Farmer and the Planet Venus," "From Plane to Plane," "Kitty Hawk," and "How Hard It is to Keep from Being King When It's in You and in the Situation.")

But while Frost's Yankee identity may have impaired his composition of effective long poems and encouraged his output of brief and often frivolous pieces, it also had serious consequences for the originality and imaginative vigor of his regional work. Although he could still produce short and medium-length poems that engaged his full lyric genius and called his dramatic gifts into play, and although he occasionally presented responses to his region that were deeply felt and brilliantly evoked, he more frequently spent his considerable powers in vain attempts to glorify and take advantage of the Yankee role that he and many of his readers found so attractive.

All too often in the collections following *Mountain Interval*, the regional poetic identity became an end in itself. In the verse with the strongest "Yankee" accent— pieces like "New Hampshire," "Good-By and Keep Cold," "A Hillside Thaw," "Acceptance," "A Drumlin Woodchuck," "A Roadside Stand," "Build Soil," "To a Young Wretch," "A Young Birch," "Peril of Hope," and "The Objection to Being Stepped On"[55]—what we find is a testimonial to the rustic New Englander, not to his admirable poetic traits, but to his prosaic side. In "New Hampshire,"

---

[55] Many poems in addition to those already cited in the text exemplify Frost's reliance on the voice and perspective of the Yankee farmer. For some of the most extreme examples, see "A Star in a Stoneboat," "A Brook in the City," "The Kitchen Chimney," "Evening in a Sugar Orchard," "A Hillside Thaw," "Our Singing Strength," "The Freedom of the Moon," "The Last Mowing," "The Birthplace," "The Bear," "A Blue Ribbon at Amesbury," "In Time of Cloudburst," "The Strong Are Saying Nothing," "There are Roughly Zones," "A Nature Note," "Trespass," "Of the Stones of the Place," "A Serious Step Lightly Taken," "Something for Hope," "Closed for Good," "The Draft Horse," "Clear and Colder," and "Unharvested."

the long title poem of his fifth collection, Frost seemed to be trying to convince himself no less than his audience that he was on the right road, the one that "made all the difference"; but the crucial choice, as he described it in this poem, was far indeed from being "reckless." After entirely too much preparation, and after tiresome, snide remarks against anyone who might question his decision, he chose a role that he apparently thought might solve all his problems:

> I choose to be a plain New Hampshire farmer
> With an income in cash of, say, a thousand
> (From, say, a publisher in New York City).
>
> (408-410)

We may question what kind of poetry such a self-satisfied individual would write. And we may suspect after finishing this sprawling, self-indulgent poem that it is a partial answer to our question.

Although six or eight of the poems gathered in New Hampshire certainly rank with Frost's best, the personae in these masterpieces are fundamentally different from the outspoken, almost arrogant speaker exemplified in the title poem. Such oft-anthologized and critically esteemed pieces as "The Star Splitter," "The Ax-Helve," "The Grindstone," "The Witch of Coös," "Stopping by Woods on a Snowy Evening," "For Once, Then, Something," "The Onset," and "The Need of Being Versed in Country Things" are reminiscent of the most vivid poems from North of Boston and Mountain Interval: "Mending Wall," "The Death of the Hired Man," "The Mountain," "A Hundred Collars," "A Servant to Servants," "The Wood-Pile," "An Old Man's Winter Night," "Putting in the Seed," "The Hill Wife," and " 'Out, Out—.' " What links all these poems is that they are more concerned with problems than solutions; they focus on an experience instead of a philosophy. Accordingly, their personae are tentative and ruminative rather than confident and didactic. They convey tension, uneasiness, even a sense of distress and transgression. The speaker of "New Hampshire," by contrast, is an exaggeration of the prototype heard faintly at first in "Birches" and then more clearly in poems like "Christmas Trees," "A Time to Talk," and "Brown's Descent." He has finally become little more than an extension of the conventional Yankee sage, the rustic bard, the renowned poet of New England who knows where he stands and what he stands for. And there he stands, a bit too monumental and statuesque for many readers, pointing the way to a better life.

Because the Yankee persona is a self-conscious spokesman for his region, his tone in many of the poems in *New Hampshire* is tendentious and domineering. He insists much too oppressively on his authority as one "versed in country things." The first line of "A Hillside Thaw" asserts his claim "to know the country," while "A Brook in the City" demands recognition for "one who knew" about brooks. Similar professions appear throughout the collection, explicitly in "A Star in a Stoneboat" (ll. 46-54), "The Ax-Helve" (l. 1), "Fire and Ice" (l. 6), and "The Onset" (l. 13), and implicitly in such poems as "Nothing Gold Can Stay," "Good-By and Keep Cold," "A Boundless Moment," and "Evening in a Sugar Orchard." The speaker in "New Hampshire" is of course the most partisan apologist, insisting that New Hampshire is one of the "best states in the Union" (l. 175) while making the rather paranoid assumption that his audience may wish "to score against the state" (l. 66). His shrill jests at the sophisticated world represented by Boston and New York (ll. 126-137, 358-405) suggest that he cannot ignore the "narrow choice the age insists on" (l. 403) as casually as he claims. Ultimately, his claims—whether for the purity of New Hampshire's apples (ll. 158-162), the superiority of its people (ll. 248-261), or the restful, uncommercial virtue of its environment (ll. 7-8, 33-38, 61-63, 119-123, 355-357, 411-412)—are neither convincing nor interesting. This great monument to the Yankee farmer is indeed an imposing piece of statuary, but the pose seems familiar and does not stimulate our deepest emotions. It is a commanding pose, yes, but hardly a poetic one, and hardly, when we reflect on it, in keeping with the figures we meet in Frost's most impressive verse.

It is clear that in Frost's best regional work, New England is part of the conflict and confusion amid which the speaker seeks a momentary stay. When in "New Hampshire" and many of the later poems the Yankee pose led him to regard the region as a solution, his poetry suffered. In committing himself most extravagantly to a regional identity, he could even go beyond his vision of the shrewd Yankee's rustic refuge and imagine himself as a bird swooping "just in time" to the safety of his nest ("Acceptance," l. 10) or a woodchuck hiding in his "strategic retreat" ("A Drumlin Woodchuck," l. 5). Here, regional subjects are deftly rendered, but the purpose to which they are put is far from compelling. The didacticism is too contrived and smug, the philosophy too facile and not a convincing or worthy complement to the skillful prosody, the clever imagery, and the supple strength of language with which these poems are endowed. It is disappointing to realize at the end of "A Drumlin Woodchuck," for instance, that Frost is satisfied merely to affirm his woodchuck-speaker's cunningly defensive durability. The poem demands more approbation than we really feel for this creature, whose chief distinction lies in being "so instinctively thorough / About his crevice and burrow" (ll. 31-32).

Within the framework of Frost's own imagery, it might be suggested at the end of this chapter on his role as regionalist that his approach to New England ranged between two poles or extremes that can be represented by the woodchuck and the butterfly. The one burrows down into the rocky crust of the region, thus sacrificing flexibility and variety of experience in order to obtain security and protection. He becomes so much a part of the region that he loses much of his sensitivity to it. The other flutters abroad in the region, buffeted by storms and threatened by violence, yet also sensitive to the diverse beauty of sweet flowers, balmy breezes, and warm shafts of sunlight.

Ironically, the poet who planned to put together a "Moth and Butterfly Book" in 1912 (SL, 45) had lowered himself to the woodchuck's more down-to-earth position twenty-five years later. While he gained confidence and security as the poet *of* New England, his poetry was limited by a lack of lofty vision. It was when he set himself free as a poet *in* New England that he came closest to fulfilling his extraordinary potential. The next chapter attempts to follow some of of these precarious and unpredictable flights, which carry forward, "on tremulous wing," both the tradition of New England regional literature *and* the spirit of poetry.

Five: The Poet in New England

The preceding chapters have offered an overview of Frost's New England poetry and the developmental process through which it took shape. If the conclusion seems to be that the power of his regional art gradually lessened, this fact should not keep us from appreciating the triumphs that make his work one of the great accomplishments and one of the great treasures of early twentieth-century American literature. The purpose of this chapter is to explore the characteristics of his most distinguished New England poetry. Produced over a span of four decades and exhibiting a wide range of poetic forms and techniques, these compositions nevertheless evince a fundamental unity that is artistic rather than merely regional.

The trouble with Frost's adoption of a Yankee identity is that it falsified a deep tension arising from his position as an outside observer of a rural world in many ways closed to outsiders. Having established his reputation as New England's farmer poet in 1915, he made literary use of his regional pose for the first time in *Mountain Interval* and embarked on the strenuous round of personal appearances, lecture tours, and academic positions that occupied and supported him for the rest of his life. His remarkable decline in creativity during the three or four years after the publication of *Mountain Interval* is attributable not just to the excitement and unfamiliar demands of being a celebrity, but to an underlying doubt and dissatisfaction about his seemingly successful role as the Yankee poet.

Years later, in an unrhymed sonnet titled "The Fear of God," Frost evinced uneasiness about rising "from Nowhere up to Somewhere, / From being No one up to being Someone"; surely he was most aware of his own rise during the period after his return to New Hampshire. He had only been back a half year—*North of Boston* was just making its way onto the best-seller lists—when he began to disclose his restiveness. Reflecting on his days in Gloucestershire in a letter (17 July 1915) to his British friend John Haines, he speculated, "Next thing you know I shall be reversing my machinery and writing of England from America. What would my friends all say to that? Shall I be allowed to write of anything but New England the rest of my life?" (SL, 183). This is a fascinating attempt to externalize motivation. It was Frost himself, not his friends, who insisted on the Yankee mask, and it was only his own concern for his reputation that "allowed" or disallowed his artistic freedom. Yet in this letter and in many others written in the following years we can see his anxiety about the delicate artistic process he referred to as "reversing my machinery."

He seems to have been troubled in several ways. There was the primary question of his ability to reverse his "machinery": assuming he *could* do it, he was uncertain whether or not he *should*; and beyond that, if he should, did he dare? By and large, he kept these doubts well concealed, but in a letter to Untermeyer (4 May 1916), the correspondent with whom he was most frank, he spoke with melodramatic exaggeration about one of his deepest fears: "something I never but once let out of the bag before . . . a very damaging secret. . . . It is this: the poet in me died nearly ten years ago" (SL, 201). Evidently, the "machinery" that had brought him so much renown might not only be irreversible, but also highly destructive—lethally so—to his creativity, to the poet within. He went on to confess: "I am become my own salesman." Perhaps, in this light, the "machinery" could be held responsible for the birth of a salesman and the death of a poet.

During such periods of doubt and distress Frost occasionally chafed under the mantle of the Yankee farmer poet. The publication of Amy Lowell's essay on him in *Tendencies in Modern American Poetry* disturbed him,[1] he wrote to Untermeyer (27 Oct. 1917), because of "Amy's theory that I never got anything except out of the soil of New England" (SL, 221). He contemplated, "for a joke," writing an essay on himself, "shifting the trees entirely from the Yankee realist to the Scotch symbolist" (SL, 225). Such an iconoclastic reevaluation could *only* be a joke, of course, and only to be shared with a trusted confidant like Untermeyer. Amy Lowell, after all, merely reflected the popular view of "the Yankee realist"—a view that Frost's "machinery" and shrewd salesmanship had propagated. What is significant is that in seeking a contrasting image he turned to a phrase so reminiscent of his mother, whose Scottish birth and visionary sensibilities he always remembered fondly.

Insofar as Frost seriously considered himself a "Scotch symbolist," he must have felt that this side of his artistic makeup had been overshadowed, perhaps harmfully, by the "Yankee realist." Thus, from a chronological or developmental point of view, his original self was the fundamentally Romantic self nurtured by Belle Moodie Frost (whose Scotch symbolism had encouraged his appreciation of such diverse poets as Poe and Emerson, Browning and Wordsworth). The "Yankee realist" was a late accretion, a beneficial accretion in many ways, but one that Frost had begun (as his letters would indicate) to regret.

It would be an oversimplification and a psychological distortion to suggest that Frost suffered from a split personality; it would even be unfair to such a complex man to place too much emphasis on any *single* polarity or opposi-

---

[1] Lowell, "Robert Frost," in Lowell, *Tendencies in Modern American Poetry* (New York: Macmillan Co., 1917), pp. 79-136.

tion in his character. Yet, given the attention that has been paid to his association with New England, there is a definite need for recognition that his identity as a Yankee farmer was counterbalanced by a persistent uneasiness about his tendencies as an outsider. For although the role of the rustic was appealing, it was in many ways uncongenial to Frost, and not just because of his background as a California-born, mill-town-raised, college-educated poet. Deeper, temperamental factors made him uncomfortable and dissatisfied with the farmer's life. He was not as practical, as down-to-earth, or as hardy as he would have liked; nor, when compared with the familiar Yankee farmer who appears in New England regional literature, did he possess the composure, the impassivity, or the single-minded sense of responsibility associated with the role. Above all, where the conventional Yankee farmer was dogmatic and wedded to tradition (like the neighbor in "Mending Wall"), comfortable with common practices, fond of apothegms and folk wisdom, and distrustful of new ideas and speculative questioning, Frost was a complex, frequently equivocal metaphysician, given to analysis, evaluation, and contemplation, and incapable—like Brad McLaughlin in "The Star-Splitter"—of either satisfying or dispelling his "lifelong curiosity / About our place among the infinities."

Though assuming his regional pose in public, Frost sometimes let his uncertainty and ambivalence about the role show through in his letters. Often he spoke longingly about farm life. He was proud, for instance, when his son Carol took over the family farm in Vermont in 1924. "Fun to look on at," he wrote Untermeyer (12 August 1924), "I've always so dreamed of being a real farmer: and seeing him one is almost the same, as being one myself" (SL, 303). Eight years later, in another letter to Untermeyer (13 May 1932), he implied that farming was, or could be, more than a dream: "I haven't got through with the farming yet. When I get these sick children rounded up, we are going to make another big attempt at the almost self-contained farm. Almost. No nonsense" (SL, 387). If there were times when farming seemed to be a salvation, there were other times when Frost's lack of Georgic commitment made him feel sinful. After a period of family troubles and ill health, he viewed his irresolution in the terms of Calvinistic morality: "All this sickness and scatteration of the family is our fault and not our misfortune or I wouldn't admit it. It's a result and a judgement on us. We ought to have gone back farming years ago or we ought to have stayed farming when we knew we were well off" (RF/LU, 178).

His failure to be the farmer he felt he "ought" to be was deeply distressing, and Frost was inordinately sensitive to any questioning of the role. Apparently E. A. Robinson at some point made an injudicious remark on the subject, and Frost's outraged response in another letter to Untermeyer (6 June 1930) may have been exacerbated by his sense of rivalry and his fear of letting the "other" New England poet get any advantage on him: "Robinson spoiled farming for me when by doubting my farming he implied a greater claim on my part to being a farmer than I had ever made. The whole damn thing became disgusting in his romantic mouth. How utterly romantic the old soak is" (RF/LU, 200).

Tensions Between Inside and Outside

As his correspondence indicates, Frost was not only ambivalent about his identity as a farmer, he was also deeply emotional on the subject. In 1916, as his doubt concerning the rustic pose increased, he produced one of the strangest—and one of the most intriguingly suggestive—works of his career: the anomalous and generally disregarded one-act play, A Way Out.[2] Of the two major

---

[2] Frost mentioned the play in a letter (7 Aug. 1916) to Untermeyer (RF/LU, 40). It was not published until February 1917, in the fourth number of The Seven Arts. It is reprinted in P&P, 272-282. Except for a plot summary by Thompson (YT, 108-109) and a brief discussion in

characters, one is an exaggeratedly regional figure, a reclusive bachelor farmer, Asa Gorrill, whose most characteristic expression is "dunno," as in "Dunno's I did" and "Dunno's I have" (*P&P*, 278, 279). Like the figure in "An Old Man's Winter Night," he tries to "keep a house, a farm" alone, and this lonely farmhouse is the setting for the play. The second character is mysteriously anonymous: "A Stranger." A conventionally sinister interloper, he enters Asa's house at the beginning of the play and announces, "I want some of your supper" (*P&P*, 273). Before long, he reveals that he is a murderer in flight from the law.

Given the melodramatic context, it seems proper to assume—as do Lawrance Thompson and Radcliffe Squires—that the stranger succeeds in his plan to murder Asa and, by assuming his identity, fool the search party. As Thompson sees it: "By the time the posse begins hammering at the door, the intruder has killed Asa and hidden the body offstage. Shuffling to the door, and opening it cautiously, he successfully deceives the posse by playing the role of Asa Gorrill very well" (*YT*, 109). According to Squires, "the play suggests that the murderer then strikes Asa and drags him from the room, returning in time to pass himself off to the arriving posse as Asa Gorrill. . . ."[3] However, the end of the play is much more complicated than this. The truly important point is that Frost's primary concern was not merely with the melodramatic confrontation of farmer and interloper, but with an almost surrealistic mergence of these seemingly opposed identities.

As the play draws to its disconcerting close, the stranger notes that his reluctant host "ought not to be hard to give an imitation of" (*P&P*, 279). Then, donning Asa's clothes and imitating his rustic voice and walk, he announces:

Radcliffe Squires, *The Major Themes of Robert Frost* (Ann Arbor: University of Michigan Press, 1963), pp. 83-84, the play has received little critical attention.

[3] Squires, *Major Themes of Robert Frost*, p. 84.

I'm going to mix us up like your potato and string beans, and then see if even you can tell us apart. The way I propose to do is to take both your hands like this and then whirl round and round with you till we're both so dizzy we'll fall down when we let go. Don't you resist or holler! I ain't a-going to hurt ye— yet. Only I've got to get up some sort of excitement to make it easier for both of us. And then when we're down, I want you should wait till you can see straight before you speak and try to tell which is which and which is t'other. Wait some time. (P&P, 280-281)

After the two whirl each other about and collapse on the floor, Frost indulges in some willful obfuscation. Instead of continuing to identify his characters as "Asa" and "Stranger," as he has up to this point, he suddenly resorts to indefinite attributions, assigning the crucial lines and the final murderous actions to characters identified only as "First to Speak," and "Second."

There is a brief silence as the two dizzied antagonists lie on the floor. Then the "First to Speak" insists, "I ain't lost track. It's you that done the crime," to which the character labeled "Second" responds with a scream, "It's not!" The "First," in turn, claims not to be afraid of his opponent anymore, and a struggle ensues in which, according to the stage directions, the "First" strikes down the "Second" and drags him away. Just at this moment the posse rushes into the empty room and waits for the return of the character (it might be Asa or the stranger), who is now identified in the stage directions both as the "Hermit"—an appellation not previously used in the play—and as Asa. When told of the posse's search, he replies that he has just escaped from the murderer, and he directs them off on their chase. All these actions and statements are ingeniously ambiguous and allow two contradictory interpretations.

The more we study the text, the more we are likely to be convinced that Frost sought not merely to obscure the identity of his characters but to prevent us from unraveling the mystery. Since Asa has previously been instructed to "try to tell which is which," we expect that he should be the "First to Speak," an expectation justified when the character so identified begins, "I ain't lost track." Furthermore, his subsequent claim that he is no longer afraid seems a logical statement for Asa to make after his earlier betrayals of fear. Thus, contrary to what Thompson and Squires have written, the play does *not* suggest that the Stranger is "First to Speak" or that he "strikes Asa and drags him from the room." Instead, it seems to be Asa who speaks first and then commits the play's climactic violence on the intruder.

On the other hand, the terrified scream with which the character labeled "Second to Speak" protests his innocence is also most appropriate for Asa (the Stranger never denies or appears remorseful about his crime). And since Asa would have no motive to lie to the posse about the outcome of the struggle, we must accept the possibility that the character labeled "First to Speak" is not Asa, but the Stranger, who (according to this interpretation) is skillful at lying *and* at anticipating the thoughts that we would expect to hear from Asa.

In the confusion of identity at the end of *A Way Out*, one thing seems clear: the mergence of simple farmer and sinister stranger occurs *before* the final struggle. Thus the crime is less the cause of an alteration in identity than it is the result. The play's ambiguity implies not only the intended violence (stranger kills farmer) but also the possibility of punishment and revenge (farmer kills stranger).

To the self-described "fugitive from the world" (SL, 158), who went as a stranger to the Derry farm in 1900 and who later adopted a regional identity as "a way out" of anonymity, depression, and financial difficulties, this extraordinary play may have had much more meaning than it is likely to have for most readers. Indeed, Frost may have decided that it was *too* revealing (Squires mentions his desire to "discourage discussion" of it).[4] As the re-

[4] *Ibid.*, p. 85.

morseful tone at the end of *North of Boston* suggests, he had reason to appreciate the element of transgression or "profanation," that is, the outsider's betrayal of the countryman whose rustic identity he had usurped. Additionally, the letters of the period indicate that he might have been especially sensitive to the horror of a loss of personality. It is not the farmer of *A Way Out* who loses his personality (Asa can only be killed) so much as it is the stranger: to succeed in his plan, the interloper must give up his personality and become an impersonation. Hence the appellation "Hermit"—if we take it as a hint of the stranger's fate—takes on lugubrious overtones. Trapped in the "old-stone savage" world envisioned in "Mending Wall" (l. 40), he would live as a Neanderthal man, as a gorilla (Asa Gorrill). If Frost imagined that sickness and family misfortunes were, as he said in the letter to Untermeyer, "a result and a judgement" brought down on him by his failure as a farmer, then he could also have feared that his public pose as a rustic was a transgression, like the stranger's crime against Asa: as a crime causing the demise of the true farmer, it left Frost liable to a punishment of artistic confinement and inanition.

This play provides a valuable counterpoint to the self-assurance with which Frost is often assumed to have played the Yankee role. Critics from the teens down through the present time might have understood his regionalism better had they given careful consideration to the strange relationship of Asa and his alien *Doppelgänger*. But more important, *A Way Out* dramatizes—grotesquely exaggerates—the tension that gave a unique poignance to Frost's experience in New England.

This tension energizes his most effective regional poetry. We will not find another work in which the conflict is as extreme or overt as it is in *A Way Out*, but a surprising number of his poems involve a house and someone (or something) outside—usually a stranger, a tramp, a thief—who wants to get in. Consider, for example, "Love and a Question," "Storm Fear," "The Oft-Repeated

Dream," "Locked Out," "The Lockless Door," "The Thatch," "The Old Barn at Bottom of the Fogs," and "An Unstamped Letter in Our Rural Letter Box."[5]

The same basic tension between inner and outer is less obvious but still readily apparent in an equally large number of poems presenting the relationship between strongly regional characters and less-experienced individuals, often outsiders or newcomers. Several such poems are in *North of Boston* ("Mending Wall," "The Death of the Hired Man," "The Mountain," and "The Code"), but many more appear in the later collections: "Christmas Trees," "The Smile," "The Ax-Helve," "The Witch of Coös," "Two Tramps in Mud Time," "Build Soil," and "From Plane to Plane." It should be noted, too, that in England in 1912 Frost began a novel built on "the differences of opinion between two farm workers: a young man fresh out of college and an old man rich with first-hand experiences on the farm." Years later he told Lawrance Thompson that when the novel fell through (after a chapter or so), he tried to use the material for a play, but again failed because "he had only the idea of the tension between two opposite points of view and . . . he could never find adequate situations to represent, dramatize, and develop this tension" (*EY*, 583-584).

Frost said that he finally worked the relationship of the old farmhand and the college graduate into the poem "From Plane to Plane" (1949). But of course Silas and Harold Wilson in "The Death of the Hired Man" fit the two character-types perfectly, and in a broad sense this "tension between two separate points of view"—although it did not provide an effective basis for a novel or a

---

[5] Eben Bass discusses the polarity between inner and outer in Frost's work. He finds Frost generally afraid of the outer and concerned to keep what is outside out and inside in. Bass, "Robert Frost's Poetry of Fear," *American Literature*, 43 (Jan. 1972), 603-615. Richard Poirier explores this dichotomy in his chapter "Home and Extravagance" and elsewhere in *Robert Frost: The Work of Knowing* (New York: Oxford University Press, 1977).

play—had much to do with the success of *North of Boston* and of the most impressive regional poems in the later collections. It was not as novelist or dramatist but as poet that Frost found the "adequate situations to represent, dramatize, and develop this tension."

So sensitive was Frost to the relationship of regional and nonregional, insider and outsider, that he created a wide range of characters and personae representative of the gradations between the opposing poles represented by Asa—the autochthonous, exaggeratedly rustic farmer— and the stranger—the faceless, homeless fugitive. As suggested in Chapter Three, the *dramatis personae* of *North of Boston* displays a complete spectrum of old-timers and newcomers, visitors and locals, with "The Death of the Hired Man" particularly noteworthy for its deftly balanced cast of characters: Silas and Harold Wilson at the extremes of regional and nonregional experience, and Mary and Warren in the middle. Throughout Frost's work there are echoes of all four of these characters. Even the distant Harold Wilson seems to reappear not only in the pedantic, college-educated Dick of "From Plane to Plane," but also in the scientists and learned types—like the geologist in "Trespass"—who speak or are referred to in the later poems. (Significantly, as Frost assumed the guise of Yankee sage in pieces like "Why Wait for Science," "The Planners," and "Bursting Rapture," he regarded scientists with increasing disdain.)

But "The Death of the Hired Man" succeeds because Frost avoided the extremes of regional and nonregional identity that make "From Plane to Plane" a trite, stagy, and unconvincing portrait of regional character. He restricted his focus to the dialogue of Mary and Warren, who, though definitely separated by the inner-outer tension (Warren being a more regional figure than Mary), are comparatively neutral. Using their perceptions of Silas and their subtly evolving dispute over his plight, Frost produces a masterful portrait of the wayward hired man that is forcefully elegaic without lapsing into sentimentality (it is, of course, simultaneously a portrait of Mary and Warren). Given the subject, the potential for a maudlin poem is immense; but by keeping Silas offstage and by exploiting the tension between Mary and Warren, Frost never has to insist on his emotions. If there is pathos, it is objectified as an aspect of Mary's response, and it is restrained by Warren's more impassive and pragmatic presence.

When Frost became too concerned with the extremes of regional character, too self-consciously committed to rustic personae, his poetry suffered, tending either toward the melodramatic (as in *A Way Out*) or the sententiously smug and pompous (as in "Christmas Trees," "Brown's Descent," "A Roadside Stand," "Build Soil," and "From Plane to Plane"). But at his best—and he remained capable of his best until he was in his seventies—he controlled the tension between his sense of belonging to the region and his sense of being alien to it, and he brought his complex and heightened sensitivity to bear on the rural world. The resulting poetry is not a platform for the regional spokesman and philosopher; rather, it evokes an imagined world and a poet *in* that world—a situation that, when things are right, gives rise to song. It may not be a gay melody, for this singer "knows in singing not to sing," but it is something altogether different from the regionalist's prosy lesson. In truth, the regional speaker's authority as a poet of New England, comforting though it may be, is an *ignis fatuus* compared with the hard, gemlike flame that only the imagination can authorize.

One reason for the wide disagreement among Frost's critics is that in many of his poems the tension between inner and outer is so subtle that it is easily overlooked, especially by readers who have preconceptions about the New England poet. The recent controversy over "Two Tramps in Mud Time" provides interesting evidence of this problem. Many readers mistakenly consider the poem's woodchopping persona a typical Yankee farmer. Laurence Perrine has called attention to the issue, citing seventeen critics and challenging the dominant assumption that the poem ends with the speaker's refusal to let the tramps chop his wood.[6] Perrine very correctly stresses the penultimate stanza as evidence that the speaker accepts (with some reluctance) the tramps' "right" (ll. 52, 60) to the job. Since the final stanza contains no reference to the tramps or the question of their taking a "job for pay," the speaker's explanation of his "object in living" (l. 66) has no direct bearing on his decision about "woodchopping"—a specific choice that seems increasingly trivial in the context of mortality and immortality created by the closing lines. Instead, Perrine maintains, the conclusion reveals that the speaker is a poet, and one for whom poetry is neither vocation or avocation but a way of life—a quest for the union of love and need. For him, woodchopping is an act of love that strengthens, as stanzas two through six demonstrate, his love of life itself. Of course, many other kinds of work—from cleaning springs, mending walls, and putting in the seed, to mowing, apple picking, and gathering leaves—also constitute "play for mortal stakes" (l. 70). And, in a general way, all are needed—urgently needed. That is the point of the poem. Thus the particular decision about hiring the woodsmen is irrelevant. To attach importance to it is to miss the final stanza's thrust toward an ideal.

It is sad to think that so many readers have misconstrued this poem, sadder still to realize that Frost is often regarded and respected as a hard-bitten Yankee who would size up the tramps and contemptuously send them on their way. Yet the poet's performance as rustic bard might well encourage this view. Indeed, reading poems like "Christmas Trees," "The Bonfire," "Brown's Descent," "New Hampshire," and "Acceptance," is surely a good preparation for misunderstanding "Two Tramps in Mud Time." In the context suggested by "The Death of the Hired Man," there is evidently an inclination on the part

[6] Perrine, " 'Two Tramps in Mud Time' and the Critics," *American Literature*, 44 (Jan. 1973), 671-676.

of Frost's readers to assume that the most characteristic voice in his work is one like Warren's. Certainly, the hardy, self-reliant Warren would be likely (were Mary not there to remonstrate with him) to turn the tramps away (as he had been ready to turn Silas away) and to do the job himself.

To be sure, Warren's voice is heard in many of Frost's poems. But it is a prosaic voice; once divorced from Mary's, it evolves toward the regional extreme represented by Asa Gorrill. Insofar as Warren is a lover of aphorism, his voice is potentially that of the neighbor in "Mending Wall": a voice devoid of imagination and originality. Similarly, Mary's voice, divorced from his, would tend toward the hypersensitivity, the instability, and finally the insanity of Amy in "Home Burial," the wives in "A Servant to Servants" and "The Hill Wife," and the witches of Coös and Grafton. Hence it was highly important for Frost to maintain the marriage of these two voices, which he later characterized not only as male and female, but also as fatherly and motherly and as Republican (austerely conservative) and Democrat (sympathetically New Deal).[7]

To pursue the analogy between "The Death of the Hired Man" and "Two Tramps in Mud Time," there can be no doubt that the latter poem echoes both Warren's *and* Mary's voices, and that to hear only Warren, to hear only the crusty, sententious farmer and not the poet, is to miss much of the poem, particularly the force of the third, fourth, and fifth stanzas. In those three stanzas Frost reveals that by chopping wood his speaker becomes a poet, a figure every bit as sensitive and sympathetic to the seasons, the bluebird (l. 25), the flowers and streams (ll. 28, 33) as Mary was to the moonlight in "The Death of the Hired Man."

Although the tension between regional and nonregional, inner and outer (and, as suggested here, Mary and

[7] Frost offered these interpretations of Warren and Mary in his interview with Richard Poirier, *Paris Review*, 6 (Summer-Fall 1960), 109.

Warren) has often been overlooked in "Two Tramps in Mud Time," it is actually more obvious, though no more significant, here than in many other poems. In fact, if the three highly lyric stanzas (three, four, and five), were more congruent with the rest of the poem, they might testify to the speaker's poetic nature more persuasively, and the likelihood of misreadings would be lessened. Yet, in all honesty, we must recognize that the uninhibited poetic sensibility of these three stanzas is not convincingly compatible with the self-consciousness and prosy didacticism of the woodchopper, who at the end claims, perhaps a bit too prosily and didactically, to be a poet.

An even more memorable poem in which the tension between Frost's regional and nonregional identity plays an important, though almost imperceptible, role is "Stopping by Woods on a Snowy Evening." The incantatory simplicity of the verse, the masterful economy of image, the thematic depth and resonance of this poem need no elaboration. What makes the piece particularly noteworthy as a regional work is that it was composed in a moment of inspiration after the poet had struggled all through a summer's night with the much longer (and much less successful) poem, "New Hampshire."[8] Although Thompson asserts that "there is no connection between either the themes or the subject matter of 'New Hampshire' and 'Stopping by Woods' " (EY, 597), the poems are linked antithetically as contrasting attempts to define a regional identity.

"New Hampshire" was an excruciatingly ostentatious and affected attempt on Frost's part to come to terms with his adopted regional personality. But after sustaining a posture of shrewd Yankee independence and droll self-assurance for some four hundred lines (one of his longest works, aside from the Masques), and after seeking to banish all the doubts, fears, and frustrations that were part of his regional experience, he could not sleep. Perhaps his

[8] Thompson describes the composition of these two poems on a summer's night in 1922 (EY, 595-597; YT, 231-237, 596-599).

imagination would not let him rest until he had righted the balance. Following such prolonged operation of intellectual "machinery" to produce the desired blend of Yankee wit and rustic virtue, the imaginative vision that finally forced its way through came on in a rush of musicality that counterpoised the Yankee's summery smugness with the wintry, rather gloomy experience of "Stopping by Woods."

In the latter poem we find restraint, economy, and gracefully tuned cadences—a far cry indeed from "New Hampshire," with its rambling blank verse and implausible modulations of banter, complaint, confession, and downright cant. Moreover, Frost produced a persona for "Stopping by Woods" who contrasts sharply with the expansive, partisan speaker of the earlier work. Instead of showing off and seeking recognition, he shares a very private moment with us, a moment when he did *not* want to be seen or recognized. Were the owner of the snowy woods present (to "see me stopping"), or were his house nearby (instead of "in the village"), the persona would be reluctant to pause by the roadside. Like the speaker in "The Pasture," he feels that his desire to stop should not be revealed too openly.

Having spent most of the night impersonating a crusty, dauntless Yankee, Frost suddenly turned about to create another persona, one who not only wishes to avoid notice but who also applies the words "queer" and "mistake" to his own actions (ll. 5, 10). His strange mood—expressed by his subdued song—is in some sense a violation of local codes. There is a subtle tension in each stanza between his contemplative inclination to wait and watch the woods fill up with snow and his feeling, or suspicion, that such activity is inappropriate, perhaps reprehensible. In the first stanza, the owner of the woods, who stands *for* local households and villages, seems also to stand *against* the speaker's desire to observe the snowy scene. But then the second quatrain offers only the horse and the possibility of a distant farmhouse to countervail the appeal of woods, frozen lake, and "darkest" evening. In the third stanza, the human world is lost from sight, evoked only by the deft symbolism of the harness bells. Finally, the last quatrain pivots on the word "promises," a word that links the speaker to the world he has left and simultaneously reveals his conscious choice to go back.

Thus a major contribution to the depth and complexity of this seemingly simple poem is the tension between a regional world, with its conventions and responsibilities, and the meditative, seclusive character of the persona. Though he is stationary, his utterance adumbrates two potential journeys: one in the countryside, a second in the realm of the imagination. In the first three quatrains, the emblems of the countryside fade away (village to farmhouse to harness bells) as the speaker approaches a personal experience, perhaps visionary, perhaps suicidal, perhaps merely recreational. With the word "but" in the last stanza, however, he stops moving in this ruminative direction and prepares instead to resume his other journey through the locale he had seemed to leave behind. Evidently, travel is an appropriate mode of experience for a speaker so sensitive to the relationship of inner and outer; in many of Frost's most effective regional poems some sort of journey is at least implicit.

Two other distinctive winter poems, "The Onset" (1921) and "Desert Places" (1934), display the same tensions and patterns of inner and outer travel seen in "Stopping by Woods." In "The Onset" the speaker reaffirms his relationship to the regional world (the "clump of houses with a church" [l. 24]) more vigorously than in the other two poems, but not before "almost" stumbling, giving up "his errand," and letting "death descend / Upon him" (ll. 6-9). "Desert Places," on the other hand, vividly demonstrates the power of the imagination to influence the traveler's perception of the region he observes. "I have it in me," he says (l. 15) of the fear that arises from his bone- and spirit-chilling meditation. As a result of his voyage toward the "blanker whiteness" (l. 11) of his imagination, he can barely continue that other journey across the countryside, at least not in the spirit with which he began. His vision of loneliness will dominate any future travel he undertakes, and we should recognize that this poem may represent a frightening extension of the imaginative journey implicit in "Stopping by Woods." If so, the two works testify to the poet's growing reluctance in the twenties and thirties to launch off on the speculative, figmental explorations that a decade or two earlier had animated such brilliant pieces as "Mending Wall," "After Apple-Picking," and "The Wood-Pile."

The two most powerful dramatic poems Frost wrote after *North of Boston* also derive power from the tension of travel or exploration in a regional world, a world that makes the traveler aware of his identity as a stranger or alien. Like many of the poems in *North of Boston*, "The Witch of Coös" (1922) and "West-Running Brook" (1928) use the traveler as auditor ("The Witch of Coös") and speaker ("West-Running Brook"). In the former poem, Frost's brilliant evocation of the "witch's" voice heightens our sensitivity to the visiting narrator's experience by stimulating our perception that she is performing for her guest's benefit as well as for her own. Presented as a dramatic monologue (using only the "witch's" voice) or as a narrative (her story told in the third person) this poem would lose its peculiar intensity. We need our intermediary, the outsider who has sought "shelter at a farm / Behind the mountain" (ll. 1-2) and who will verify the name "Toffile" on the letter box when he leaves (ll. 154-155). His astonishment and uneasiness as a visitor to this "haunted" house are crucial. Without him, and without the tension he brings to the poem, we would take the "witch" less seriously (as we take the pauper witch of Grafton), and we would not see or hear her as vividly as we do.

"West-Running Brook," Frost's most effective philosophical poem, benefits from the circumstance that its speakers are explorers, newcomers apparently taking a

first walk on their newly purchased property. Their dis-
cussion of the brook's westerly flow is actually an artful
indication of their innocence and their tenuous relation-
ship to the region they are moving into (this point has
never been properly appreciated). Since New England's
Appalachian ridges run north-south, brooks and streams
in the back-country are as likely to flow west as east. In
fact, the three regions north of Boston that Frost knew best
are on the west side of mountain systems and hence
drained by rivers and streams flowing westerly. All the
brooks near the Frost farm in Derry, for instance (includ-
ing Hyla Brook, as well as the original West-Running
Brook), drain west from Warner Hill into the Merrimac.
Similarly, in Franconia, New Hampshire, the Gale and
Ammonoosac rivers flow west from the White Mountains
into the Connecticut, and near Ripton and South
Shaftsbury, Vermont, the Batten Kill and the Walloomsac
run generally west to the Hudson. Thus, by having the
husband and wife base their conversation on the assump-
tion that "country brooks flow east / To reach the ocean"
(ll. 5-6), Frost subtly disclosed their naive inexperience.
Being both "young" *and* "new" (l. 10), they speak of more
"contraries" (ll. 7, 38) than they know; their philosophy
rides not only on the ice of its own melting, but also on
the impulse of fresh discovery.

Furthermore, "West-Running Brook" derives unusual
force from the interplay of male and female voices that
Frost had previously exploited in "The Death of the Hired
Man," "Home Burial," and "The Fear." Here, Frost begins
by establishing tension between the wife's inquisitive,
speculative, visionary character and the husband's prag-
matic rationalism. But after developing their opposing
points of view toward the brook in the first half of the
poem, Frost fashioned one of his most eloquent passages
in the husband's climactic speech (ll. 38-72): an astonish-
ing, yet persuasive blend of the two voices. Although
seeming at first to reject his wife's fantastic suggestion
about marrying the brook (ll. 11-15) and her poetic in-

terpretation of the wave that appeared to be "waving" (l. 16), the husband actually shows that his voice also can "trust itself to go by contraries" (l. 7), shifting from conversational to philosophical tones, from scientific (even Darwinian, in line 41) to poetic language. The burden of his argument is that in the "universal cataract of death" human life must be a contrary force, a "backward motion" (ll. 56-69). To be humanly contrary is to imagine meaning in a wave or a brook or a marriage, love itself being the most contrary vision of all (where "most we see ourselves" [l. 69]). His conclusion is a defense of his wife's intuition: we *must* marry the west-running brook. We must be faithful to that backward motion, that contrary spirit. It is our imagination, our love, our life. Evoking a poetic marriage of the husband's solid logic and factual precision with the wife's unconstrained emotions and fantasies, Frost made this remarkable nuptial poem one of his most moving and popular achievements.[9]

At Home Like a Traveler

By dramatizing a variety of outsiders—travelers, visitors, and newcomers—Frost imbued his regional poems with a complexity lacking in most local-color writing (Sarah Orne Jewett's *Deephaven* and *The Country of the Pointed Firs* are notable exceptions). But we should note that both the work and the career of Henry David Thoreau provided broad precedent for Frost's unusual approach to New England. A man of extraordinarily wide interests, Thoreau is not generally classified as a regional writer; nevertheless,

[9] The popular accessibility of *West-Running Brook* has elicited an attack from Richard Poirier, who links the piece with "New Hampshire" and claims that it is "genteel to a fault . . . slightly vulgar . . . written for an audience of literary clubs . . . over-clarified and relatively complacent . . ." (*Robert Frost: The Work of Knowing*, pp. 223-225). However, "West-Running Brook" should surely not be written off with "New Hampshire." Although it is not Frost's subtlest or most complex work, its broadly affirmative eloquence merits the respect of sensitive readers, be they literary club members or not.

as a careful observer, an energetic naturalist, and the author of numerous books and essays dealing with New England, he appealed to Frost as "the chief advocate since the Old Testament of making the most of the home town and township."[10]

Frost was particularly concerned with Thoreau's special mode of exploratory observation within a restricted area. As early as 1934, he linked *Walden* with *Robinson Crusoe*,[11] and he later observed that these two books, along with another record of travel and exploration, Darwin's *The Voyage of the Beagle*, "have a special shelf in my heart."[12] His approach to New England has more in common with Thoreau's exploratory attitude than it does with the insider's perspective, that is, the perspective of the experienced local spokesman, which is favored by most regionalists. It was the outsider—or at least an individual aware of the outsider's point of view—who appreciated the "white wave" running "counter to itself," the snow-filled wood or field, the forgotten woodpile, the strange traits of local character found in *North of Boston* or "The Witch of Coös."

There was no need to travel far: if one traveled in the right way, with the right exploratory and contemplative spirit, one would make the important discoveries. "Live at home like a traveler," Thoreau counseled his friend Harrison Blake in 1859. Surely the poet who was born in San Francisco fifteen years later grew up to understand and to exemplify Thoreau's philosophy that "It should not be in vain that these things are shown us from day to day. Is not each withered leaf that I see in my walks something which I traveled far to find?—traveled, who can tell how

[10] Frost, in "Thoreau's 'Walden': Discussion between Robert Frost and Reginald Cook, introduced by J. Isaacs," *The Listener*, 52 (26 Aug. 1964), 319.

[11] Frost submitted a list of his ten favorite books to the Massachusetts Library Association in 1934. He specifically compared *Walden*, the third book on his list, with *Robinson Crusoe*, the second. The list is reprinted in *P&P*, 355.

[12] Frost, in "Thoreau's 'Walden,' " p. 319.

far? What a fool must he be who thinks that his El Dorado is anywhere but where he lives!"[13] By living "at home like a traveler," one could make strange and exotic discoveries. And where the conventional regionalist, lacking the traveler's perspective, was satisfied to discover the essence of the region, of Tiverton or Winesburg, Tilbury Town or Spoon River, Thoreau and Frost felt, or hoped, that by exploring in the region, by analyzing, contemplating, and speculating, they might discover at least a vision of the extraordinary, of El Dorado. "Thoreau saved himself a journey to the Arctic to see red snow," Frost was interested to note, "by waiting at home till red snow fell in Concord."[14]

Of course, the exploring traveler could not expect that the exotic would be easy to find, or even, if found, easily recognized. All too often the extraordinary thing would seem trivial at first glance, merely commonplace to an unperceptive eye. One must know what to look for and, more important, *how* to look. Being close to the soil or "saturated" with a region is intrinsically no more useful than traveling far and wide. The issue is one of vision. Thus for Thoreau, even the "withered leaf" demands close scrutiny and profound contemplation. For Frost, the pasture spring, the woodpile and old patch of snow, the butterfly and "dimpled spider" are meaningful because of what the observer brings to them, because of what he has learned to see and to appreciate by traveling "who can tell how far?" And this is why the poetic power of his regional verse derives not just from New England, but from his and his speakers' exploration *in* it. Even those poems that lack a clearly dramatized explorer or outsider (like the visitor in "The Witch of Coös" and the personae in "West-Running Brook") depend for their force on Frost's skill at capturing the drama of exploration and discovery.

[13] Thoreau to Harrison Blake, 1 Jan. 1859, *The Writings of Henry David Thoreau*, ed. Horace E. Scudder, 20 vols. (Boston: Houghton Mifflin Company, 1906), VI, 347.
[14] Frost, in "Thoreau's 'Walden,' " p. 320.

The sonnet "Design" fully deserves the unusual compliment Randall Jarrell has paid it—"The most awful of Frost's smaller poems"[15]—because it so skillfully and movingly recreates the observer's response to what he finds in his walks. And we should not forget that Thoreau also realized that nature could be frightening. In *The Maine Woods*, for instance, he wrote of his discovery on the lonely peak of Mt. Katahdin that "Nature was here something savage and awful, though beautiful," and he described the killing of a moose as a "tragedy" that "affected the innocence, destroyed the pleasure" of his adventure.[16] Similarly, the speaker in Frost's "Design" has found in his travels not El Dorado but a tragedy (or, as he presents it, a kind of Gothic horror story) enacted by the spider and the moth, which has indeed "affected the innocence, destroyed the pleasure" of his morning walk.

The discovered tragedy of "Design," the lugubrious "morning rite" (to respell the pun at the end of line 5), elicited from Frost one of his most brilliantly crafted and vividly imagined poems. Its technical sophistication and imagistic complexity have received wide critical attention (most notably from Randall Jarrell, Reuben Brower, and Richard Poirier).[17] But as an example of his approach to his region, his living "at home like a traveler," it shows how much he could accomplish when, instead of posing as regional spokesman, he concerned himself with a speaker in the process of responding to things found through Thoreauvian exploration.

The obvious contrast in "Design" is between declarative and interrogative. The octave is a single, smooth-flowing, descriptive sentence. We can associate its tone of

---

[15] Jarrell, *Poetry and the Age* (New York: Random House, 1953), p. 42.

[16] Thoreau, "Ktaadn," in *Writings*, III, 67-71, 132.

[17] Jarrell devotes four pages to "Design" in *Poetry and the Age*, pp. 42-45; Brower gives the poem five pages in *The Poetry of Robert Frost: Constellations of Intention* (New York: Oxford University Press, 1963), pp. 104-108; and Poirier spends sixteen pages on it in *Robert Frost: The Work of Knowing*, pp. 244-259.

detachment and objective restraint with the voice of the conventionally impassive New Englander. The sestet, however, is a series of questions that reveals a strikingly idiosyncratic blend of emotions: horror, dismay, passionate curiosity, and agonized bewilderment. But in light of Frost's comments on "The Death of the Hired Man" in his *Paris Review* interview, especially those concerning the opposition of Warren's masculine, paternal attitude and Mary's feminine, maternal sympathy, we might contrast the rather stern stoicism at the beginning of "Design" with the distressed compassion that dominates the sestet. In the ninth line, for the first time, an emotional response to the observed situation is suggested, and the language becomes more urgent and more overwrought than it was in the octave—more like the language of Mary, Amy, and the other wives in *North of Boston*:

> What had that flower to do with being white,
> The wayside blue and innocent heal-all?
>
> (9-10)

The triple modification of line 10 is a meaningful gauge of the persona's grief and distress. Shifting from the physical ("wayside blue") to the metaphysical ("innocent"), from concrete, descriptive accuracy to abstract, attributive exaggeration, the line constitutes a brief lament, a plea that establishes once and for all the speaker's sympathies. This prolonged appositive structure heightens the impact of the preceding line's interrogative outburst, reaching a climax of anguished intensity in the pathetic fallacy of "innocent." Innocence might seem an irrelevant issue: the flower, after all, is neither innocent nor guilty. Only to the human imagination could this natural scene involve criminality and evil. Only the anthropomorphizing mind would dispute whether the flower was an innocent bystander or a sinister accomplice, luring victims to the scene of the crime. What Frost ingeniously reveals in these lines is that his speaker's innocence is at stake, threatened not so much by evil as by his own ability to create a sense of villainy and malevolence in the universe. And the central issue is the speaker's ability to withstand the experience of evil, an experience greatly strengthened by his own imagination.

The sestet's repetitious questions (ll. 9, 11, 13) are slightly strained in diction, syntax, and logic—evidence of the speaker's horror and dismay at the sinister force deducible from the observed scene. This emotion is conveyed by strange predicate structures: "What had that flower to do with. . . . What brought the kindred spider . . . then steered the white moth thither. . . ." Curiously, but with telling effect, the reference of the pronoun "what" changes: first it pertains to essentially natural (botanical, horticultural) causes for the color of the flower (l. 9); but then it relates to an awesome, supernatural power— perhaps a godlike being, perhaps a sinister anthropomorphic force—capable of "bringing" the spider and "steering" the moth to their horrifying encounter.

As the speaker phrases his questions in the sestet, the cause of his tormented response to what he has seen becomes clear. We realize that he expects no answers. His mode of questioning betrays both his sense of futility and his reluctance to admit defeat. Thus Frost prepares us effectively for the ambivalent conclusion of the final couplet: what has happened bespeaks either a sinister design or, worse, the *absence* of design.

If the sestet's speaker is not explicitly an outsider, he at least reveals sympathies and emotional commitments that make it difficult for him to accept things as they are. The octave, however, much lighter in tone, shows touches of wit and what Brower terms "joking discovery."[18] Yet even within these lines there is something of the same tension that is responsible for the contrast of octave and sestet, although it is evident here only insofar as the speaker's matter-of-fact tone (the tone we might associate with Warren) is threatened by his fascination with the terrifying

[18] Brower, *Poetry of Robert Frost*, p. 105.

symbolism of what he has found. Faintly, but significantly nonetheless, he reveals sympathies more appropriate to Mary than Warren, sympathies exposed more openly in the sestet. He shows the tendency to "overdo it a little" of which Amy was accused in "Home Burial" (l. 62). His four similes ("Like a white piece of rigid satin cloth," "Like the ingredients of a witches' broth," "like a froth," "like a paper kite") and several of his other images ("holding up a moth," "Assorted characters," "mixed ready to begin," "a snow-drop spider," "dead wings") are not as offhand as they seem. The ironies and the complex ambiguities of the language converge on an entirely human sense of evil and dark design. The persona who compares a dead moth with a "white piece of rigid satin cloth" can hardly be as lighthearted as his casual, unemotional tone might suggest—not given the deathly connotations of rigidity and the funereal associations of satin cloth.

Ultimately, the octave of "Design" has such imagistic force that it asks "in all but words" the same fundamental questions posed in the sestet. The speaker is reluctant to pose these questions and to face them openly, and we suspect that his wittily disguised reticence in the first eight lines arises from his underlying fear, which he discloses only (and tentatively even then) in the sonnet's final line, that there is less design in the world than he can bear. His tendency as an explorer and observer is to make too much of the "design of darkness" he discovers in the world around him. Unable to convince himself that the pattern he sees is mere whimsy, he is deeply distressed by it. As a practical insider, however, he sees the futility of overinterpretation and of too much emotional involvement with what he observes. His final doubt—"If design govern in a thing so small"—is doubly ironic. First of all, it concludes this poem about "Design" with a seemingly casual yet—because of its climactic position—very forceful suggestion that design does not govern *anything*. But, it is also ironic that a rejection of design should be couched in such an ingeniously designed sonnet (one of

English poetry's most intricate forms, especially when only three rhymes are employed). Surely design *has* governed the speaker's mind, and as a Thoreauvian traveler, he has responded deeply to it; yet, simultaneously, as a practical, hardheaded Yankee, he disapproves of his own response. Throughout nine of the sonnet's fourteen lines, he resists the appallingly dark design, first by making light of it (through the octave's wit and whiteness), and finally (l. 14) by suggesting that it is at most a figment of his own imagination. This complex work blends regional and nonregional perspectives so effectively that the piece will not seem to be a New England poem at all unless we recognize that much of its crucial tension derives from the poet's sensitivity to a subtle conflict of voices (or tones of voice), a sensitivity nurtured by his regional experience.

While Frost's deftness at synthesizing different points of view contributes to the distinctive power of "Design," a similar skill is at work in several masterpieces that seem to have regional personae yet still succeed in preserving some trace of the outsider's perspective—just enough to save the speaker from becoming the predictable, doctrinaire Yankee spokesman of poems like "Christmas Trees," "New Hampshire," or "A Roadside Stand." We meet this regional speaker, who is somehow slightly in conflict with local values, in many of Frost's best New England poems: "The Pasture," "Mending Wall," "After Apple-Picking," "The Ax-Helve," "The Grindstone," "Stopping by Woods," and "The Onset." Another very impressive regional piece is the medium-length narrative " 'Out, Out—,' " which avoids the liabilities of sentimentality and moralistic posturing because its speaker keeps himself at a slight distance from the drama.[19] Specifically identified neither as outsider nor insider, he displays elements of each. He is familiar enough with regional values to provide insights into the mind of a country boy:

[19] Frost wrote " 'Out, Out—' " roughly six years after an accident similar to the one in the poem took the life of a boy he had met while vacationing in Franconia (EY, 566-567).

his love of a half-hour "saved from work" (ll. 11-12) and his immediate comprehension of what it means to lose a hand in a world where labor is largely manual.

The most obvious device establishing the speaker's stance toward New England in " 'Out, Out—' " is his use of the third-person plural. By focusing on *them* and *they*, rather than *us* and *we*, he separates himself from local people. Occasionally we hear the emotion and the imagination of Frost's "feminine" voice, the voice that wants to say "I sympathize," as Mary does in "The Death of the Hired Man" (l. 76). Yet we enter the regional world of the poem in a burst of down-to-earth images of sound and smell:

> The buzz saw snarled and rattled in the yard
> And made dust and dropped stove-length sticks of
>   wood,
> Sweet-scented stuff when the breeze drew across it.
>
> (1-3)

The *z*'s and *s*'s, *t*'s and *d*'s give us the sound; the dust and "sweet-scented stuff" give us the smell of the local here and now. Immediately, however, the speaker offers a vision, for "those that lifted eyes" (l. 4), of another world: the mountain ranges toward the sunset. It has been suggested that these sun-reddened mountains foreshadow the bloodied teeth on the saw,[20] but particularly following the "lifted eyes," they seem instead to evoke a transcendent world, radiant, serene, and distant—a magnificent contrast to the busy local setting of the poem.

The speaker's awareness of other worlds is again evident when he makes one of those futile wishes that Frost's feminine speakers are prone to sigh: "Call it a day. I wish

---

[20] William S. Doxey, "Frost's 'Out, Out—,' " *Explicator*, 29 (Apr. 1971), 70, argues that the boy's accident is "an inarticulate and self-destructive protest against the insensitivity of the family which wishes to hurry him into the responsibilities of adulthood." For a similar approach, see Weldon Thornton, "Frost's 'Out, Out—,' " *Explicator*, 25 (May 1967), 71.

they might have said" (l. 10). Then he describes the acci-
dent so speculatively and contradictorily that the lines
dramatize his search for its meaning, its design:

> the saw,
> As if to prove saws knew what supper meant,
> Leaped out at the boy's hand, or seemed to leap—
> He must have given the hand.
>
> (14-17)

In the closing lines, after the boy's death, Frost gives the
regional apothegm, "No more to build on there" (l. 33).
Yet he neither elaborates it nor lets it stand as a lesson to
the reader. Instead, he turns attention to the regional
people, and in so doing, reaffirms his speaker's separation
from them: "And they, since they / Were not the one dead,
turned to their affairs" (ll. 33-34). Having seen the
speaker's imaginative sympathies earlier in the poem, we
appreciate that his response is not the same as the re-
gional response. Rather, he feels the need—much as did
Amy in "Home Burial" and the persona in "Design"—to
release the emotions aroused by tragedy. He cannot turn
himself, as Amy's husband was able to do, to "everyday
concerns" (l. 86). Thus, like "Design" and like the best of
Frost's lyrics, this poem is its own explanation—at once a
record of and a response to the drama from which it arises.

In "The Grindstone," "The Ax-Helve," and "The Star-
Splitter," though using a more regionally oriented
speaker than he did in " 'Out, Out—,' " Frost still man-
aged to control the tension of inner and outer perspec-
tives. The first two of these poems pivot on a dramatic
confrontation of the persona—a countryman, but of the
whimsical, speculative, reflective cast generally found in
North of Boston—and an extreme, almost mythopoeically
exaggerated Yankee: the "Father-Time-like man" of "The
Grindstone" (l. 29) and the French-Canadian master
craftsman of "The Ax-Helve."

"The Star-Splitter" has special significance in this
study because it demonstrates how much Frost could gain

for his regional poetry by adopting the countryman's stance—but only if he kept control of it. This is one of his most brilliant and profound studies of New England. A complex survey of rural codes and standards and of Brad McLaughlin, who chose "heavenly stars" over "hugger-mugger farming" and was thus a misfit in the regional world, it is also a study of the speaker himself, who, caught between Brad and the local community, is both the source and in many ways the focal point of the observations, the insights, and the ironies that distinguish the poem.

Frost weaves a rich fabric of skillfully coordinated images around the simple narrative frame of "The Star-Splitter." From his central concern with stars and with Brad's quest for vision and enlightenment about "our place among the infinities," he branches out into a series of interrelated images involving light and sight, fire and warmth, darkness and coldness, and so back to night and the mystery of the stars. In terms of the imagery, the poem's conflict can be described as a disagreement about seeing or about vision (ll. 33-37). The townspeople are content not to go out in the dark at all; at most, they fumble about in the blackness, trying to see what they can by the feeble light cast from a lantern. Brad, on the other hand, is not satisfied with the limited vision provided by a "smoky lantern" (ll. 8, 98); instead of carrying a small flame around in the darkness with him, he tries a great conflagration, burning down his next-to-worthless farmhouse for the insurance money and buying himself a telescope with which to look out into the dark and find the light.

Although Brad is given a few lengthy passages in which to express his unorthodox but highly stimulating point of view, our impression of him is deeply influenced by the persona's attitudes. At the beginning and end of the poem the latter associates himself with the townspeople and against Brad (ll. 40-58, 87-99). One reason the piece is so powerful is that the persona's sympathy for Brad gradually increases during the first seventy-five lines. Then, in an impressively climactic eleven-line passage just before the poem's end (ll. 76-86), the two share an almost mystical vision as they peer through the telescope's "brass barrel, velvet black inside, / At a star quaking in the other end" (ll. 77-78). It is a transforming experience, carrying the speaker momentarily beyond his customary regional horizons and giving him a sense of union both with Brad and with a higher reality:

> We spread our two legs as we spread its three,
> Pointed our thoughts the way we pointed it,
> And standing at our leisure till the day broke,
> Said some of the best things we ever said.
>
> (83-86)

This transcendent moment is shattered as the speaker reverts to his regional standards, pointing out that the telescope "didn't do a thing but split / A star in two or three" (ll. 88-89) and noting that splitting stars cannot be compared with splitting wood. What he seems to forget—but what we cannot—is the importance of "some of the best things we ever said."

Without the speaker's vacillation from regional to nonregional and back to regional attitudes, "The Star-Splitter" would have less depth than it does. Brad McLaughlin is an intriguing individual so long as he remains an ambiguous blend of the Promethean hero and the Yankee eccentric. But had the speaker taken his side too strongly or condemned him too vigorously, the poem would have been likely to degenerate, either into transcendental hero-worship, or into the sort of pious moralizing found in Alice Brown's "At Sudleigh Fair," a story dealing very sternly and punitively with an insurance-motivated house burning like Brad's.[21]

By maintaining tension between inner and outer views of rural New England, Frost avoided the priggishness and

[21] Brown, "At Sudleigh Fair," in *Meadow-Grass: Tales of New England Life* (Boston: Houghton Mifflin Company, 1895), pp. 191-228.

sentimentality to which regional literature is vulnerable. His transcendence of the tradition is perhaps most evident in three highly original poems devoted to a favorite, indeed trite, local-color theme: the desolate, abandoned New England house.[22] "An Old Man's Winter Night," "The Need of Being Versed in Country Things," and "Directive" represent Frost at about the ages of thirty, fifty, and seventy;[23] certainly his ability to produce memorable contributions to such an unpromising genre throughout his long career is a tribute to his unusual powers as a regional artist. In each of the poems he finds a different way of establishing the interplay of inner and outer that provides the original force for a new working of the old theme.

In "An Old Man's Winter Night," he goes into the house and deals with inside and outside in relation to the solitary occupant. It seems significant, considering the pattern of Frost's career, that the earliest of these pieces should convey the strongest sense of isolation and despair, the most vigorous opposition of man and region. Here the inner and outer forces are profoundly at odds with one another, and they represent not only the regional and nonregional worlds, but the human and the natural, the sensate and the insensate, the living and the dead.

In later years Frost seemed to shun such dynamic, and perhaps threatening, evocations of this tension. He did dramatize the disturbing conflict of inner and outer in *A Way Out*, but the result may have taught him a lesson: he was in danger of losing control of his material and falling into the abyss of melodrama if he confronted his deepest fears too openly. It was better for him to represent the ter-

---

[22] Among myriad trivial, sentimental poems on old houses, one might compare not only Frost's early "Ghost House" and "The Generations of Men," but also E. A. Robinson's "The House on the Hill" (another early piece), and R.P.T. Coffin's "Old Cellar."

[23] "An Old Man's Winter Night" was begun about 1906 (*YT*, 450); "The Need of Being Versed in Country Things" appeared first in 1920 (*YT*, 153-154); and "Directive," Frost's last poem of true genius, was apparently written late in 1945 (*LY*, 134).

ror of opposing forces as they impinged on an individual consciousness. The violent confrontation of Asa Gorrill and the sinister stranger is actually less compelling than the tension Frost makes us feel by imagining that "all out of doors looked darkly in" at an old man facing the solitude of a winter's night.

The Thoreauvian rambler appears in "The Need of Being Versed in Country Things." In the sensitive, highly sympathetic voice associated with Frost's female and nonregional figures, he imagines the birds sighing for the burned house (l. 15) and envisions the lilac, the elm, the dry pump, and the fence post (ll. 17-20) all playing a part in an elaborate pathetic fallacy to console the weeping phoebes. The tension in this poem is between the need to be versed in "New England Ways" and this speaker's failure (as demonstrated in the poem) to conform with local attitudes.[24] The poem is a testament to his inability to be a practical, hardheaded Yankee who will not let the evil or sad design of things disturb him.

The gently lilting rhythms in this subdued piece, and the poignant images of grief and sympathy, predispose us to imagine that the phoebes do weep. The soft, sympathetic voice gains strength throughout the first five quatrains, building toward a vision of compassionate nature in stanzas four and five. The speaker reverses himself in the final couplet, using the Yankee's homiletic voice to assert, "One had to be versed in country things / Not to believe the phoebes wept." But the very fact of his poetic utterance violates the impassive New Englander's wisdom. This is not the verse of a well-versed Yankee; it is rather an instance of "too much dwelling on what has been" (l. 16). In spite of what Yankees are supposed to believe, the persona felt—could not completely escape feeling—that the phoebes wept. And the poetic power of his words makes us feel it too.

In "Directive" Frost found an especially advantageous

---

[24] Early drafts of this poem used the phrase "New England Ways" instead of the later "country things." See *RF/LU*, 105.

218 THE POET IN NEW ENGLAND

way of presenting a speaker who could at once reflect re-
gional and nonregional concerns. His persona is a well-
intentioned, ultimately ineffectual guide, one whose
directive should be taken in the modest adjectival sense
("tending to direct") and not as a noun ("specific instruc-
tion or command"). This is a relaxed and good-humored
piece, full of gentle ironies, and neither as challenging
nor, despite its Christian symbolism and biblical allu-
sions, as profound as some of Frost's earlier work. Though
he lavishes attention on the regional setting, the
persona-guide's primary objective is not a place he wants
us to visit but an experience he wants us to have. Since
the old rustic world he describes is evanescent—"made
simple by the loss / Of detail" (ll. 2-3)—much of what he
says is almost immediately gainsaid. The poem is shot
through with negatives and equivocations, and its many
rhetorical flourishes are counterbalanced by a whimsical
self-deprecation. Instead of mapping a specific journey *to*
the region, the speaker encourages us to move *through* the
region toward a vaguely defined ideal—it seems to in-
volve personal discovery and spiritual regeneration—an
ideal never fully attained in the poem.

Accordingly, how one travels in "Directive" is more
important than where one goes. The verse itself, with its
long, meandering sentences, its discursive, parenthetical
remarks, and its fragments and hesitations, leads the
reader on an unparalleled imaginary expedition. We must
ramble along observantly and contemplatively for nearly
fifty lines before coming up against a "destination and . . .
destiny" (l. 49), which will leave us puzzled and un-
satisfied because it is only a "brook that was the water of
the house" (l. 50). Once we are there, the final goal of
being "whole again beyond confusion" (l. 62) seems an
elusive mystery requiring further, perhaps endless, pur-
suit.[25] Allusions to the Holy Grail and St. Mark convey the

[25] The implications of "Directive" as a Thoreauvian exhortation are
highly significant and have been explored by S.P.C. Duvall, who cites
Walden as a source for several images and metaphors in Frost's poem.

difficulty as well as the importance of this quest; but such ceremoniousness is considerably undercut by the persona's irreverent confession (in the playful parenthesis of line 60) that he has stolen his Grail-like cup "from the children's playhouse." Here is evidence that should make us wary of being too serious or doctrinaire about "Directive." It is not a dogmatic work. The speaker makes no claim to take us "beyond confusion." On the contrary, by providing a fragmentary, disjointed vision of New England, and by injecting a capricious incongruity into the closing lines, he demonstrates that confusion is itself the inescapable source of our perennial desire for integrity (to "be whole again"). He does not encourage us to imagine a simple escape from "all this now too much for us" (l. 1) into an idyllic rustic world. Rather than offering such a naive itinerary, he invites and conjures us toward a process of imaginative exploration, toward a rejuvenated and reinvigorated dedication to those highest ideals that seem most impossible to realize. We will find no Yankee farmer on the "farm that is no more a farm" (l. 6), nor will we be directed by such a regional figure. In fact, the poem indicates more clearly than any other why Frost's truest and most memorable verse always pushed through the region toward a purer, more original, and more universal imaginative vision than the region itself could offer.

Many years before writing "Directive," Frost produced another traveling or hiking poem, "The Road Not Taken," which, because it is a poem of tantalizing beauty and rich musicality, and because it seems to express the philosophy of the Yankee farmer poet, has received considerable attention.[26] As we look back on Frost's career as a regional

---

Duvall, "Robert Frost's 'Directive' out of *Walden*," *American Literature*, 31 (Jan. 1960), 482-488.

[26] The most helpful information on the genesis of "The Road Not Taken" is in YT, 88-89, 544-548. Thoughtful interpretation has been made by Ben W. Griffith, Jr., "Frost's 'The Road Not Taken,' " *Explicator*, 12 (June 1954), 55, and James M. Cox, "Robert Frost and the Edge of the Clearing," *Virginia Quarterly Review*, 35 (Winter 1959), 76.

poet, this piece provides an important comparison with "Directive." Although apparently written in response to the wistful indecisiveness of Frost's friend Edward Thomas (*YT*, 88), the poem has often been taken as a credo of the independent Yankee who takes the "less traveled" road because he knows it makes "all the difference." Yet this is to overlook the irony of the piece. The speaker actually cannot distinguish which path is "less traveled," and he does not evince pride or satisfaction about his choice. Instead he sighs over his failure to take the "other" road, and he laments his inability to "travel both": he is only "one traveler."

In fact, if we put aside the extraneous Yankee stereotype and let ourselves respond to the graceful images, forceful language, and mellifluent lyricism of "The Road Not Taken," we will find that it conveys a poignant sadness, a haunting sense of life's limitations. This is not so much an exhortatory poem about choice (Moral: "Take the less traveled road") as it is a wistful meditation on the consequences of choice for a creature whose vision runs beyond the realm of possibility. Not only does the imaginative mind yearn to take those infinite untraveled paths that no mortal can ever follow, but it also thrusts itself forward and back into the future and the past (the poem is a demonstration of this visionary mobility). In response to our mortal weakness, the imagination invents palliative fictions. One example is the self-deception of line 12: "Oh, I kept the first for another day!" More important is the speaker's attempt to console himself with the idea that he had made a correct choice in taking the "less traveled" road—though he knows full well that both roads "*equally* lay / In leaves no step had trodden black" (my emphasis). Such fictions are a subtle gauge of grief that the speaker cannot bring himself to express openly. The emotion is implicit in the poem's many images of yearning, of inability, of frustration: "I *could* not travel both"; "*long* I stood"; "as far as I *could*"; "I *doubted* if I should *ever* come back"; "a sigh / Somewhere *ages* and *ages* hence" (my emphasis).

Frost happened to write "The Road Not Taken" just as he mounted his campaign for recognition as the poet of New England. Evidently, as suggested in Chapter Four, he recognized the poem's unintended applicability to his situation as a Yankee poet, and in setting up his next collection, *Mountain Interval*, he placed it prominently in italics before the table of contents as a prologue. Readers turning from that piece to "Christmas Trees," at the beginning of the collection, were likely to conclude that this was the work of a poet who had taken the regional road and secluded himself on the mountain interval farm.

In the years following 1915 the regional pose became an increasingly elaborate costume—all too frequently, a suit of armor. In 1951, when Louis Untermeyer adopted the title "The Road Not Taken" for his heavily annotated anthology of Frost's work, he placed the poem at the very end of the collection, and in the concluding paragraphs of his commentary he asserted that Frost's road "was not only the 'different' road, the right road for him, but the only road he could have taken."[27] This is a grave distortion. As "Directive" affirms, and as Frost's best regional poetry demonstrates, he succeeded not by taking the "right" road (which, Untermeyer implied, was a rustic or country road), but by traveling in the right way, that is, by carrying himself as a poet. Ultimately, if we make too much of his being on the "right" road, we will misjudge the complexity and depth of his verse. It is his concern with that *other* road—the road *not* taken, the road of the imagination—that assures his eminence as a New England writer.

Untermeyer was also wrong to suggest that Frost had followed the "only road he could have taken." This poet was in some ways a victim as well as a beneficiary of his Yankee identity; had he been less dependent on his regional role, had he been less satisfied with his tendency toward stereotypical posturing, he might have done more to explore his particular genius, his full potentiality. As a

[27] Untermeyer, *The Road Not Taken: An Introduction to Robert Frost* (New York: Henry Holt and Company, 1951), p. 270.

result, we might now have more collections of the caliber of *North of Boston*, more imaginative and perceptive explorations truly worthy of Thoreau, more carefully conceived and dramatically sustained long poems, more study of character, more variation of voice, more restraint of facile sentiment, and perhaps more nonregional verse to stand with such triumphs as "Once by the Pacific," "Acquainted with the Night," "Neither Out Far nor In Deep," "Provide, Provide," and "Never Again Would Birds' Song Be the Same."

This is a good deal to ask, of course. Yet, on surveying the artistic record, are we not likely to feel that Frost deserves a more solid position among the first rank of American authors? Surely we may suspect that his vision of himself as a Yankee poet was an important factor in his most noticeable—and most remediable—shortcomings. Although his association with New England assisted his career, it was not the primary source of his most impressive poetry. It enhanced the commercial value of his verse, and it strengthened his confidence and provided the sense of artistic purpose that his early work generally lacked. But by itself it could not assure—indeed, it seems to have inhibited—the full development of his literary powers.

A survey of the Frost canon will perhaps seem disappointing in view of what might have been. Yet it also reveals that there is a large body of work to appreciate. As a complete volume, *North of Boston* is a notable landmark in the history of American poetry. Vivid in its language, well crafted in its metrical forms and overall structure, stimulating in imagery, unified in vision, and profound of theme, this work alone would assure Frost's eminence among his nation's regional writers. But beyond it there are enough first-rate poems to stake two or three literary reputations. How many poets have produced a dozen medium-length poems that can rank with a selection of Frost's best narratives and dramatic poems *aside* from those in *North of Boston*? Imagine a gathering of the following pieces: "Love and a Question" and "The Tuft of Flowers" from Frost's early period; "An Old Man's Winter Night" and "The Ax-Helve," apparently begun at Derry; "Birches," " 'Out, Out—,' " "The Witch of Coös," "A Star in a Stoneboat," "The Star-Splitter," "Two Look at Two," and "The Grindstone" from the teens and early twenties; and "West-Running Brook," "Two Tramps in Mud Time" and "Directive" from the later period. How many other poets could set aside their best collection and then find fourteen other poems as substantial and unforgettable as these? They average some sixty lines in length, yet they contain few weak phrases, faults of tone or image, or lapses of inspiration. Though centered on New England, they offer a variety of tone, situation, setting, and emotion that few poets can rival. Among the pieces listed are love poems, poems of joy and fraternal affection, poems of conflict and competition, poems of reverence, solitude, and deep sadness, poems of fear, death, and ultimate loneliness.

Yet, aside from the brilliant feat of *North of Boston* and the solid achievement of the poems just cited, we could turn again to Frost's collected verse and pull out a grouping of short poems that only one or two of his contemporaries could match. Indeed, for his success with the sonnet alone, Frost deserves a special ranking among modern poets. After reading such works as "Mowing," "Meeting and Passing," "Hyla Brook," "The Oven Bird," "Putting in the Seed," "On a Tree Fallen Across the Road," "Acceptance," "The Investment," "The Flood," "Design," "Unharvested," and "The Silken Tent," what other poet could we turn to for a comparable set of sonnets or variations on the form? Where else can we find such fine examples of prosodic dexterity, compression and lucidity, verbal power and metaphorical suggestiveness? For worthy comparisons we must look to Keats, to Wordsworth, and to the great masters of the Renaissance.

But Frost's sonnets are only a portion of his extensive output in short verse forms. There is also a significant body of widely recognized masterpieces, poems that rightly appear in anthologies and textbooks: "Reluctance," "The Road Not Taken," "The Sound of Trees," "Nothing Gold Can Stay," "The Aim Was Song," "Stopping By Woods," "For Once, Then, Something," "The Onset," "The Need of Being Versed in Country Things," "Spring Pools," "On Going Unnoticed," "Bereft," "The Last Mowing," "Desert Places," "A Leaf-Treader," "The Most of It," "Away!" Here is another distinguished gathering of poems. It might be altered or supplemented according to individual taste, but the point is that by itself such a gathering would justify Frost's rank as a leading American poet.

Along with *North of Boston*, then, some three dozen poems provide the basis for Frost's prominence as a New England author. Yet, in addition, more than a dozen pieces of nonregional poetry deserve great respect and attention. For its intensity, its craftsmanship, its consistently high level of imaginative performance, this is another notable body of verse that finds its match in the work of only the greatest modern poets. When we read poems like "Fire and Ice," "Once by the Pacific," "Acquainted with the Night," "The Lovely Shall Be Choosers," "A Soldier," "Departmental," "Neither Out Far nor In Deep," "Provide, Provide," "All Revelation," "Never Again Would Birds' Song Be the Same," "The Fear of God," and "Escapist—Never," we know we are in the presence of a great artistic force.

Altogether there are roughly fifty regional poems and at least a dozen nonregional pieces that we should consider in trying to reach an estimate of Frost's place in literary history. The question that seems to trouble many observers is whether or not this poet is, ultimately, a major or minor figure in modern literature. David Perkins, for example, in an important piece of recent scholarship, is reluctant to rank Frost with "major writers" like Eliot, Joyce, Yeats, and Lawrence, owing to the New England poet's restricted artistic scope and tendency toward an ironic evasiveness that prevents us from taking him seriously.[28] However, after discussing the other authors' "commitment" to serious beliefs (typified for him by Eliot's awe-inspiring vision in *The Waste Land*), Perkins notes that such seriousness often led to extremism and mental instability. From this point, he hastily concludes his discussion of Frost with the backhanded compliment that he is one of the few modern authors· "whose work seems consistently to preserve poise and sanity of mind" (p. 251). We are left with the implication that Frost probably is not a true major figure, but that there is nothing wrong with enjoying his work since it is so sane.

Perhaps this is conceding too much in one direction and claiming too much in another—a lamentable situation indeed, because the claim for Frost's poise and sanity is much better supported by the stance of the sturdy Yankee farmer who dominates the mediocre verse than by that of the contemplative, uncertain, often distressed persona whom we meet in the most vivid and forceful poems. Furthermore, insofar as this claim is tacitly biographical, it is considerably undercut by the Thompson-Winnick volumes, which do not allow us to imagine that Frost's poetry made him more sane or mentally balanced than, say, Eliot, or even Ezra Pound.

If Perkins's claim for the healthiness of Frost's verse hardly puts this poet in his best light, the concession that he lacks fundamental seriousness raises a number of consequential issues that deserve close attention. Before accepting such a concession we must make certain that it is called for in relation to the poet's greatest work.

Perkins is correct: seriousness is a highly important issue (in truth, he provides a fair and reasonable survey of prevailing views on the poet). Regional writers have a special obligation to prove their seriousness: they must demonstrate that their work is not escapist, trivial, or irrelevant. And in order to be fully convincing, they cannot

[28] Perkins, *A History of Modern Poetry* (Cambridge, Mass.: Belknap Press of Harvard University Press, 1976), p. 250.

be too partisan about their regions; instead, maintaining a degree of objectivity, they must show understanding of the fundamental humanity observable in the local world. Regional novelists like Faulkner and Hardy have been accorded "major" status by literary historians because they display an artistic detachment that makes their universality hard to miss. Faulkner's immense prestige as a modern novelist springs in large part from his reputation as an analyst and critic of the South. In this light, Frost's popular role as the Yankee poet is a severe liability. Critics have often had trouble recognizing that he is more than a chauvinistic regional spokesman, as Lionel Trilling explained so honestly and movingly in his essay, "A Speech on Robert Frost: A Cultural Episode."[29] In fact, Frost's performance of the Yankee role may well have been another of his many ways of challenging and taunting the critics. He disliked being appropriated by scholarly interpreters as a "serious" author. Yet serious he was: in that corpus of some three score poems on which his reputation should rest and on which he deserves to be judged, he was deeply, mortally serious. If he is ironic, if he seems playfully evasive or ambiguous, his great poems are in some crucial sense not mere play but "play for mortal stakes."

Frost's treatment of rural New England is no less serious than William Faulkner's treatment of the rural South, and we should not let superficial differences blur the fundamental similarity between these two artists. Faulkner's position as a major figure, a serious, dedicated artist, is no longer in doubt: first, and most important, owing to his brilliant perception and evocation of life in Yoknapatawpha County; and second, owing to his reputation for stylistic innovation. The latter is not, most critics agree, a reliable indication of an author's seriousness; yet it conveys a certain aura of fashion that has worked in Faulkner's favor. Conversely, and unjustifiably, this factor has

[29] *Partisan Review*, 26 (Summer 1959), 445-452.

worked against the stylistically conservative Frost. But the former reason seems to offer a more plausible contrast between these two authors of North and South. Frost, some readers feel, is little more than a mouthpiece for appealing Yankeeisms. At the core of his art there is no deep understanding of the region, no well-integrated view of the human condition there, no decisive commitment to the human values that George W. Nitchie has taken as the central concern of his probing study, *Human Values in the Poetry of Robert Frost*.[30]

Where Faulkner—or Eliot, Yeats, and other recognized major authors—may be given credit for illuminating human existence, the New England poet is often criticized as equivocal, evasive, opaque. Nitchie, perhaps the most persuasive proponent of the theory that Frost's poetry is "less than absolutely first rank," builds the conclusion of his book around a discussion of the poet's "fundamental indecisiveness," summarizing his objections thus: "Distrusting intelligence, emphasizing will, he offers us a world in which those difficulties that cannot be resolved by an exercise of the will simply cannot be resolved, and had better be left alone." This view reduces Frost to little more than a voice, a manner of speaking, what Nitchie calls an "aptness." Perkins seems to agree, maintaining that "the form is the major content" in Frost's verse. By appreciating the poet's poise and ability to keep "his balance, not coming down on one side or the other of arguments that cannot be settled," Perkins gives such faint praise that it is tantamount to Nitchie's condemnation.[31]

But if we read Frost's very best regional work (Nitchie gives much too much emphasis to the Masques and such inferior pieces as "A Roadside Stand," "To a Thinker," and "The Bear"), we find that his commitment to the discovery of human values in his region is entirely worthy of

[30] Nitchie, *Human Values in the Poetry of Robert Frost: A Study of a Poet's Convictions* (Durham: Duke University Press, 1960).

[31] *Ibid.*, pp. 219-223; Perkins, *Modern Poetry*, pp. 250-251.

comparison with Faulkner's. And what he was most serious about is one of the central problems that confronts the modern mind: the problem of meaning.

In the post-Darwinian, post-Freudian world this problem has been important to a wide range of individuals and to many intellectual and artistic movements. From surrealism and cubism to abstract impressionism, from existentialism and phenomenology to logical positivism, among psychologists and linguists, among philosophers and artists—the concern has been to investigate the nature of meaning and the processes through which human beings create it and make use of it. By dramatizing situations that involve perceptions, questions, and problems of meaning, Frost placed his work much more directly in the mainstream of modern thought than many observers have realized.

In a profoundly serious way, each of Frost's great poems explores the human condition, the universal experience of an individual located in New England, who struggles to find meaning in his or her life and in the surrounding natural and social worlds. There is no lack of commitment here, and at bottom no evasiveness or irony. Frost's speaker may doubt his ability to find meaning in the situation; he may express an ironic awareness that the meaning he finds, or thinks he may find, is unreliable or inappropriate. But the very existence of the poetic utterance, and of the care it implies, establishes commitment to the persona (or personae) and provokes strong sympathy with his search for meaning.

There may be an element of indecision in Frost's poems, but they do not express "fundamental indecisiveness." A sensitive reading of the darkest pieces (and actually they are few), even those in which the speaker fails to find any shred of useful meaning, does not lead to such a conclusion. Frost takes a humble view of intelligence, a very humble view, but that is not the same as "distrusting" it. His Yankee persona indeed does distrust it, and that is the chief deficiency of the regional voice. Poetry cannot be willed into existence. But in his best work Frost refuses to give in to blind willfulness, recognizing the inadequacy, even danger, of the belief he ascribes to Len in "A Servant to Servants": "one steady pull more ought to do it. / . . . the best way out is always through" (ll. 55-56). As I have emphasized, this Yankee stance is fundamentally different from the poetic stance that characterizes Frost's most effective personae. The speakers in "Mending Wall," "After Apple-Picking," "Mowing," "Stopping by Woods," and "Directive" never regard will as a replacement for intelligence or vision. Much the opposite: for such precious, though admittedly weak and limited, faculties, the will provides much-needed support, strengthening the desire to struggle on—not in a meaningless quest (though it may appear that way, even to the speaker), but in an admirable quest for meaning itself.

Hence Nitchie's summary is wrong on two counts. First, even in a dark poem like "Design" or an ironically evasive one like "For Once, Then, Something," Frost never suggests that "those difficulties that cannot be resolved by an exercise of the will simply cannot be resolved." That is not his point at all. His speakers seem to know that difficulties can only be resolved by intelligence. The poems do not testify to blind will alone (such poems would be dull and uninspiring); they are instead marvelous evidence of a questing, exploring, unpredictable, *almost* magical, *almost* divine—but so, so fallibly human— intelligence. Second, although the intelligence may be aware that "difficulties had better," as Nitchie claims (p. 221), "be left alone," the whole purpose of the poem is to demonstrate, intriguingly, inspiringly, the human miracle of *not* leaving alone what indeed might be left that way, but what is much better attempted, much better tried for, even in a seemingly hopeless situation. Thus the human value, the universal human trait to which Frost commits himself, is that seeking, sensitive, and appreciative—one might say loving—spirit exhibited by his truly memorable personae. The compelling lyric force of their utterances evinces a depth and intensity of commitment that neither frustration nor fearful cynicism can nullify. Frost treasures—and encourages us to treasure—both the intelligence and the willingness "to go by contraries," an ability (as "West-Running Brook" and many other poems show) most fully exhibited in exploration, in aspiration and devotion, in love and visionary experience, in poetry itself.

Frost's most powerful inspiration seemed to take shape in visions of struggle. The speakers in his three score greatest poems, regional and nonregional alike, are explorers, seekers, questioners. What they long for is understanding, confidence, and a sense of form or order: what he called a "momentary stay against confusion." All his great works draw on this vision. As a young man (in fact, until he was approaching forty), his personal lack of confidence was so great and his sense of uncertainty and aberrancy so strong that he could hardly find effective ways to express his imaginative impulses. His quest for an attractive and imposing vantage point led him to adopt a variety of essentially Romantic poses; yet they elicited no sincere commitment and provided no satisfactory stance from which he could objectify his visions and give voice to his inspiration.

It was New England that first provided him with a way of approaching and gaining artistic control of the confusing emotional and imaginative forces that nearly overwhelmed him during the early years. Yet his tendency toward Romantic postures remained a hindrance to his development throughout the Derry period, until, having moved to England, he began to see himself and his special characteristics more clearly. There he discovered that his experience in New England provided imagery, dramatic conflict, lyric stimulation, and a variety of vocal tones that he could combine with his own personal visions and emotions to create highly effective poetry. Thus he became capable of the extraordinary achievement embodied in some fifty regional masterpieces—a poetic equivalent of

Faulkner's Yoknapatawpha fiction or Hardy's Wessex novels.

As part of his New England experience, however, Frost was familiar with (and capable of imitating) an image of the conventional Yankee, an image that was popular with readers and critics, especially in the mid-teens, and that also gave him a feeling, for the first time in his life, of confidence and worthiness. The more he adopted this stance of the conventional Yankee, the more stilted and uninspired his work became. Nevertheless, personal anxieties and encouragement from many friends, most commentators, and the audience that bought his books and attended his lectures made this the role he apparently preferred after 1914, at least when he felt an impressive performance was called for.

In the fifteen years since Frost's death, an extensive process of reevaluation and "demythifying" seems to many observers to have reduced his stature as a great man and a great poet. The interest aroused by Thompson and Winnick's biography is significant, especially as it involves considerable shock, dismay, and even outrage. Perhaps we should expect some trauma with the shattering of a cherished myth. Many recent observers, however, have resorted to extremes of invective against a man whom they see as not merely dishonest and vain but cruel and morally repulsive—a hateful, terrifying, inhuman figure. Surely this falsifies a biography in which Thompson remains even-tempered, compassionate, and generally respectful. Of course he expresses disapproval and dismay at some of Frost's actions and attitudes, but at no point does he evince hatred or terror concerning his subject, a man he knew intimately.

If the various facts and documents Thompson has amassed are put to thoughtful and constructive use, the effect will not be simply to deprive us of a pleasant and reassuring figure on the poetic landscape. Instead, the biography can help us to gain understanding of the poet in Frost; this is a worthy purpose indeed, for this poet does not need so much to be better known as to be known better. The loss of the "mythical" Frost, the renowned, noble Yankee bard, is accordingly no real loss. The poems are still there, still alive each time a reader finds them so. And for those with a deep interest, Thompson provides information about the circumstances and the process through which the poetry was created, information that contributes to an understanding of the significant patterns in the poet's life and artistic development. The mythical Yankee bard is important as an aspect of Frost's personality and as an indication of his imaginative tendencies, but it is not necessary as a support for the poems, nor should its loss in any way undercut the validity and integrity of his achievement. If the great poems are works of art that also stand in some sense as words to live by, it is not because they come from a saint, or even from a rustic national hero, but because they show us something about human nature, about ourselves.

Nevertheless, those of us who believe in Frost's greatness as a poet must confront the widespread opinion among readers and reviewers that the Thompson-Winnick biography portrays a man who could be mean, vindictive, selfish, and hypocritical. We must recognize also that the conventional regional approach to his poetry apparently fits with and corroborates this view: such a small, perverse man could only have found a place in a minor—or moribund—tradition. It has been my goal to demonstrate that Frost was in fact a very large poet, large in the possession of two qualities that contribute to the greatest poetry, whether regional or nonregional: first, an extraordinary verbal genius, and second, a powerful and meaningful vision of the human condition.

Of Frost's verbal genius there has never been much doubt, although he is too often praised merely for a lucid, conversational simplicity, as if he lacked depth and complexity. On a variety of strengths, however, he can stand comparison with the great poets of his language. For that oft-mentioned conversational quality, for instance, we might go back to Robert Burns, or still further to Shakespeare and Chaucer, to find such an exceptional gift of idiom and such a hearty, natural vigor. But that is to suggest only one dimension of Frost's prosodic ability. Surely we should not forget that he was also a master of the keen wit and linguistic dexterity that we associate with the Metaphysical poets. Nor, if we respect his command of the technical skills, the Augustan grace and balance of Pope and Dryden, should we overlook his ability to conjure with the lush natural imagery and intense emotions of the early Romantics, and even to touch the harsh chords, the malaise, the existential gloom of the late-Romantics and the moderns.

Throughout this study readers will find analysis and explication of many examples from Frost's verse that are intended to demonstrate anew the high order and wide range of his verbal genius. On the other hand, this chapter and the discussion of *North of Boston* in Chapter Three are primarily attempts to investigate the thematic depth, the remarkable vision and insight, and the wealth of human understanding found in his greatest New England poems. Now, since the chief reservations of those who would deny him major rank in the literature of our age pivot on the issue of seriousness, we must decide whether his best work engages our deepest concern with the experience of life itself. Does it enlarge our awareness and understanding of human nature? Does it move us in the unforgettable, unfathomable way we expect great art to move us? In arguing that Frost lacks the "seriousness, profundity, and commitment" of a major poet, David Perkins has summarized the most influential assumption about the poet's limitations, an assumption that hardly contributes to a full understanding and appreciation of his most serious work:

At his best Frost is never unqualified, final, and merely in earnest. As a result, some poetic or imaginative effects are not open to him. At the mysterious ethical and religious commands that conclude *The Waste Land* (doubly mysterious because they are in Sanskrit), we feel a certain awe, a piety in the presence of something ultimate. We never feel this in reading Frost. However irrational the effect may be, we feel for a moment that with Eliot's Sanskrit— DATTA, DAYADHVAN, DAMYATA—we have been given a basis for ordering our existence.[32]

This passage goes to the heart of the contrast often made between Frost and the "major" modern authors. The Yankee poet's aversion not only to Sanskrit religious texts but also to foreign languages and the allusive eclecticism typical of modern verse may predispose us to agree that he is a limited poet. Yet Perkins's claim is that while reading Frost we will never feel awe and piety "in the presence of something ultimate." The assertion seems dangerously categorical. And when it is followed by the charge that Frost cannot match Eliot's "quasi-moral, quasi-religious satisfactions for the imagination," our awareness of the difficulties faced by the Yankee poet's critics should make us realize that the comparison needs more thought. For it is precisely this "quasi-moral, quasi-religious" quality in Frost's work that is most easily overlooked. Especially if we have in mind the rustic New Englander or the shrewd performer exposed by Thompson—and it is significant that Perkins leads into his final estimate of Frost by discussing his irony and "Yankee wariness" (p. 250)—we may fail to recognize a seriousness that in Frost's handling was at once subtle and profound. There are no signposts, no Sanskrit quotations to announce the "quasi-moral, quasi-religious" element in his poetry, yet the element is there: it is central to the greatest poems. Consider Frost again, as Perkins says, "at his best." Consider "Mowing," "The Death of the Hired Man," "Home Burial," "After Apple-Picking," "The Wood-Pile," "Birches," "An Old Man's Winter Night," "The Star-

---

[32] Perkins, *Modern Poetry*, p. 250.

Splitter," "Stopping by Woods," "The Onset," "Desert Places," "Design," "The Most of It," and "Directive." Perhaps the most important unifying trait of the speakers in these pieces and in many others is that they indeed *do* feel "the presence of something ultimate." They feel it in the New England countryside, in the fields and walls and trees and living creatures. They feel it in their fellow men and in themselves, in their work and play, in their love and fear and grief. As we read and reread, this feeling is reflected to us—in some sense a religious feeling, a feeling of awe, of reverence, of sacredness.

The voices we hear in Frost's major work may be indecisive, occasionally tinged with the Yankee's wary skepticism; yet they also show a deep concern for New England and for a particular response to experience there. The force of these poetic utterances overrides any self-deprecating ironies and equivocations, bearing witness to an earnest mission in search of meaning.

To read or hear or recite Frost's great poetry is to share in the pursuit of a profound vision of human life. As we observe his speakers undertake physical, intellectual, and imaginative exploration, the power of their words and the beauty of their song persuades us that they deserve not only our attention, but also our commitment and fullest appreciation. Few modern American authors have more to offer us. Whether in America, or around the world in Europe, Africa, or Asia, we may find rewarding fields for our own exploration as we turn and turn again with increased understanding and enjoyment to those poems in which Frost made best use of his literary gifts and his extraordinary imagination, his special sensitivity to life in New England and his insight into human nature.

Appendix: A Chronological Listing of Commentary on Frost's Regionalism

This appendix provides a chronological listing of critical and scholarly studies that involve discussion of Frost's regional identity. The list is not intended to be comprehensive, but it includes the major regional interpretations, as well as many derivative and less distinguished offerings by both American and British commentators. The most significant items are annotated.

The prevalence of Frost's regional reputation is evident both from the number of items listed and from the prominence of many of the writers cited. Unfortunately, the tendency among many of these writers has been to accept Frost as the indigenous Yankee farmer he imitated so adeptly. All too often, commentators have been swayed by what James Dickey (1966) calls "the Robert Frost Story, a secular myth of surprising power and tenacity." And all too many reviews and studies of the poetry have shown a deplorable resemblance to the movie scenario that Dickey has facetiously proposed for a Hollywood version of the "Robert Frost Story": "It might open, for example, with a sequence showing Frost moving among his Properties— apple trees, birch trees, stone fences, dark woods with snow falling into them, ax handles, shovels, woodpiles, ladders, New England brooks, taciturn neighbors. . . ."

Frost's critics have favored regional catalogues of this sort, and their commentary frequently involves little more than a rehearsal of New England stereotypes—a litany of rural images interlarded with pertinent epigrams from the Yankee sage. Even Sidney Cox, who knew Frost well, wrote an essay on Frost and New England (1934) without mentioning the poet until more than halfway through the piece. A description of New England, according to Cox, *was* a description of Robert Frost; the poet's peculiar métier mattered little. No more important statement could be made than the fundamental characterization: "he is a New Englander."

From 1913 on, writers on Frost have engaged in a running debate over the value of being a New Englander. To summarize briefly, it is clear that after the initial burst of enthusiasm that greeted the Yankee farmer poet in 1914 and 1915, an opposing hostility and skepticism began to build, as much against the New Englander's identity as against the poetry itself. It was barely noticeable at first, but some of the praise that greeted *Mountain Interval* in 1916 and 1917 was damningly faint (see the brief notice in the *New York Times Book Review* of 7 January 1917, for instance). In the twenties and thirties, *New Hampshire* (1923), *West-Running Brook* (1928), and *A Further Range* (1936) provoked significant opposition to the sagacious New Englander, opposition that took on a Marxist tinge during the heyday of American radicalism. Frost's ostensibly rustic stand against New Deal liberalism was most overt in *A Further Range*; consequently, this work received more abuse on publication than did any of his other books. In addition to left-wing impatience with his lack of revolutionary zeal, there was also condescension and hostility from members of the literary avant-garde, who condemned his unwillingness to experiment and his conservative attachment to traditional meter and rhyme.

In the late thirties, with the Marxists disenchanted and disarrayed, with Eliot in England and Pound already in disgrace, with Robinson dead and Frost's nigh-seventy-year-old head getting whiter and craggier, the literary community seems to have revived a "good grey poet" a century after his time. Bernard DeVoto took a lead article in the *Saturday Review* (1938) to mount a major counterattack against Frost's detractors. He presented Frost as "the finest American poet, living or dead," implying that he had achieved "the only major affirmation that modern American literature has made" simply by being true to "the generations of men in New England" and by exploiting such regional gifts as the "traditional habit of Yankees" and the "characteristic of the Yankee mind." What is most amazing about DeVoto's essay is that it elicited no appreciable response. The opponents of the Yankee bard apparently no longer cared to enter the lists against him, and despite such isolated demurrers as Malcolm Cowley (1944) and Yvor Winters (1948), Frost was generally accepted during the forties and fifties as a poet of "major affirmation." Some might wonder whether he had written himself out; others might question his relevance to the new directions in poetry pioneered by Pound, Eliot, and Williams. But such deprecations rarely appeared in print.

In the late 1940s, Randall Jarrell's "The Other Robert Frost" (1947) stimulated a new concern and appreciation for a darker and bleaker side of Frost than DeVoto (and the numerous readers he spoke for) wanted to see. Similarly, W. G. O'Donnell's "Robert Frost and New England: A Revaluation" (1948) suggested that Frost's relationship to the region was far more complex than the anthologies and the poet's public performances indicated. Nevertheless, in the last few decades, despite continuing efforts by a few commentators to strike through the rustic mask, the regionalist hypothesis can still be found in historical surveys like Spiller's (1948), Bogan's (1951), and Quinn's (1951), in scholarly studies like Cook's (1958), Lynen's (1960), Morrison's (1969), Westbrook's (1973), and Cox's (1973), and in widely marketed anthologies of Frost's poetry by Untermeyer (1943, 1946, and 1951) and Graves (1963).

The list that follows emphasizes reviews from the teens, twenties, and thirties and books and scholarly studies from the last thirty to thirty-five years. Reviews since 1940 have generally been less thoughtful and original than the books and articles cited. Needless to say, however, many such pieces deal with Frost as a regionalist much as the earlier reviews did.

1913

Douglas, Norman. Review of *A Boy's Will*. *English Review*, 14 (June 1913), 505.
Flint, F. S. Review of *A Boy's Will*. *Poetry and Drama*, 1 (June 1913), 250.
  Like Pound, Flint had been carefully primed by Frost. Thus he stressed "simplicity of utterance" and insisted that "Frost's poetry is so much a part of the life that to tell his life would be to explain his poetry. I wish I were authorized to tell it, because the one is as moving as the other."
Pound, Ezra. Review of *A Boy's Will*. *Poetry: A Magazine of Verse*, 2 (May 1913), 72-74.
  The first review influenced by Frost's myth making and the first to view the poetry in relation to the poet's supposed background in "the New Hampshire woods"—a background, Pound incorrectly assumed, of "utter simplicity" (p. 72).
Review of *A Boy's Will*. *Bookman* (London), 44 (Aug. 1913), 189. Frost is depicted "on a lonely farm in a forest clearing."

1914

Abercrombie, Lascelles. "A New Voice." *Nation* (London), 15 (13 June 1914), 423-424.
Aldington, Richard. Review of *North of Boston*. *Egoist*, 1 (1 July 1914), 248.
Gibson, W. W. "Simplicity and Sophistication." *Bookman*, 46 (July 1914), 183.
Henderson, Alice Corbin. "Recent Poetry." *Dial*, 57 (1 Oct. 1914), 254.

A good example of the pervasiveness of Frost's early reputation as a regional poet. Henderson, in one of the first negative reviews, finds Frost liable to bore many readers and decries his "insistent monosyllabic monotony." Nevertheless, she gives credence to his identity as a Yankee farmer and is pleased that his poetry "gives us a direct sense of the earth; that close connection between nature and man which is only gained by constant companionship or by that intimacy of toil in which the earth gives up only that which is demanded of her."

Hueffer, Ford Madox. "Literary Portraits—XLII: Mr. Robert Frost and 'North of Boston.' " *Outlook* (London), 33 (27 June 1914), 879-880.

Pound, Ezra. "Modern Georgics." *Poetry: A Magazine of Verse*, 5 (Dec. 1914), 127-130.
Frost labeled a "parochial" talent (p. 127).

Thomas, Edward. Review of *North of Boston*. *English Review*, 18 (Aug. 1914), 142-143.

1915

Adams, Franklin P. "The Conning Tower." *New York Tribune*, 11 June 1915, p. 9.

Baxter, Sylvester. "New England's New Poet." *American Review of Reviews*, 51 (Apr. 1915), 432-434.
Considering Frost "New England in every fiber" (p. 433), Baxter credits him with "farming in northern New Hampshire" (p. 432) *before* the trip to England and with coming back in 1915 "to return to farming on his beloved soil" (p. 434).

"Books of the Week." *New York Globe and Commercial Advertiser*, 17 Apr. 1915, p. 8.

Braithwaite, W. S. "A Poet of New England: Robert Frost a New Exponent of Life." *Boston Evening Transcript*, 28 Apr. 1915, pt. 3, p. 4.

———. "Robert Frost, New American Poet." *Boston Evening Transcript*, 8 May 1915, pt. 3, pp. 4, 10.

Garnett, Edward. "A New American Poet." *Atlantic Monthly*, 116 (Aug. 1915), 214-221.

Alone among the early reviewers, Garnett doubted that Frost's special talent and even "his genuine New England voice" were the "pure product of the New England soil." He maintained that Frost, like Cooper, Poe, Hawthorne, and Melville, benefited from "the ferment of foreign influence" (pp. 214-215).

Howells, William Dean. "The Editor's Easy Chair." *Harper's Monthly Magazine*, 131 (Sept. 1915), 165.

Perhaps America's leading literary arbiter in 1915, Howells linked Frost with Sarah Orne Jewett, Mary Wilkins, Alice Brown, and the New England regional movement.

Lowell, Amy. "North of Boston." *New Republic*, 2 (20 Feb. 1915), 81-82.

This influential but misleading early praise for Frost emphasizes that he is "saturated with New England" (p. 81) and that his poetry is "of a color so local as to be almost photographic." Viewing Frost as an "uncompromising New Englander" (p. 82), Lowell compares him with Whittier and Alice Brown.

"A New Poet of the Hills." *Brooklyn Daily Eagle*, 24 Apr. 1915, sec. 2, p. 5.

Rittenhouse, Jessie B. "North of Boston: Robert Frost's Poems of New England Farm Life." *New York Times Book Review*, 16 May 1915, p. 189.

Untermeyer, Louis. "Robert Frost's 'North of Boston.'" *Chicago Evening Post*, 23 Apr. 1915, p. 11.

Wheeler, Edmund J. "Discovered in England—A Real American Poet." *Current Opinion*, 58 (June 1915), 427-428.

1916

Colum, Padraic. "The Poetry of Robert Frost." *New Republic*, 9 (23 Dec. 1916), 219-222.

"The New Books: Verse and Verse-Makers." *American Review of Reviews*, 54 (Dec. 1916), 674.

This review concludes: "One feels that his revelation of the poesy of this rustic locality shows the immense dignity of a man's human cleavage to the spot where he was born, and to the ordinary happenings of his daily life."

"Poetry of Axe Handles Urged by Robert Frost." *Philadelphia Public Ledger*, 4 Apr. 1916, p. 11.

Smith, Geddes. "Four Pioneer Poets." *Independent*, 88 (25 Dec. 1916), 533-534.

Frost is viewed as a neighborly "poet of New England folks" in *Mountain Interval*: "Much of what he has to say is frankly agreeable conversation about the New England countryside . . ." (p. 533).

Wilmore, Carl. "Finds Famous American Poet in White Mountain Village." *Boston Post*, 14 Feb. 1916, p. 16.

1917

Johonnot, Rodney F. "Robert Frost, New England Poet, As He Impresses a Maine Clergyman." *Lewistown Journal* (Maine), 10 Feb. 1917, magazine sec., p. 12.

Lowell, Amy. "Robert Frost." In Lowell, *Tendencies in Modern American Poetry* (New York: Macmillan Co., 1917), pp. 79-136.

Monroe, Harriet. "Frost and Masters." *Poetry: A Magazine of Verse*, 9 (Jan. 1917), 202-207.

Monroe was concerned with the regional spokesman: "In Frost Puritan New England speaks with a voice as absolute as New Hampshire's granite hills" (p. 203).

Review of *Mountain Interval*. *New York Times Book Review*, 7 Jan. 1917, sec. 6, p. 2.

Although Frost wrote more than two-thirds of *Mountain Interval* before moving to Franconia, this reviewer, like many others, was convinced that the collection deals with "the region under Franconia Notch."

1919

Elliott, G. R. "The Neighborliness of Robert Frost." *Nation*, 109 (6 Dec. 1919), 713-715.

One of many attempts to extrapolate regional moral standards from Frost's work.

Untermeyer, Louis. "Robert Frost." In Untermeyer, *The New Era in American Poetry* (New York: Henry Holt and Company, 1919), pp. 15-39.

1920

Benjamin, P. L. "Robert Frost—Poet of Neighborliness." *Survey*, 45 (27 Nov. 1920), 318-319.

1921

Anthony, Joseph. "Robert Frost: The Farmer Poet." *Farm and Fireside*, 45 (June 1921), 4.

An exaggerated testimonial to "the farmers' own poet."

1923

Farrar, John. "The Poet of New England's Hill-men." *Literary Digest International Book Review*, 1 (Nov. 1923), 25.

Littell, Robert. "Stone Walls and Precious Stones." *New Republic*, 37 (5 Dec. 1923), supplement, 24-26.

New Hampshire is seen as "a journey across country in the company of a wise, shrewd, humorous person with an uncommon gift of common speech, a journey punctuated with philosophy, anecdotes, reminiscence, scandal . . ." (p. 24).

Morton, David. "The Poet of the New Hampshire Hills." *Outlook*, 135 (19 Dec. 1923), 688-689.

Morton disapproves of Frost's "choice of direction among several tendencies discernible in the earlier books." *New Hampshire* is disappointing because "the whole aim is special and peculiar and restricted" (p. 688).

Review of *Selected Poems*. *Times Literary Supplement* (London), 29 Mar. 1923, p. 213.

A good example of how Frost's ostensibly regional identity was used against him. This critic found

Selected Poems uninspired and prosy: "He knows his people, his farms, his solitudes. . . . But he avoids poetry."

Untermeyer, Louis. "Robert Frost." In Untermeyer, *American Poetry Since 1900* (New York: Henry Holt and Company, 1923), pp. 15-41.

Although Untermeyer recites at great length purported evidence of Frost's "intimacy with New England" (p. 15), he never gets beyond regional stereotype. His portrait of the hardy, rustic man of the soil ignores intellectual, academic, and literary aspects of Frost's background. Furthermore, it offers no hint of tension between poet and region.

Van Doren, Mark. "Robert Frost." *Nation*, 117 (19 Dec. 1923), 715-716.

Van Doren oversimplifies Frost's identification with New Hampshire in "New Hampshire."

1924

Monroe, Harriet. "Robert Frost." *Poetry: A Magazine of Verse*, 25 (Dec. 1924), 146-151.

Van Doren, Carl. "The Soil of the Puritans." In Van Doren, *Many Minds* (New York: Alfred Knopf, 1924), pp. 50-66.

1925

Elliott, G. R. "An Undiscovered America in Frost's Poetry." *Virginia Quarterly Review*, 1 (July 1925), 205-215.

Van Doren, Carl and Mark. *American and British Literature Since 1890*. New York: Century Co., 1925.

Frost "kept close to the soil of New England" (p. 20) and "lived much of his life as a farmer" (p. 21), according to this historical survey. Hence, he "has been content to write of Yankee matters in a Yankee idiom" (p. 21), and he has no need to deal with anything other than "familiar objects" and "familiar emotions" (p. 23).

Wood, Clement. "Robert Frost: The Twilight of New England." In Wood, *Poets of America* (New York: Dutton, 1925), pp. 142-162.

1927

Farrar, John. "Robert Frost and Other Green Mountain Writers." *English Journal*, 16 (Oct. 1927), 581-587.
Frost is seen as a Vermont poet and is linked to Dorothy Canfield Fisher, Bertha Oppenheim, and Zephine Humphrey; Willa Cather and Edna Ferber are also mentioned for comparison.

Munson, Gorham. *Robert Frost: A Study in Sensibility and Good Sense*. New York: Doran, 1927.
In *Robert Frost: The Years of Triumph*, Lawrance Thompson devotes Chapter 22 ("Helping to Shape an Image") to Frost's "spoon-feeding" of material to Munson. This first book-length study is a showcase for the "Derry myth."

1928

Deutsch, Babette. "Inner Weather." *New York Herald Tribune Book Review*, 18 Nov. 1928, pp. 1, 2.
Disappointed with Frost's turn (in *West-Running Brook*) from dramatic poetry toward personal, regional philosophy, Deutsch also had difficulty accepting his dark side ("Bereft," "Acquainted with the Night"): "It was rather as one acquainted with the look of dawn on fresh turned soil, with the smell of the barn and harvest time . . . that one thought of Frost" (p. 2).

Untermeyer, Louis. "Still Robert Frost." *Saturday Review of Literature*, 5 (22 Dec. 1928), 533-534.
Trying to defend *West-Running Brook* against criticism like Deutsch's, Untermeyer links it with *A Boy's Will* (prevalence of short forms), claiming that Frost's bardic art is not the sort that changes or develops, and closing with the final couplet of "Into My Own":

"They wouldn't find me changed from him they knew— / Only more sure of all I thought was true."

Whipple, T. K. "Robert Frost." In Whipple, *Spokesmen: Modern Writers and American Life* (New York: D. Appleton and Company, 1928), pp. 94-114.

An extreme instance of the influence of the farmer-poet myth. Frost is presented as a hardworking, money-making farmer.

1929

Kreymborg, Alfred. "The Fire and Ice of Robert Frost." In Kreymborg, *Our Singing Strength: An Outline of American Poetry 1620-1930* (New York: Coward-McCann, Inc., 1929), pp. 316-332.

Pierce, Frederick E. "Three Poets Against Philistia." *Yale Review*, 18 (Winter 1929), 365-366.

1930

Hicks, Granville. "The World of Robert Frost." *New Republic*, 65 (3 Dec. 1930), 77-78.

Hicks attacks Frost for failing to deal with "industrialism," "the disruptive effect that scientific hypotheses have had on modern thought," and "Freudianism."

1931

Blankenship, William R. *American Literature as an Expression of the National Mind*. New York: Henry Holt and Company, 1931. Pp. 588-594.

Blankenship links Frost and Hamlin Garland.

Moore, Virginia. "Robert Frost of New Hampshire." *Yale Review*, 20 (May 1931), 627-629.

Schneider, Isidor. "Robert Frost." *Nation*, 132 (28 Jan. 1931), 101-102.

1932

Smith, Fred. "The Sound of a Yankee Voice." *Commonweal*, 15 (Jan. 1932), 297-298.

Emphasizing Yankee speech, Smith views Frost's poetry as the utterance of a regional figure: "Unless you hear his voice in his verse you have not come fully into understanding him" (p. 298).

1934

Cox, Sidney. "New England and Robert Frost." *New Mexico Quarterly Review*, 4 (May 1934), 89-94.
Making the simplistic assumption that Frost was a New Englander, Cox argues that "New England people are like their dwelling place. . . . tough, sinewy, difficult, exacting, full of sap" (p. 90). His comments about the "absence of easy flowing sentiment" in New England (pp. 90-91) are especially misleading in light of Frost's concern with the *conflict* between sentimental, feminine sympathies and tough-minded, masculine attempts at restraint. This tension is overt in dramatic poems like "The Death of the Hired Man" and "Home Burial," yet it is no less important in interior monologues like "Design" and "The Need of Being Versed in Country Things."

Weygandt, Cornelius. *The White Hills*. New York: Henry Holt and Company, 1934.

1935

Carroll, G. H. "New England Sees It Through." *Saturday Review of Literature*, 13 (9 Nov. 1935), 519-522.

Ford, Caroline. *The Less Travelled Road*. Cambridge, Mass.: Harvard University Press, 1935.

1936

Arvin, Newton. "A Minor Strain." *Partisan Review*, 3 (June 1936), 27-28.
Like many of the leftist attacks that greeted *A Further Range*, this one uses Frost's regional identity as evidence that he is at best a minor poet. His "Yankee renunciation" is philosophically "as profitless as a dried-up well" (p. 27).

Auden, W. H. "Preface" to *Selected Poems of Robert Frost*
(London, 1936). Reprinted in Richard Thornton, ed.,
Recognition of Robert Frost (New York: Henry Holt
and Company, 1937), pp. 293-298.

Blackmur, R. P. "The Instincts of a Bard." *Nation*, 142 (24
June 1936), 524-525.
Frost's regional work is criticized as escapist.

Gregory, Horace. Review of *A Further Range. New Repub-
lic*, 87 (June 1936), 817-819.

Humphries, Rolfe. "A Further Shrinking." *New Masses*,
20 (11 Aug. 1936), 41-42.

Van Doren, Mark. "The Permanence of Robert Frost."
American Scholar, 5 (Spring 1936), 190-198.

1937

Moore, Merrill. "Poetic Agrarianism, Old Style." *Sewanee
Review*, 45 (Oct.-Dec. 1937), 507-509.

Thornton, Richard, ed. *Recognition of Robert Frost*. New
York: Henry Holt and Company, 1937.
Intended as a tribute, this collection of criticism in-
cludes an unfortunate selection of exaggerated and
oversimplified regional estimates of Frost, thus giv-
ing undue influence to some of the more misguided
interpretations by writers like Lowell, Van Doren,
Farrar, and Whipple.

1938

Coffin, Robert P. Tristram. *New Poetry of New England:
Frost and Robinson*. Baltimore: Johns Hopkins Uni-
versity Press, 1938.
Much approval but little analysis of Frost's regional
role. Significantly, Coffin lists several minor re-
gionalist poets (including himself) whom Frost sup-
posedly influenced (72), but he neither notices nor at-
tempts to explain the immense differences between
Frost and the others on the list.

DeVoto, Bernard. "The Critics and Robert Frost." *Satur-
day Review of Literature*, 17 (1 Jan. 1938), 3-4, 14-15.

DeVoto praises Frost enthusiastically, attributing his stature as a major poet to his immersion in and association with a distinctive and (to DeVoto) admirable region.

1939

Brooks, Cleanth. "Frost, MacLeish, and Auden." In Brooks, *Modern Poetry and the Tradition* (Chapel Hill: University of North Carolina Press, 1939), pp. 110-135.
Although this essay opens with the pronouncement, "Robert Frost is a regionalist" (p. 110), Brooks goes on to show some of the limitations of the definition, demonstrating that Frost has more affinities with the modern symbolists than is often thought.

Untermeyer, Louis. "The Northeast Corner." In *From Another World: The Autobiography of Louis Untermeyer* (New York: Harcourt, 1939), pp. 206-228.
Personal reminiscences of Frost as the archetypal Yankee.

Van Dore, Wade. "Poet of the Trees." *Christian Science Monitor*, 23 Dec. 1939, pp. 3, 14.

1940

Fletcher, John G. "Robert Frost the Outlander." *Mark Twain Quarterly*, 3 (Spring 1940), 3-5.

1942

Thompson, Lawrance. *Fire and Ice: The Art and Thought of Robert Frost*. New York: Henry Holt and Company, 1942.
Thompson's first study of Frost shows the influence of the poet's myth-making power. Here—especially in the section titled "The Yankee Manner"—Frost is presented as the self-confident New Englander, relying on his "ingrained Yankee manner" (p. 57) and his "Yankee instinct" (p. 58).

1943

Stovall, Floyd. "Robinson and Frost." In Stovall, *American Idealism* (Norman: University of Oklahoma Press, 1943), pp. 167-186.
Frost is seen as an optimistic idealist, closer to New England's "everyday life" (p. 179) than Robinson.

Untermeyer, Louis, ed. *Come In and Other Poems*. New York: Henry Holt and Company, 1943.
Frost's poetry is placed in the context of a Yankee bard's rustic life.

1944

Cowley, Malcolm. "Frost: A Dissenting Opinion." *New Republic*, 111 (11, 18 Sept. 1944), 312-313, 345-347.
Like many of Frost's admirers, Cowley makes the dangerous assumption that the poet is a New Englander through and through. But this is no virtue to Cowley; it is rather the source of Frost's limitations. It leads to poetry that "celebrates the diminished but prosperous and self-respecting New England of the tourist home and the antique shop in the abandoned grist mill" (p. 347).

1945

Foster, Charles H. "Robert Frost and the New England Tradition." In *Elizabethan Studies and Other Essays in Honor of George F. Reynolds*, University of Colorado Studies, Series B, 2 (Oct. 1945), pp. 370-381.
Frost is praised as the "embodier of the New England tradition," linked by his "Yankee independence and conviction" (380) with Emerson, Thoreau, Whittier, Lowell, and Holmes.

1946

Morse, Stearns. "Robert Frost and New Hampshire." *New Hampshire Troubadour*, 16 (Nov. 1946), 6-8.
Morse is deeply impressed by Frost's claim to have

slept in every town in New Hampshire: "There is no doubt that Robert Frost knows New Hampshire—at least rural New Hampshire—as well as anyone" (pp. 6-7).

West, Herbert F., ed. "Robert Frost Issue" of *New Hampshire Troubadour*, 16 (Nov. 1946).

Articles by Sylvia Clark, Stearns Morse, Sidney Cox, and others glorify Frost's New Hampshire background.

1947

Cook, Reginald. "Poet in the Mountains." *Western Review*, 11 (Spring, 1947), 175-181.

Jarrell, Randall. "The Other Robert Frost" (1947). Reprinted in Jarrell, *Poetry and the Age* (New York: Vintage Books, 1953), pp. 26-33.

Emphasizing Frost's dark side and his concern with evil and fear, Jarrell was the first commentator to challenge the mythical "Farmer-Poet" figure "who knows all about trees and farms and folks in New England" (p. 26).

1948

O'Donnell, William G. "Robert Frost and New England: A Revaluation." *Yale Review*, 37 (Summer 1948), 698-712.

One of the few attempts to distinguish Frost from the New England regionalist writers. To O'Donnell, *North of Boston* is Frost's best collection because it is the most distant from traditional regionalism.

Spiller, Robert E., et al. *Literary History of the United States* (1948). 4th ed. New York: Macmillan Co., 1974.

Not only does Willard Thorp's chapter on "The New Poetry" (pp. 1171-1196) treat Frost as a regionalist, but Malcolm Cowley and Henry Seidel Canby, in "Creating an Audience" (pp. 1119-1134), discuss the professions of modern writers like William Carlos

Williams (doctor) and Wallace Stevens (insurance
executive) and identity Frost as "a farmer" (p. 1120),
thus perpetuating the Derry myth.

Winters, Yvor. "Robert Frost: Or, the Spiritual Drifter as
Poet." *Sewanee Review*, 56 (Aug. 1948), 564-596.
Frost's regional concentration is seen as a major cause
of his philosophical confusion and obscurity.

1949

Cook, Reginald. "Frost Country." *Vermont Life*, 3 (Sum-
mer 1949), 15-17.

1950

Bowra, C. M. "Robert Frost." *Adelphi*, 27 (Nov. 1950),
46-64.

Whicher, George F. "Sage from North of Boston." In
Whicher, *Mornings at 8:50: Brief evocations of the
Past for a College Audience* (Northampton, Mass.:
Hampshire Bookshop, 1950), pp. 34-38.

1951

Bogan, Louise. *Achievement in American Poetry: 1900-
1950*. Chicago: Henry Regnery Company, 1951.

Untermeyer, Louis, ed. *The Road Not Taken: An Introduc-
tion to Robert Frost*. New York: Henry Holt and Com-
pany, 1951.

Van Doren, Mark. "Robert Frost's America." *Atlantic*, 187
(June 1951), 32-34.

Whicher, George F. "In the American Grain." In Arthur
Hobson Quinn, ed., *The Literature of the American
People* (New York: Appleton-Century-Crofts, Inc.,
1951), pp. 900-913.
Whicher aligns Frost with regionalists like Willa
Cather and Dorothy Canfield Fisher.

1952

Pearce, Roy Harvey. "The Poet as Person." *Yale Review*,
41 (Spring 1952), 421-440.

1954

Beach, Joseph Warren. "Robert Frost." *Yale Review*, 43 (Winter 1954), 204-217.

1955

Spiller, Robert E. *The Cycle of American Literature*. New York: Macmillan Co., 1955.
Spiller sees Frost "in the native grain as was no other modern poet . . ." (p. 239).

1957

Cox, Sidney H. *A Swinger of Birches: A Portrait of Robert Frost* (1957). Reprint ed. New York: Collier Books, 1961.

1958

Alvarez, A. *Stewards of Excellence: Studies in Modern English and American Poets* (1958). Reprint ed. New York: Gordian Press, 1971.
A vigorous attack on Frost's New England poetry.
Cook, Reginald L. *The Dimensions of Robert Frost*. New York: Rinehart and Company, 1958.

1959

Cox, James M. "Robert Frost and the Edge of the Clearing." *Virginia Quarterly Review*, 35 (Winter 1959), 73-88.
Jamieson, Paul F. "Robert Frost: Poet of Mountain Land." *Appalachia*, 32 (December 1959), 471-479.
Langbaum, Robert. "The New Nature of Poetry." *American Scholar* (1959). Reprinted in *The Modern Spirit: Essays on the Continuity of Nineteenth- and Twentieth-Century Literature* (New York: Oxford University Press, 1970), pp. 101-126.
An important interpretation of Frost as a New England nature poet, presenting him as a transitional figure between the Wordsworthian tradition and the "new nature poetry," which, Langbaum maintains,

conveys a sense "of the mindlessness of nature, its nonhuman otherness" (p. 102). Although giving Frost credit for occasionally approaching the modern vision (which is revealed more clearly in the work of poets like D. H. Lawrence, Marianne Moore, Wallace Stevens, and Ted Hughes), Langbaum notes disparagingly that this new "sense of nature is difficult to convey in poems about the cultivated countryside of England or New England" (p. 111). This argument overlooks the fact that many of Frost's best poems are not simply "about the cultivated countryside," but deal instead with an observer in the countryside—an observer who is often more aware of "the mindlessness of nature," and of his own alien position within it, than Langbaum seems to appreciate.

Thompson, Lawrance. "A Native to the Grain of the American Idiom." *Saturday Review of Literature*, 42 (21 Mar. 1959), 21, 55-56.

1960

Brooks, Cleanth. "Regionalism in American Literature." *Journal of Southern History*, 26 (Feb. 1960), 35-43.

Lynen, John F. *The Pastoral Art of Robert Frost*. New Haven: Yale University Press, 1960.
Lynen's theory of Frost's pastoralism is based on the debatable assumption that the poet "wrote from the point of view of an actual New England farmer" (p. 19).

MacDonald, Dwight. "Masscult and Midcult." *Partisan Review*, 27 (Spring 1960), 203-233.

Nitchie, George W. *Human Values in the Poetry of Robert Frost: A Study of a Poet's Convictions*. Durham: Duke University Press, 1960.
Chapter 4 contains significant comparisons of Frost and such New England writers as Stowe, Jewett, Freeman, Thoreau, and Dickinson; but Nitchie fails to recognize the tension between Frost and his region. Thus his complaint in the final chapter about Frost's

evasiveness and indecisiveness applies chiefly to those relatively weak poems dominated by the wily Yankee.

Sergeant, Elizabeth Shepley. *Robert Frost: The Trial by Existence.* New York: Holt, Rinehart and Winston, 1960.

A tribute to the mythical Frost.

1962

Ciardi, John. "Robert Frost: American Bard." *Saturday Review of Literature*, 45 (24 Mar. 1962), 15-17, 52-54.

Pritchard, William H. "*North of Boston*: Frost's Poetry of Dialogue." In Reuben Brower and Richard Poirier, eds., *In Defense of Reading: A Reader's Approach to Literary Criticism* (New York: E. P. Dutton and Company, Inc., 1962), pp. 38-56.

In an interesting departure from familiar regional interpretations of *North of Boston*, Pritchard argues that the book does *not* contain "faithful representations of colloquial speech" but, on the contrary, succeeds through its "dramatic intermingling of personal vision and social fact" (p. 55).

1963

Graves, Robert. "Introduction." In *Selected Poems of Robert Frost* (New York: Holt, Rinehart and Winston, 1963), pp. ix-xiv.

In his introduction to this popular paperbound edition, Graves fosters many myths about the poet's New England background.

Squires, Radcliffe. *The Major Themes of Robert Frost.* Ann Arbor: University of Michigan Press, 1963.

After brief comparisons with Emerson, Dickinson, and Robinson (pp. 7-12), Squires finds Frost to be the greatest New England poet.

1966

Dickey, James. "Robert Frost: Man and Myth." *Atlantic*, 218 (Nov. 1966), 53-56.
Commentary on the power of the Frost myth.

Thompson, Lawrance. *Robert Frost: The Early Years, 1874-1915*. New York: Holt, Rinehart and Winston, 1966.
The first volume of Thompson's heavily documented biography demonstrates how Frost's myth making falsified his background and artistic development, particularly his difficult experience as an outsider in rural New England.

1967

St. Armand, Barton L. "The Power of Sympathy in the Poetry of Robinson and Frost: The 'Inside' vs. the 'Outside' Narrative." *American Quarterly*, 19 (Fall 1967), 564-574.
Although failing to appreciate the full significance of the tension between Frost and rural New England, St. Armand is one of the few scholars to contrast the poet with other New England regionalists.

Snow, C. P. "Robert Frost." In Snow, *Variety of Men* (New York: Scribner's, 1967), pp. 130-150.
Drawing on Thompson's *Robert Frost: The Early Years*, Snow discusses "the New England myth" and examines farming as Frost's "own romantic invention" (p. 135).

1969

Morrison, Theodore. "Frost: Country Poet and Cosmopolitan Poet." *Yale Review*, 59 (Dec. 1969), 179-196.
A Harvard professor and a good friend of Frost's (his wife became Frost's secretary and "schedule planner" after Mrs. Frost's death in 1938), Morrison speaks with considerable authority. But although he comes to praise Frost as both countryman and cos-

mopolitan, he puts himself in a weak position by clearly *preferring* the former (the "country element has endeared him to most of his readers, as it has to me" [p. 181]), while arguing that the latter will have to provide the basis for Frost's future reputation. The dichotomy is false, however, since instead of alternating from countryman to cosmopolitan, Frost often incorporates both perspectives, availing himself of the tension between them to achieve the special complexity and intensity that characterize his best work.

1970

Thompson, Lawrance. *Robert Frost: The Years of Triumph, 1915-1938.* New York: Holt, Rinehart and Winston, 1970.
    The second volume of this biography details Frost's rise to fame and his struggle to project the image of the Yankee farmer poet.

1971

Sampley, Arthur M. "The Myth and the Quest: The Stature of Robert Frost." *South Atlantic Quarterly*, 70 (Summer 1971), 287-298.
    Frost as a nineteenth-century Yankee.

1973

Barry, Elaine. *Robert Frost on Writing.* New Brunswick: Rutgers University Press, 1973.
    Frost's poetics are ascribed solely to his Yankee heritage.
Foster, Richard. "Leaves Compared with Flowers: A Reading in Robert Frost's Poems." *New England Quarterly*, 46 (Sept. 1973), 403-423.
    Foster considers Frost to be a poet "who lives physically in the mountain land of New England 'North of Boston' " (420).

1974

Cox, James M. "Robert Frost and the End of the New England Line." In Jac L. Tharpe, ed., *Frost: Centennial Essays* (Jackson: University Press of Mississippi, 1974), pp. 545-561.
Frost as a descendant of Emerson and Thoreau.

Davison, Peter. "The Self-Realization of Robert Frost, 1911-1912." *New Republic*, 170 (30 Mar. 1974), 17-20.
Frost's year in Plymouth, N.H., contributed partly to his development of a regional identity.

Greiner, Donald. *Robert Frost: The Poet and his Critics.* Chicago: American Library Association, 1974.

Nitchie, George W. "Robert Frost: The Imperfect Guru." In Tharpe, ed., *Frost: Centennial Essays*, pp. 42-50.
Focusing on Frost's role as Yankee prophet or regional "guru," Nitchie extends the argument of his earlier book (1960) and reveals more clearly the extent to which his attack is based on assumptions about Frost's identity as a New Englander.

Westbrook, Perry D. "Robert Frost's New England." In Tharpe, ed., *Frost: Centennial Essays*, pp. 239-255.
Frost in the context of New England Puritanism.

1975

Tate, Allen. " 'Inner Weather': Frost as Metaphysical." In *Robert Frost: Lectures on the Centennial of His Birth* (Washington, D.C.: Library of Congress, 1975), pp. 57-68.
Frost's limited perspective and monotony of metrics and tone are attributed to his regional pose.

1976

MacLeish, Archibald. "Robert Frost and New England." *National Geographic*, 149 (Apr. 1976), 438-444.
This brief essay stresses the inadequacy of conventional attitudes toward Frost's New England poetry.

MacLeish combines deep knowledge of the poet's work and temperament with a rare sensitivity to the forces of literary history to produce a fresh and insightful estimate of the complex relationship between artist and region.

Perkins, David. "Robert Frost." In Perkins, *A History of Modern Poetry: From the 1890's to the High Modernist Mode* (Cambridge, Mass.: Belknap Press of Harvard University Press, 1976), pp. 227-251.

Frost's "Yankee wariness" is associated with his lack of "seriousness, profundity, and commitment" (p. 250).

Thompson, Lawrance, and Winnick, R. H. *Robert Frost: The Later Years, 1938-1963.* New York: Holt, Rinehart and Winston, 1976.

This final volume of the official biography demonstrates the wide impact of Frost's Yankee-poet image and analyzes the severe strain of maintaining such a public role. The miracle is that amid frightful stress in public and private life, Frost remained capable of gathering his still considerable powers in such triumphs as "The Silken Tent," "Come In," "The Most of It," "Never Again Would Birds' Song Be the Same," and "Directive."

1977

Poirier, Richard. *Robert Frost: The Work of Knowing.* New York: Oxford University Press, 1977.

Perhaps Frost's most ingenious and thought-provoking explicator, Poirier presents a major defense of the poet's importance. However, the book reflects the recent tendency among some commentators to slight Frost's position as a New Englander. Especially in light of Poirier's concern with images of home, this reluctance to deal with Frost's attitudes toward his own various dwellings in and out of New England seems unfortunate. Furthermore, the commendable attack on Frost's weakness for "contrived and stagey imaginative daring" (p. 99) would be more convincing if Poirier examined the different regional techniques in such disparate poems as "The Death of the Hired Man," "New Hampshire," "West-Running Brook," and "Directive."

Index

Morse, Stearns, 251
Morton, David, 244
Mosher, Thomas B., , 72, 100n, 147
Munson, Gorham, 10, 246

New England literature, 4-13,
27-41 passim, 58, 63, 65, 87-88,
101-104, 128, 143-162 passim,
170, 176, 184-185, 196, 204-205,
222-226. See also farmer poet;
local color; regionalism
New England Magazine, 27
Nitchie, George W., , 176n, 259;
Human Values in the Poetry of
Robert Frost, 3, 13n, 167, 227-
229, 255

O'Donnell, William G., , 239, 252

Palgrave, F. T., The Golden Treas-
ury, 47, 61
Peabody, Josephine Preston, 157n,
158
Pearce, Roy Harvey, 85, 162, 253
Percy, Thomas, Reliques, 56
Perkins, David, A History of Mod-
ern Poetry, 224-227, 233-234,
260
Perrine, Laurence, 196-197
Pierce, Frederick E., , 247
Pinkerton Academy, 66, 77, 149
Poe, Edgar Allan, 45-49, 52-58,
99, 151, 156, 187; "Al Aaraaf,"
58; "The City in the Sea," 57;
"Dream-Land," 58; "The
Haunted Palace," 55; "MS.
found in a Bottle," 56; Tamer-
lane, 53
Poirier, Richard, 198n; Robert
Frost: The Work of Knowing,
13n, 63n, 81n, 194n, 204n, 207,
260
Pope, Alexander, 143, 233
Porter, Jane, 48
Pound, Ezra L., 3, 10, 90, 92-96,
100, 140, 148, 151, 152n, 162,

171, 225, 238-239; review of A
Boy's Will, 92, 240; review of
North of Boston, 93, 241
Prescott, W. H., 48; The Conquest
of Mexico, 53
Pritchard, William H., 28n, 256

Quinn, Arthur Hobson, 239

regionalism, 5-8, 25, 87-90, 97-
104, 149-151, 158-162, 169,
183-188, 193-239 passim. See
also farmer poet; local color;
New England literature; Yankee
character
Rittenhouse, Jessie B., 150, 242
Robinson, Edwin Arlington, 7, 42,
87, 100, 103, 147-149, 157-162,
189, 238; "Aaron Stark," 15,
160; "Captain Craig," 161; The
Children of the Night, 158; "The
Chorus of the Old Men from
'Aegeus,' " 158; "Horace to
Leuconoë," 158; "The House on
the Hill," 216n; "Reuben
Bright," 15, 160; "Richard
Cory," 15, 160
Robinson Crusoe, 205
Romig, Edna Davis, 48n
Roosevelt, Theodore, 157n
Rourke, Constance, 27n, 30n

St. Armand, Barton L., 161n, 257
Sampley, Arthur M., 175n, 258
Sandburg, Carl, 149
Schneider, Isidor, 247
Scott, Sir Walter, 48, 56, 61
Sedgwick, Catharine Maria,
A New England Tale, 35n
Sedgwick, Ellery, 26, 150n
Sergeant, Elizabeth Shepley,
Robert Frost: The Trial by Exist-
ence, 16n, 171, 256
Shakespeare, William, 47-48, 233
Shelley, Percy Bysshe, 47-48, 52,

LIBRARY OF CONGRESS CATALOGING IN PUBLICATION DATA

Kemp, John C
    Robert Frost and New England.

    Based on the author's doctoral dissertation,
University of Pennsylvania.
    Includes index.
        1. Frost, Robert, 1874-1963—Criticism and
interpretation.   2. New England in literature.
3. Regionalism in literature.   I. Title.
PS3511.R94Z758   811'.5'2   78-70301
ISBN 0-691-06393-1